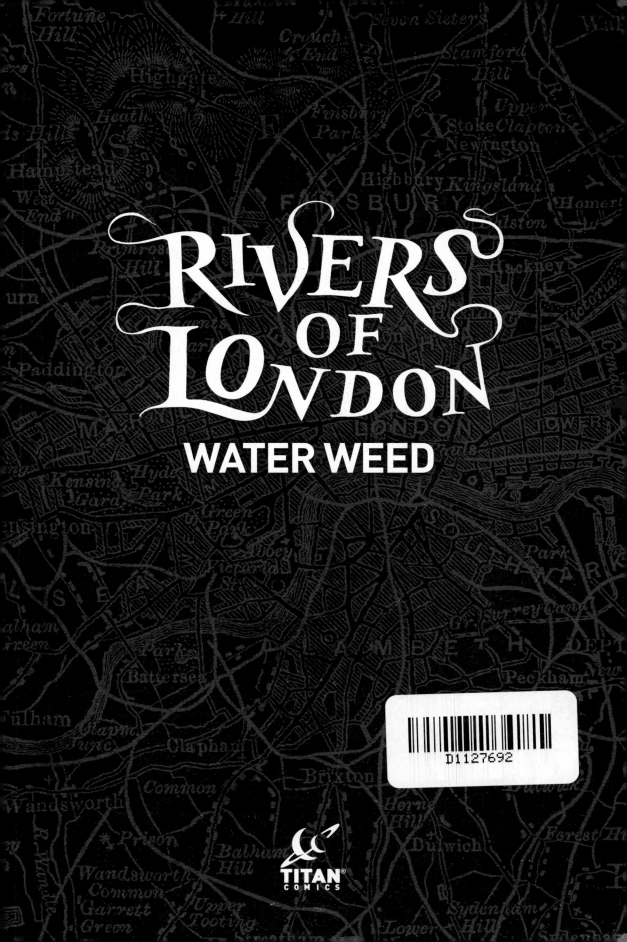

RIVERS OF LONDON
WATER WEED

TITAN
COMICS

RIVERS OF LONDON: WATER WEED
ISBN: 9781785865459
HC ISBN: 9781785866227

TITAN COMICS

EDITORS STEVE WHITE & KIRSTEN MURRAY
SENIOR DESIGNER ANDREW LEUNG

Managing & Launch Editor Andrew James
Production Assistant Rhiannon Roy
Production Controller Peter James
Senior Production Controller Jackie Flook
Art Director Oz Browne
Circulation Executive Frances Hallam
Sales & Circulation Manager Steve Tothill
Marketing Assistant Charlie Raspin
Press Officer Will O'Mullane
Publicist Imogen Harris
Brand Manager Chris Thompson
Direct Sales and Marketing Manager Ricky Claydon
Ads and Marketing Assistant Bella Hoy
Commercial Manager Michelle Fairlamb
Head of Rights Jenny Boyce
Publishing Manager Darryl Tothill
Publishing Director Chris Teather
Operations Director Leigh Baulch
Executive Director Vivian Cheung
Publisher Nick Landau

Published by Titan Comics
A division of Titan Publishing Group, Ltd.
144 Southwark St.
London, SE1 0UP

A CIP catalogue record for this title is available from the British Library.

First edition: November 2018
10 9 8 7 6 5 4 3 2 1

Printed in Spain.
Titan Comics.

For rights information contact jenny.boyce@titanemail.com

WWW.TITAN-COMICS.COM
Become a fan on Facebook.com/comicstitan
Follow us on Twitter @ComicsTitan

RIVERS OF LONDON

WATER WEED

CREATED BY
BEN AARONOVITCH

WRITTEN BY
ANDREW CARTMEL

ART BY
LEE SULLIVAN

COLORS BY
LUIS GUERRERO & PAULINA VASSILEVA

LETTERING BY
ROB STEEN

TITAN®
COMICS

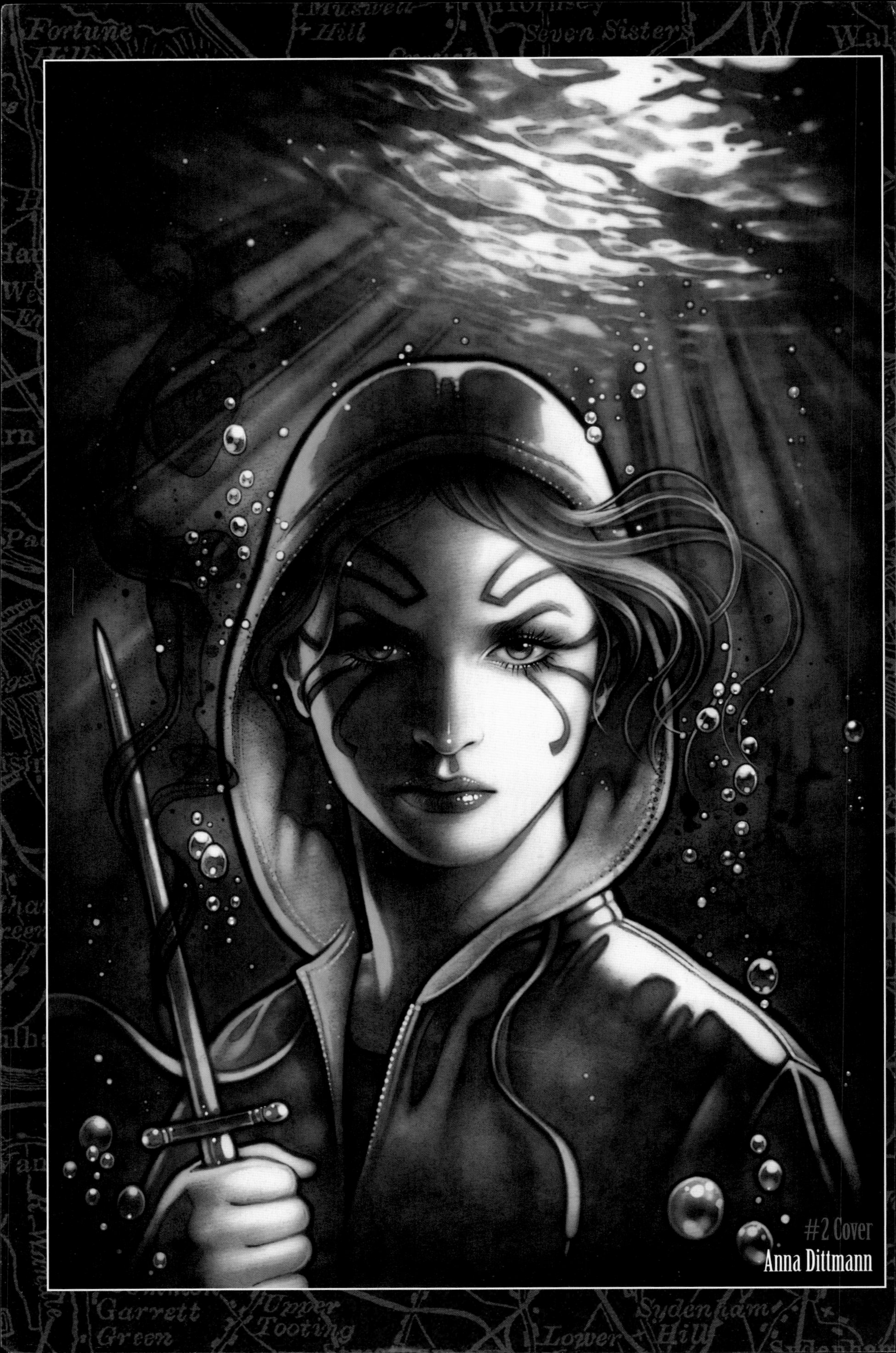
Fortune
Muswell Hill
Seven Sisters
Garrett Green
Upper Tooting
Sydenham Hill
Lower
#2 Cover
Anna Dittmann

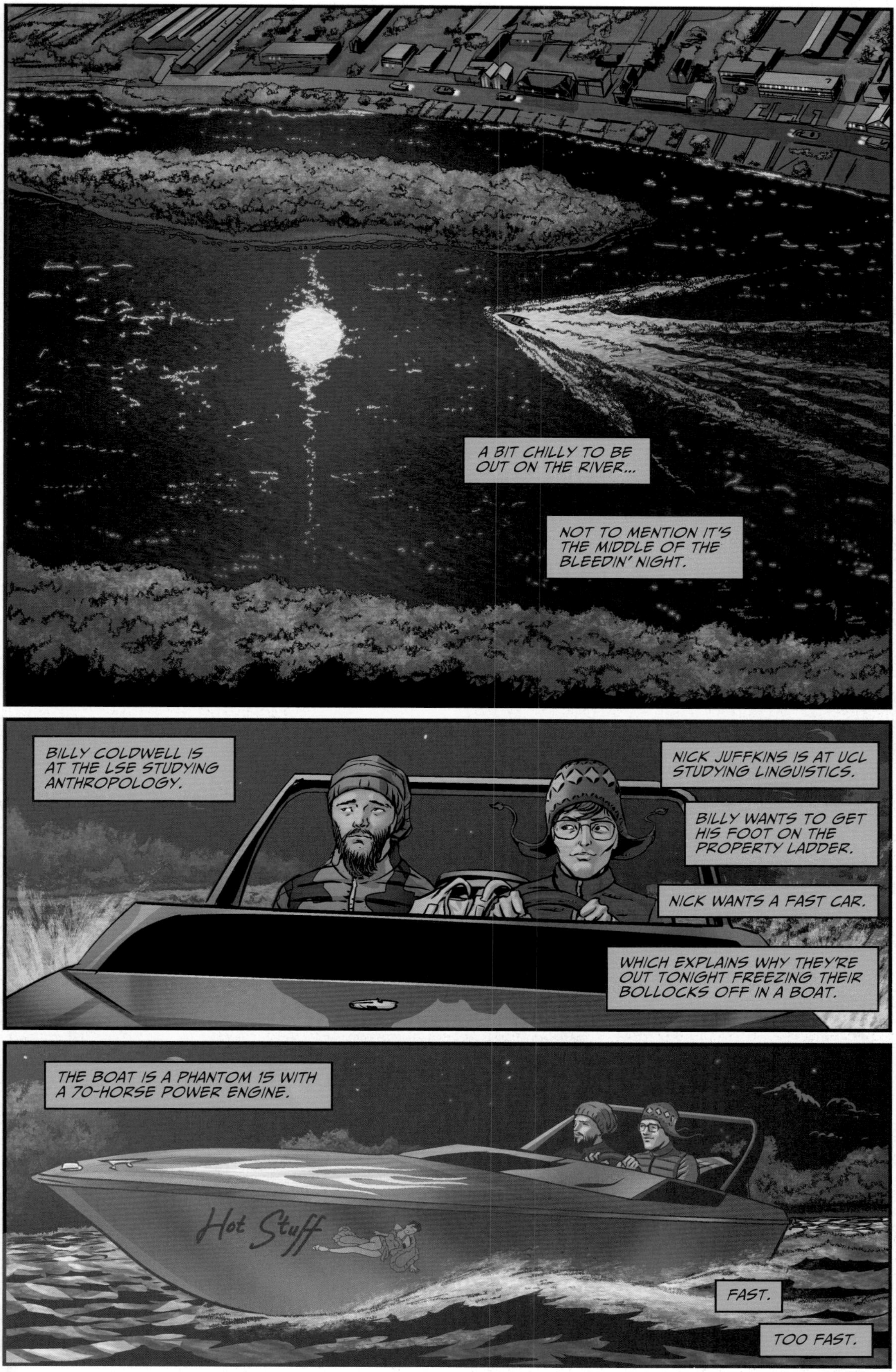
A BIT CHILLY TO BE OUT ON THE RIVER...
NOT TO MENTION IT'S THE MIDDLE OF THE BLEEDIN' NIGHT.
BILLY COLDWELL IS AT THE LSE STUDYING ANTHROPOLOGY.
NICK JUFFKINS IS AT UCL STUDYING LINGUISTICS.
BILLY WANTS TO GET HIS FOOT ON THE PROPERTY LADDER.
NICK WANTS A FAST CAR.
WHICH EXPLAINS WHY THEY'RE OUT TONIGHT FREEZING THEIR BOLLOCKS OFF IN A BOAT.
THE BOAT IS A PHANTOM 15 WITH A 70-HORSE POWER ENGINE.
Hot Stuff
FAST.
TOO FAST.

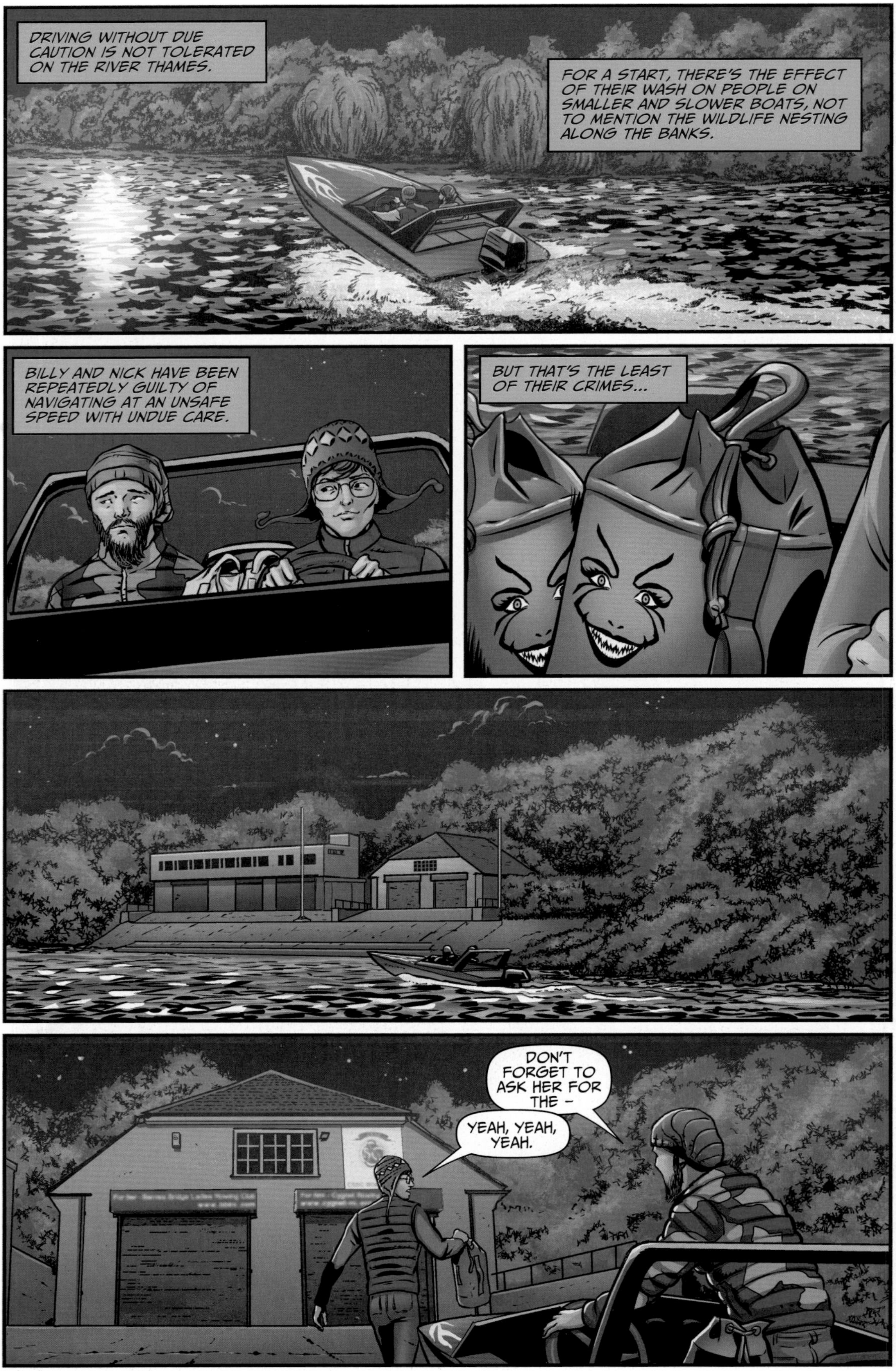
DRIVING WITHOUT DUE CAUTION IS NOT TOLERATED ON THE RIVER THAMES.
FOR A START, THERE'S THE EFFECT OF THEIR WASH ON PEOPLE ON SMALLER AND SLOWER BOATS, NOT TO MENTION THE WILDLIFE NESTING ALONG THE BANKS.
BILLY AND NICK HAVE BEEN REPEATEDLY GUILTY OF NAVIGATING AT AN UNSAFE SPEED WITH UNDUE CARE.
BUT THAT'S THE LEAST OF THEIR CRIMES...
DON'T FORGET TO ASK HER FOR THE –
YEAH, YEAH, YEAH.

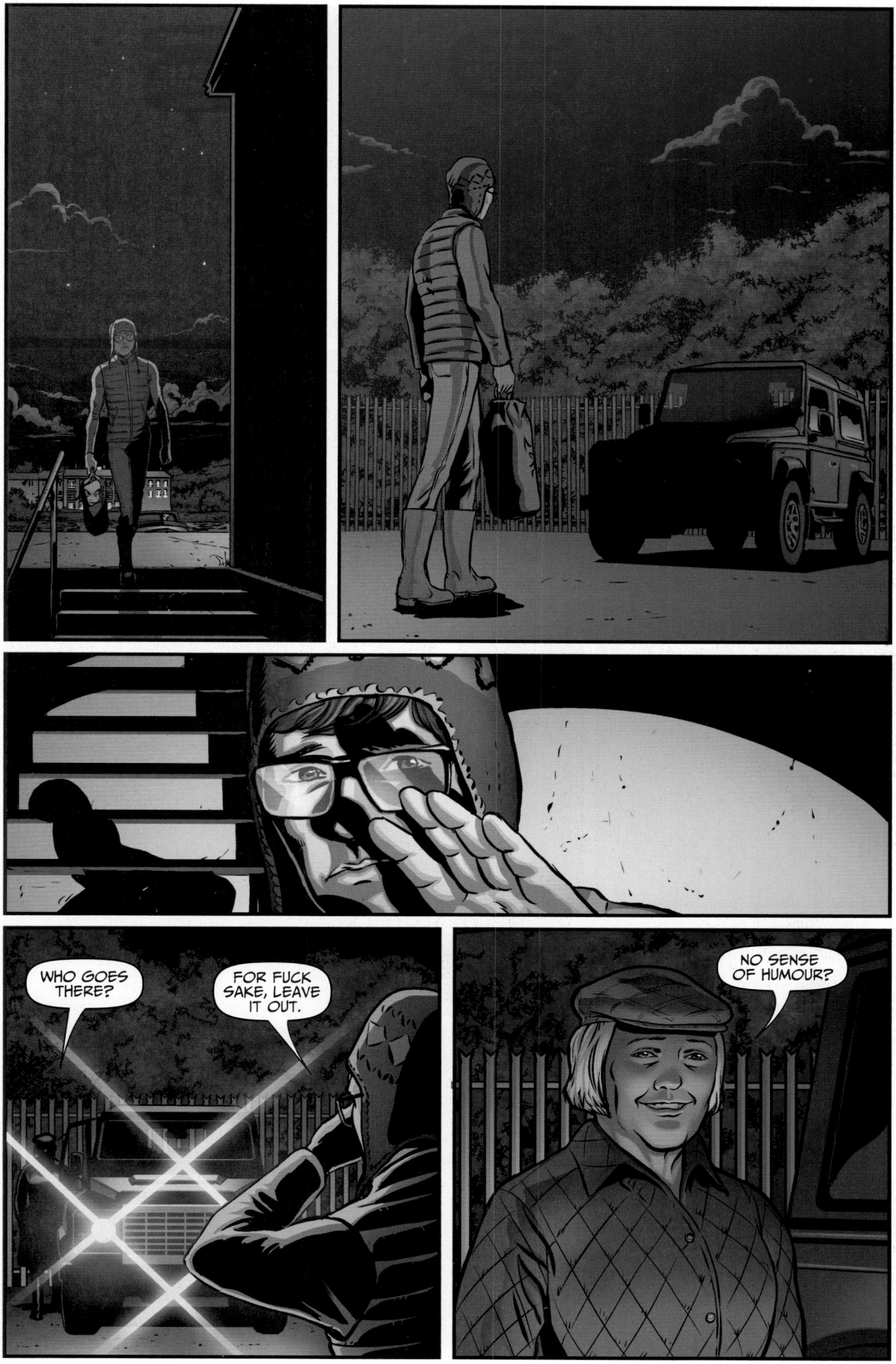
WHO GOES THERE?
FOR FUCK SAKE, LEAVE IT OUT.
NO SENSE OF HUMOUR?

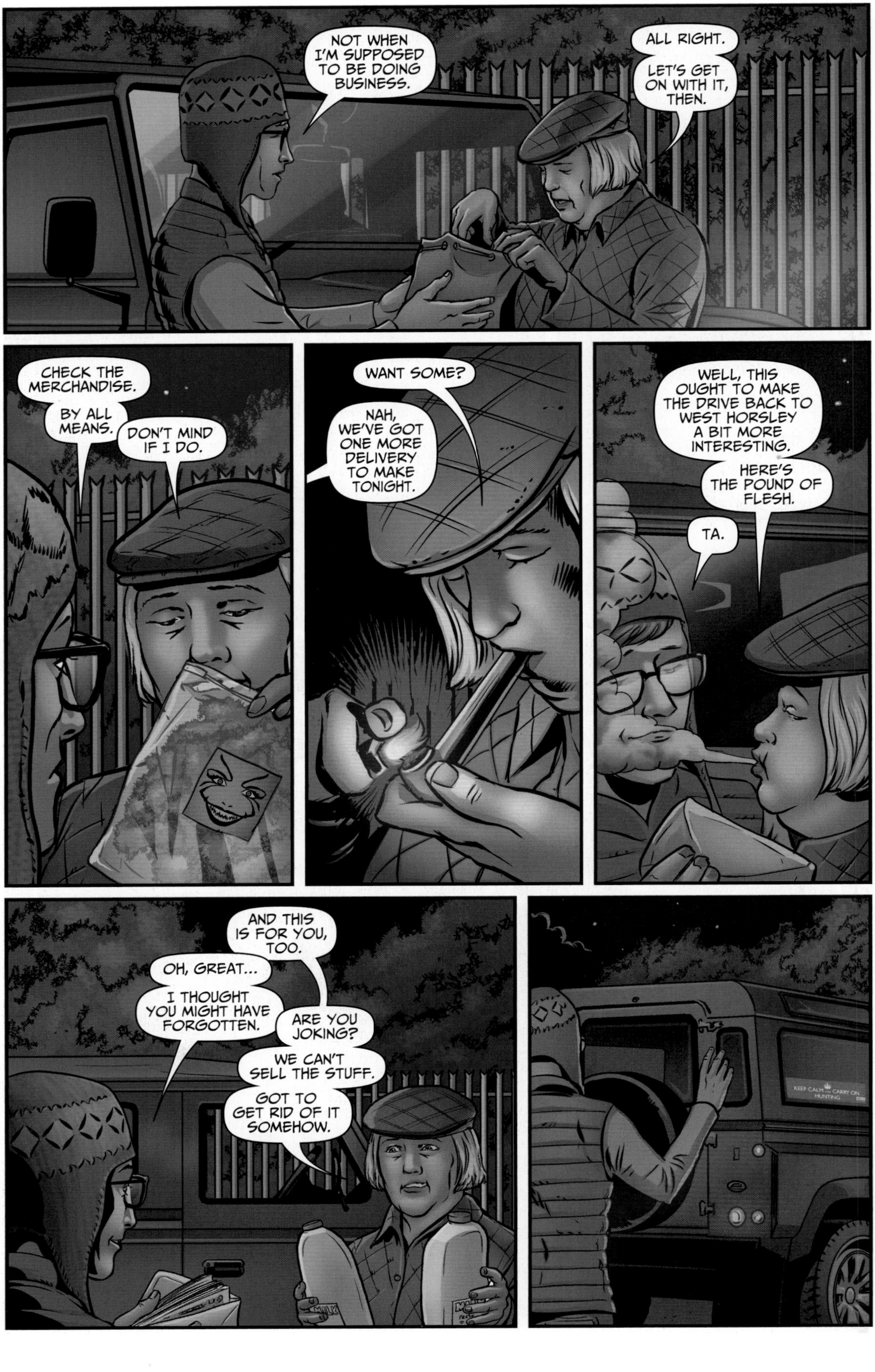
NOT WHEN I'M SUPPOSED TO BE DOING BUSINESS.
ALL RIGHT.
LET'S GET ON WITH IT, THEN.
CHECK THE MERCHANDISE.
BY ALL MEANS.
DON'T MIND IF I DO.
WANT SOME?
NAH, WE'VE GOT ONE MORE DELIVERY TO MAKE TONIGHT.
WELL, THIS OUGHT TO MAKE THE DRIVE BACK TO WEST HORSLEY A BIT MORE INTERESTING.
HERE'S THE POUND OF FLESH.
TA.
AND THIS IS FOR YOU, TOO.
OH, GREAT...
I THOUGHT YOU MIGHT HAVE FORGOTTEN.
ARE YOU JOKING?
WE CAN'T SELL THE STUFF.
GOT TO GET RID OF IT SOMEHOW.
KEEP CALM CARRY ON HUNTING

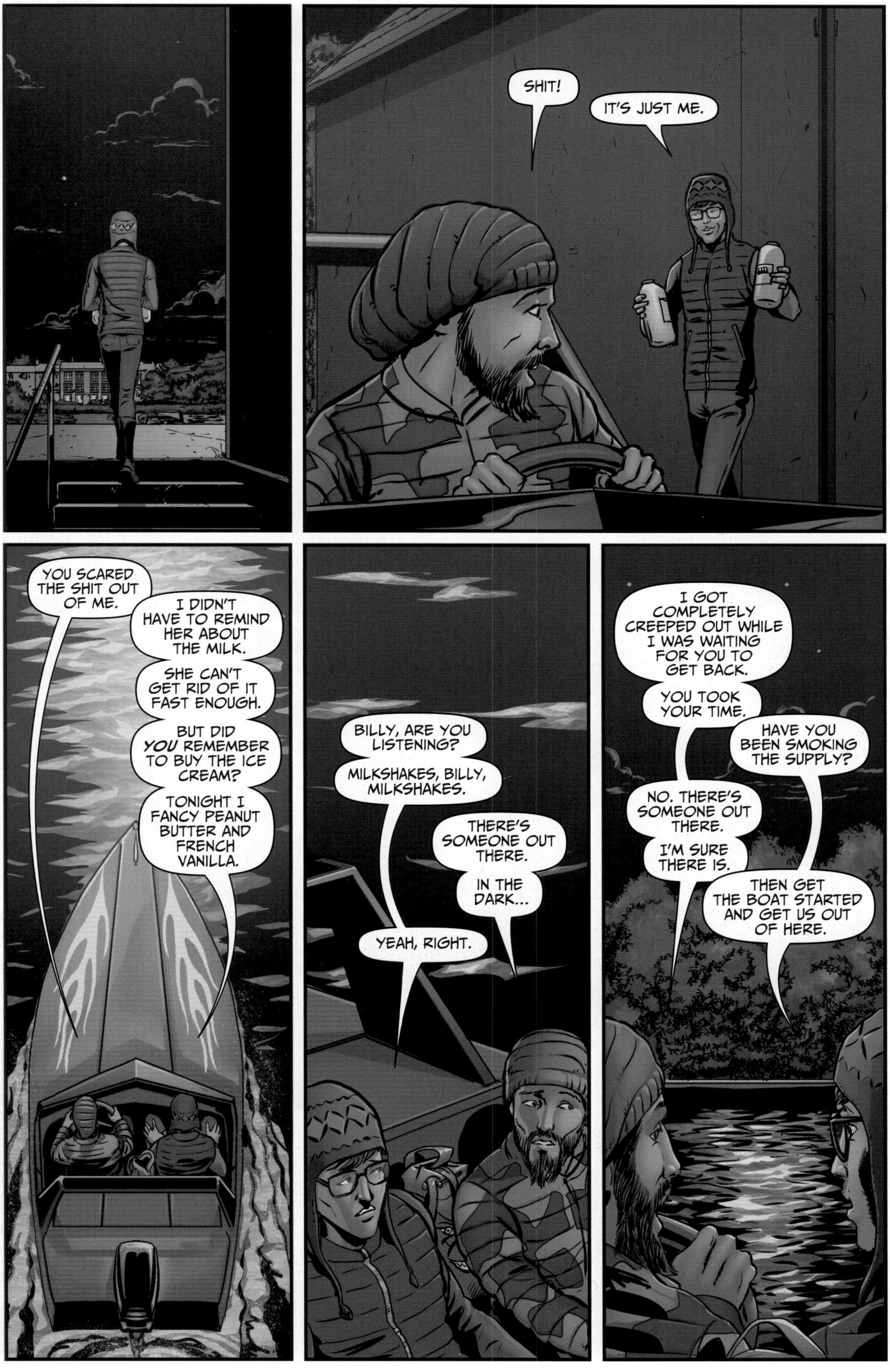
SHIT!
IT'S JUST ME.
YOU SCARED THE SHIT OUT OF ME.
I DIDN'T HAVE TO REMIND HER ABOUT THE MILK.
SHE CAN'T GET RID OF IT FAST ENOUGH.
BUT DID *YOU* REMEMBER TO BUY THE ICE CREAM?
TONIGHT I FANCY PEANUT BUTTER AND FRENCH VANILLA.
BILLY, ARE YOU LISTENING?
MILKSHAKES, BILLY, MILKSHAKES.
THERE'S SOMEONE OUT THERE.
IN THE DARK...
YEAH, RIGHT.
I GOT COMPLETELY CREEPED OUT WHILE I WAS WAITING FOR YOU TO GET BACK.
YOU TOOK YOUR TIME.
HAVE YOU BEEN SMOKING THE SUPPLY?
NO. THERE'S SOMEONE OUT THERE.
I'M SURE THERE IS.
THEN GET THE BOAT STARTED AND GET US OUT OF HERE.

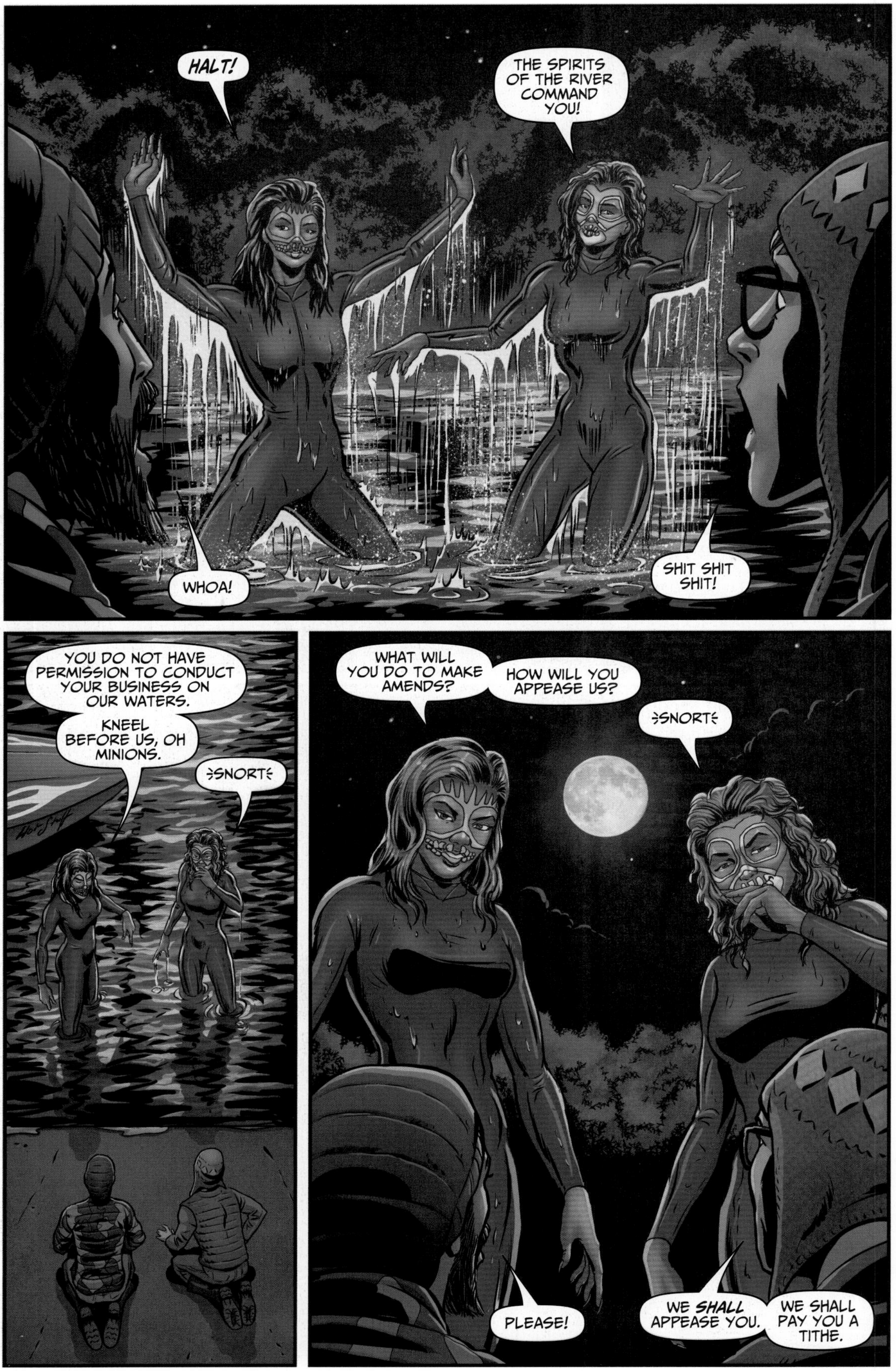
HALT!
THE SPIRITS OF THE RIVER COMMAND YOU!
WHOA!
SHIT SHIT SHIT!
YOU DO NOT HAVE PERMISSION TO CONDUCT YOUR BUSINESS ON OUR WATERS.
KNEEL BEFORE US, OH MINIONS.
SNORT
WHAT WILL YOU DO TO MAKE AMENDS?
HOW WILL YOU APPEASE US?
SNORT
PLEASE!
WE *SHALL* APPEASE YOU.
WE SHALL PAY YOU A TITHE.

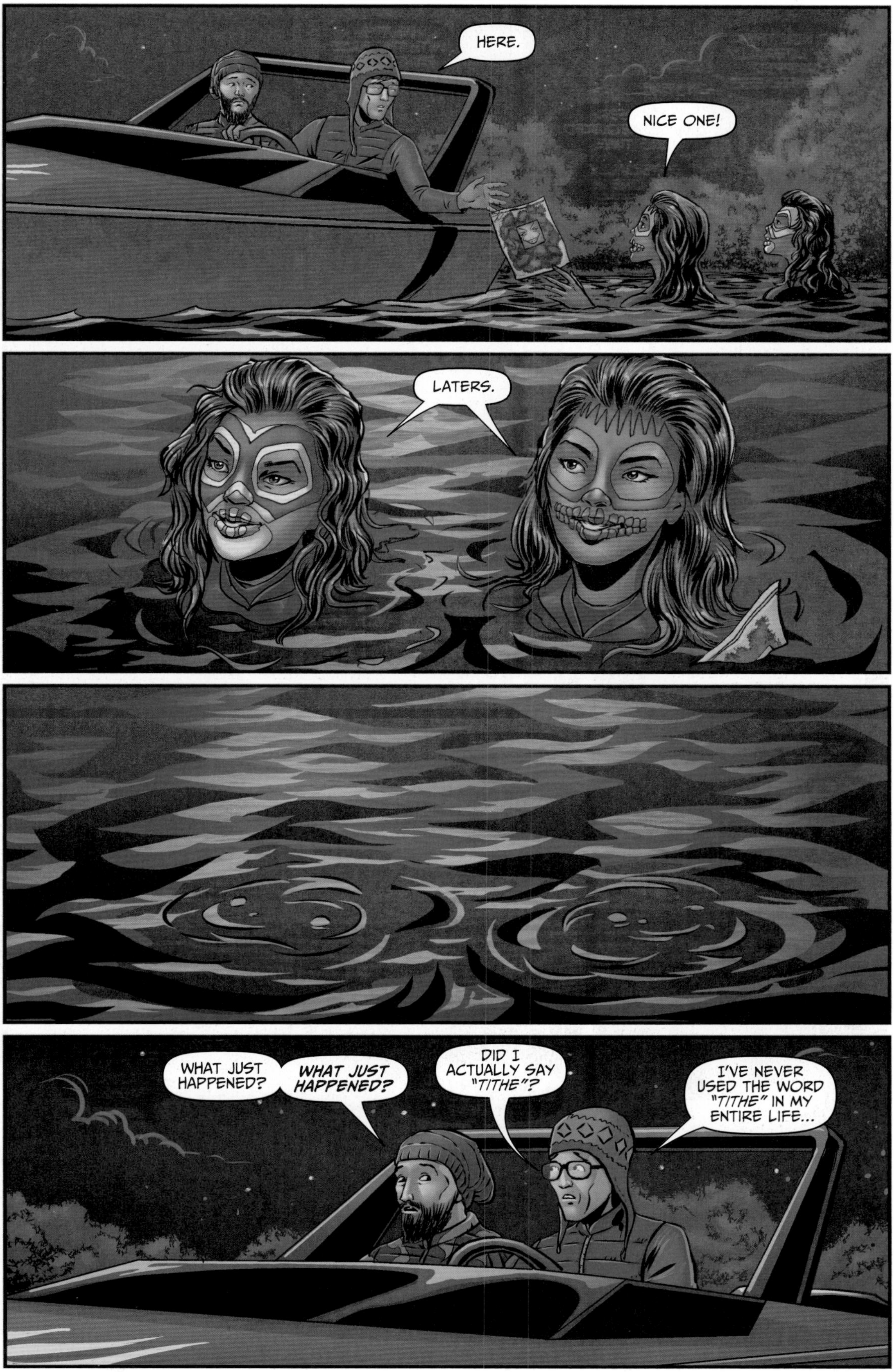
HERE.
NICE ONE!
LATERS.
WHAT JUST HAPPENED?
WHAT JUST HAPPENED?
DID I ACTUALLY SAY *"TITHE"*?
I'VE NEVER USED THE WORD *"TITHE"* IN MY ENTIRE LIFE...

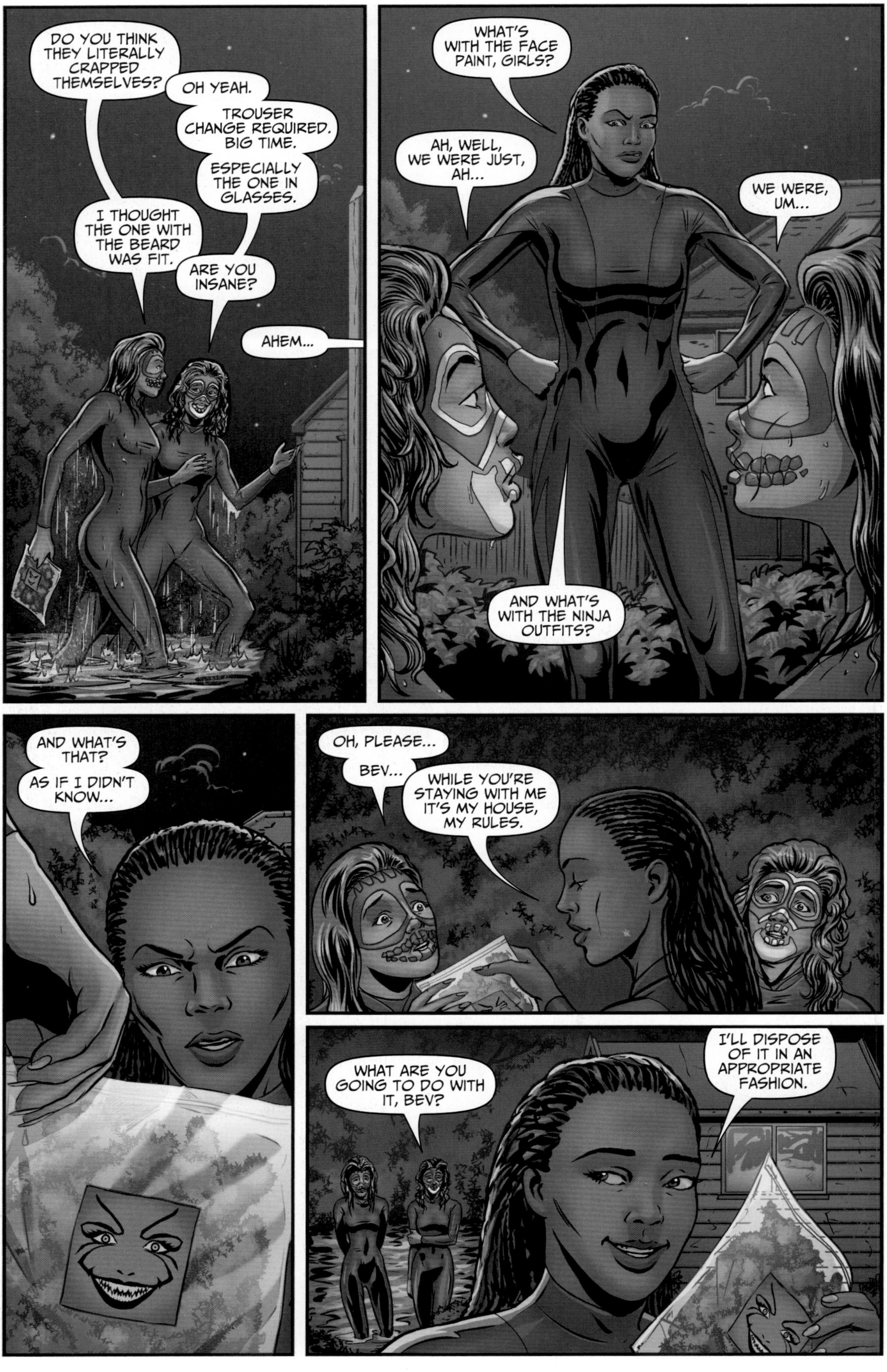
DO YOU THINK THEY LITERALLY CRAPPED THEMSELVES?
OH YEAH.
TROUSER CHANGE REQUIRED. BIG TIME.
ESPECIALLY THE ONE IN GLASSES.
I THOUGHT THE ONE WITH THE BEARD WAS FIT.
ARE YOU INSANE?
AHEM...
WHAT'S WITH THE FACE PAINT, GIRLS?
AH, WELL, WE WERE JUST, AH...
WE WERE, UM...
AND WHAT'S WITH THE NINJA OUTFITS?
AND WHAT'S THAT?
AS IF I DIDN'T KNOW...
OH, PLEASE...
BEV...
WHILE YOU'RE STAYING WITH ME IT'S MY HOUSE, MY RULES.
WHAT ARE YOU GOING TO DO WITH IT, BEV?
I'LL DISPOSE OF IT IN AN APPROPRIATE FASHION.

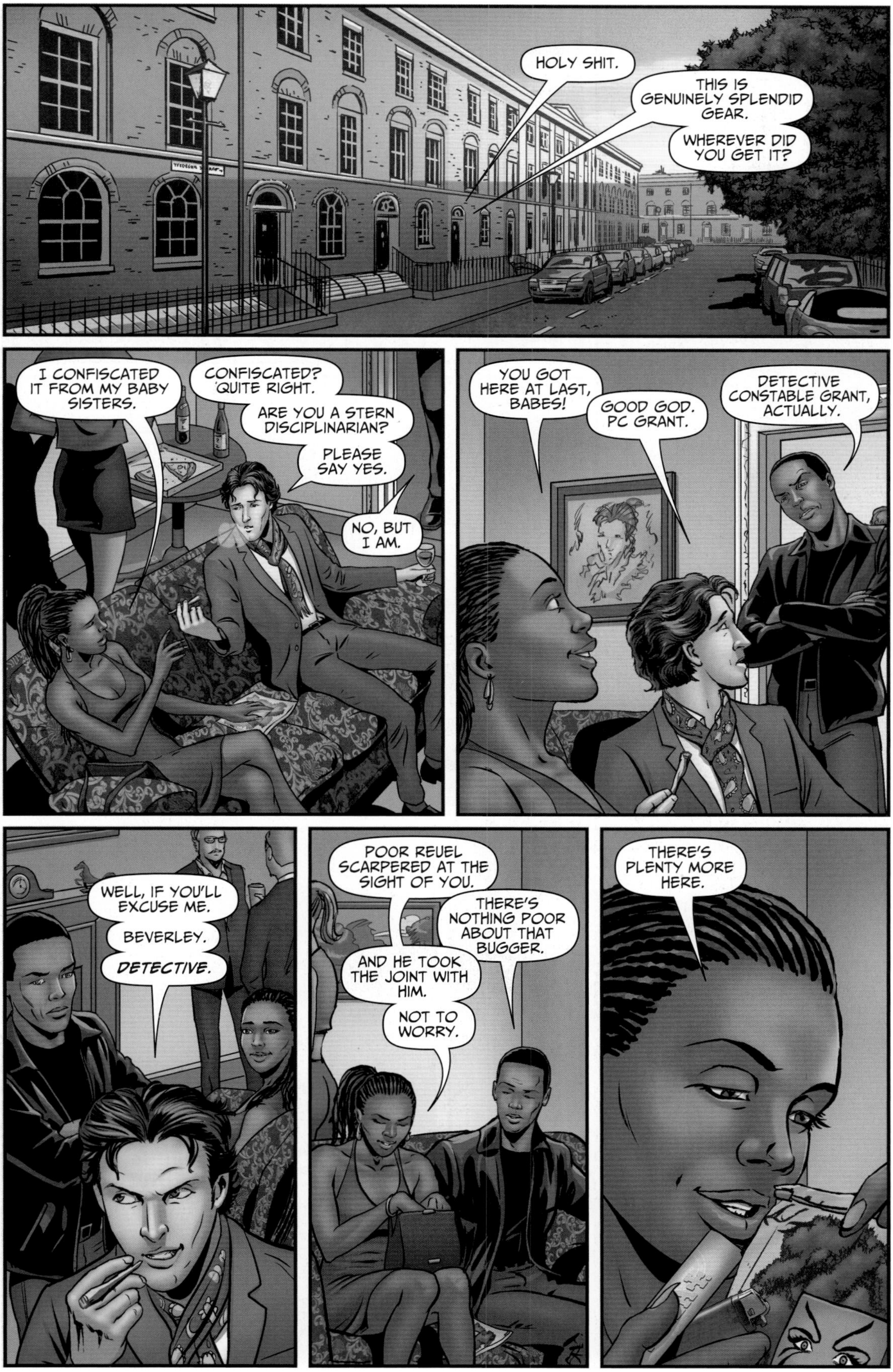
HOLY SHIT.
THIS IS GENUINELY SPLENDID GEAR.
WHEREVER DID YOU GET IT?
I CONFISCATED IT FROM MY BABY SISTERS.
CONFISCATED? 'QUITE RIGHT.
ARE YOU A STERN DISCIPLINARIAN?
PLEASE SAY YES.
NO, BUT I AM.
YOU GOT HERE AT LAST, BABES!
GOOD GOD. PC GRANT.
DETECTIVE CONSTABLE GRANT, ACTUALLY.
WELL, IF YOU'LL EXCUSE ME.
BEVERLEY.
DETECTIVE.
POOR REUEL SCARPERED AT THE SIGHT OF YOU.
THERE'S NOTHING POOR ABOUT THAT BUGGER.
AND HE TOOK THE JOINT WITH HIM.
NOT TO WORRY.
THERE'S PLENTY MORE HERE.

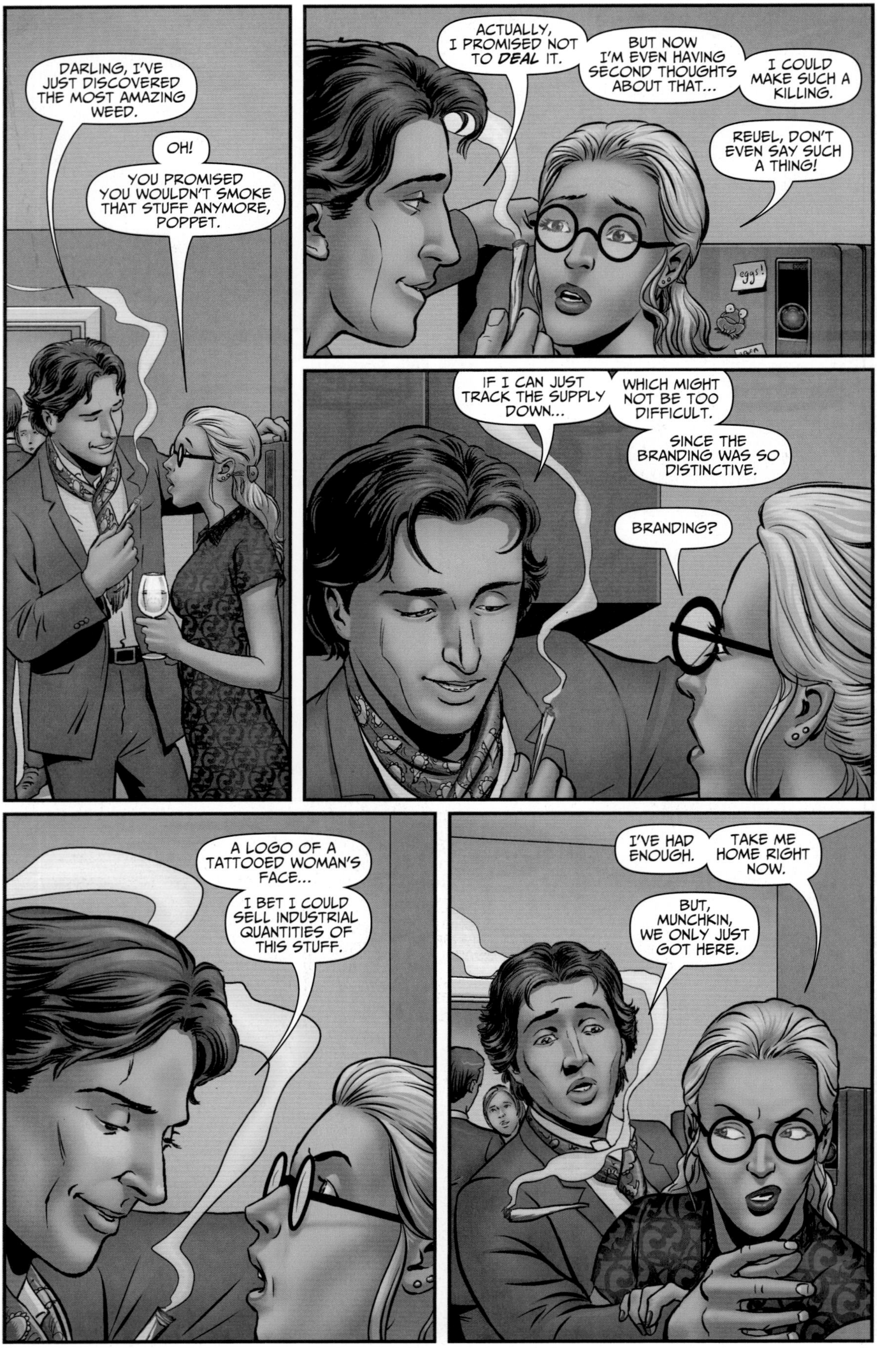
DARLING, I'VE JUST DISCOVERED THE MOST AMAZING WEED.
OH!
YOU PROMISED YOU WOULDN'T SMOKE THAT STUFF ANYMORE, POPPET.
ACTUALLY, I PROMISED NOT TO DEAL IT.
BUT NOW I'M EVEN HAVING SECOND THOUGHTS ABOUT THAT...
I COULD MAKE SUCH A KILLING.
REUEL, DON'T EVEN SAY SUCH A THING!
eggs!
IF I CAN JUST TRACK THE SUPPLY DOWN...
WHICH MIGHT NOT BE TOO DIFFICULT.
SINCE THE BRANDING WAS SO DISTINCTIVE.
BRANDING?
A LOGO OF A TATTOOED WOMAN'S FACE...
I BET I COULD SELL INDUSTRIAL QUANTITIES OF THIS STUFF.
I'VE HAD ENOUGH.
TAKE ME HOME RIGHT NOW.
BUT, MUNCHKIN, WE ONLY JUST GOT HERE.

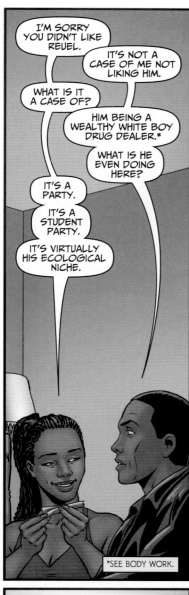

I'M SORRY YOU DIDN'T LIKE REUEL.

IT'S NOT A CASE OF ME NOT LIKING HIM.

WHAT IS IT A CASE OF?

HIM BEING A WEALTHY WHITE BOY DRUG DEALER.*

WHAT IS HE EVEN DOING HERE?

IT'S A PARTY.

IT'S A STUDENT PARTY.

IT'S VIRTUALLY HIS ECOLOGICAL NICHE.

*SEE BODY WORK.

AHA!

A COUPLE OF CONNOISSEURS, EH?

WHAT?

THAT DOPE.

I COULD SMELL IT WHEN I CAME IN.

AND I RECOGNISED IT.

OH REALLY?

YOU RECOGNISED IT?

BY THE SMELL?

YEAH, IT COMES WITH A STICKER OF A FACE.

WITH, LIKE, TATTOOS ON IT, RIGHT?

UH...YEAH.

THOUGHT SO. IT'S GREAT GEAR.

WOULD YOU LIKE SOME?

NOT JUST NOW, THANKS.

SOUNDS LIKE *SHE'S* THE CONNOISSEUR.

YEAH, AND WITH QUITE A NOSE ON HER.

STILL, SHE'S RIGHT. IT IS GREAT GEAR.

WHY DON'T YOU TRY SOME?

NO THANKS.

OH, GO ON.

HAVE A LITTLE FUN.

BEFORE I CAN STOP MYSELF, I'VE INHALED A LUNG FULL OF THE STUFF.

AND IT HITS ME.

BUT NOT LIKE DOPE...

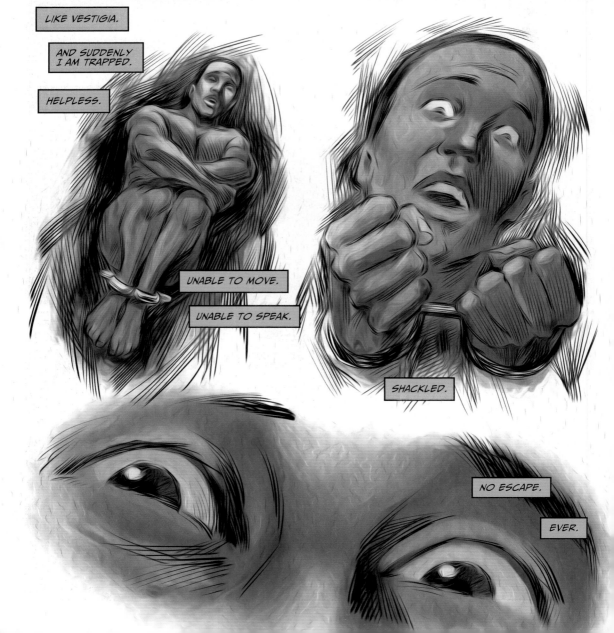

LIKE VESTIGIA.

AND SUDDENLY I AM TRAPPED.

HELPLESS.

UNABLE TO MOVE.

UNABLE TO SPEAK.

SHACKLED.

NO ESCAPE.

EVER.

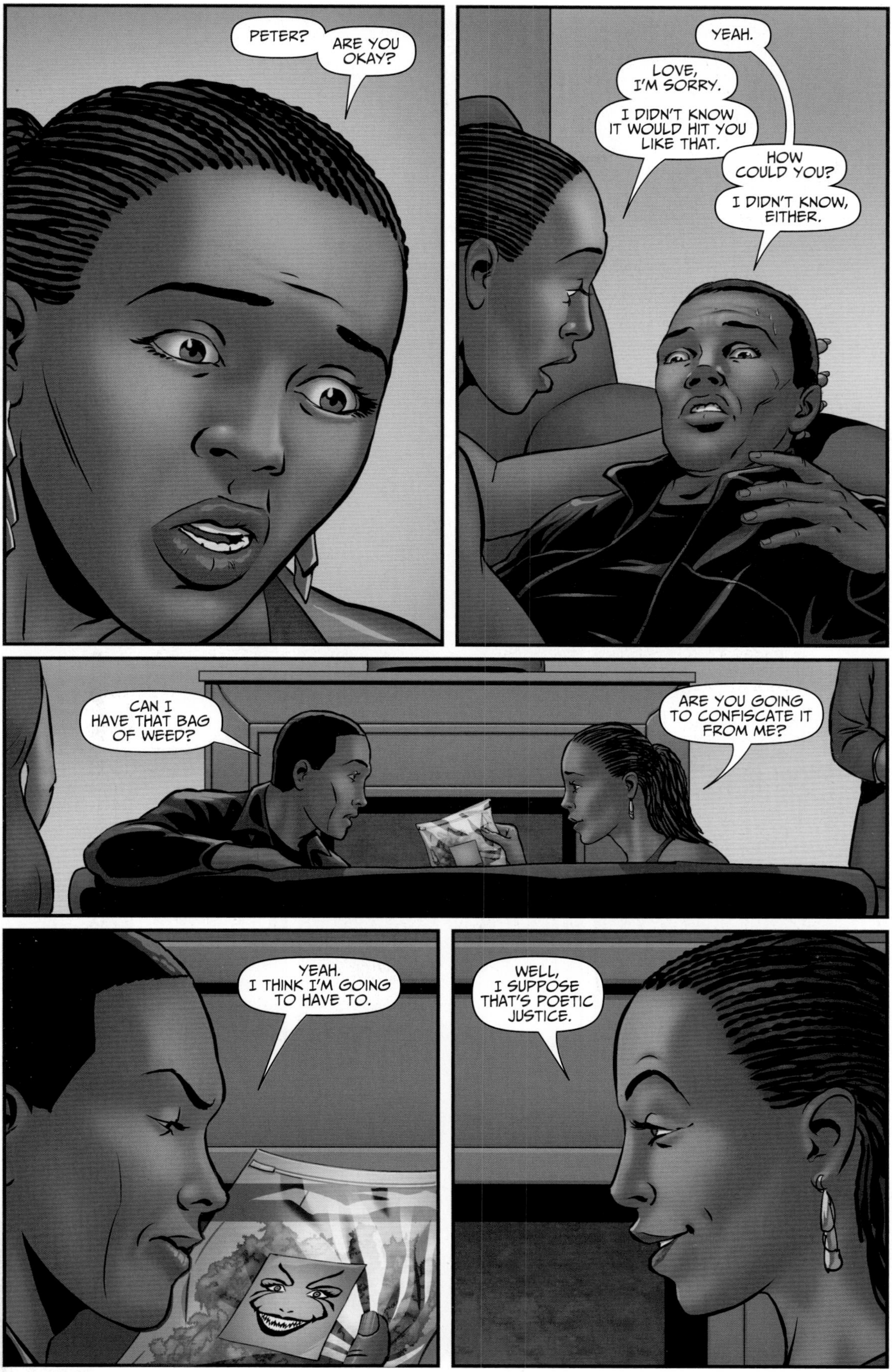
PETER?
ARE YOU OKAY?
YEAH.
LOVE, I'M SORRY.
I DIDN'T KNOW IT WOULD HIT YOU LIKE THAT.
HOW COULD YOU?
I DIDN'T KNOW, EITHER.
CAN I HAVE THAT BAG OF WEED?
ARE YOU GOING TO CONFISCATE IT FROM ME?
YEAH. I THINK I'M GOING TO HAVE TO.
WELL, I SUPPOSE THAT'S POETIC JUSTICE.

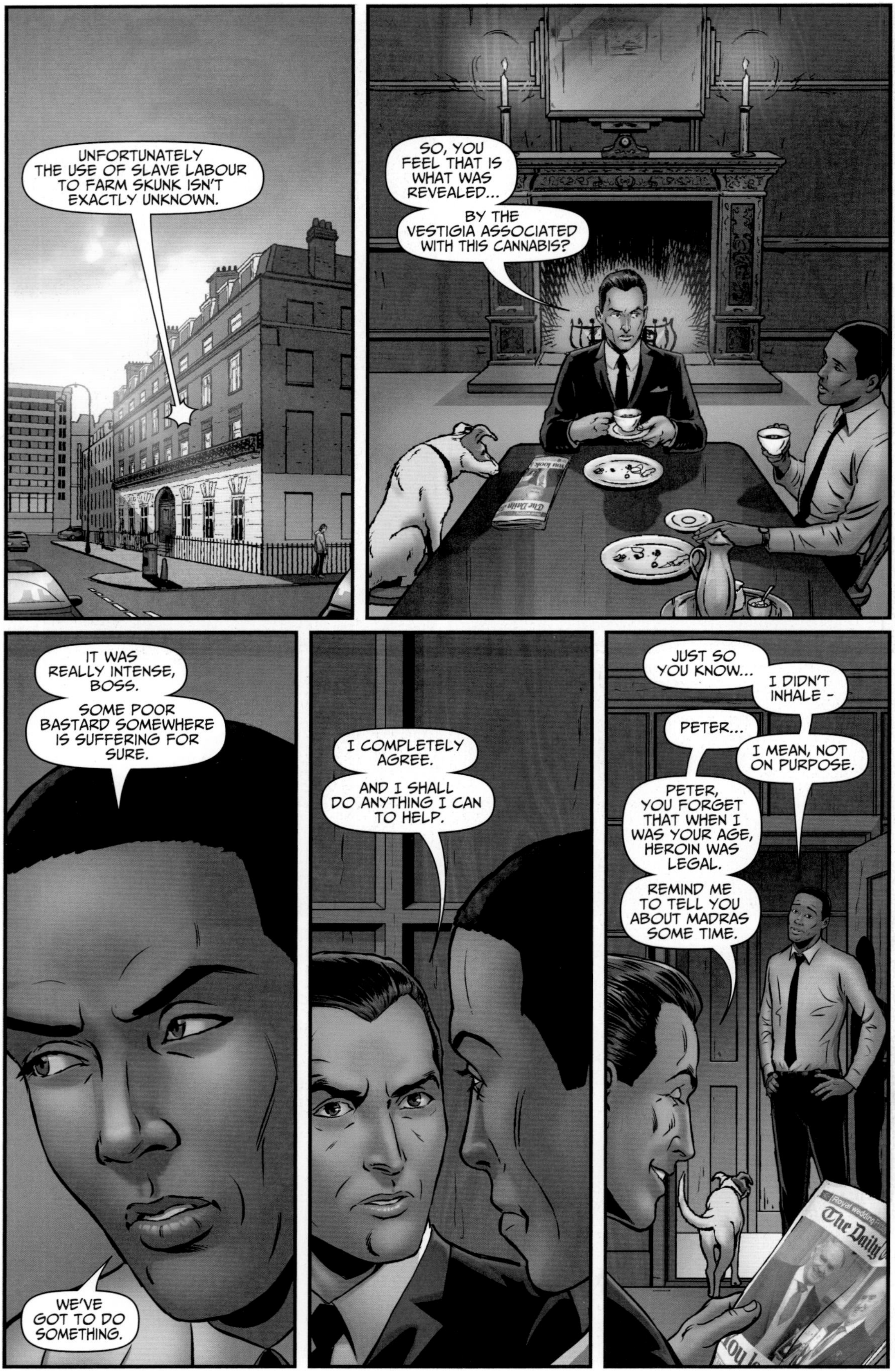
UNFORTUNATELY THE USE OF SLAVE LABOUR TO FARM SKUNK ISN'T EXACTLY UNKNOWN.
SO, YOU FEEL THAT IS WHAT WAS REVEALED...
BY THE VESTIGIA ASSOCIATED WITH THIS CANNABIS?
IT WAS REALLY INTENSE, BOSS.
SOME POOR BASTARD SOMEWHERE IS SUFFERING FOR SURE.
WE'VE GOT TO DO SOMETHING.
I COMPLETELY AGREE.
AND I SHALL DO ANYTHING I CAN TO HELP.
JUST SO YOU KNOW...
I DIDN'T INHALE -
PETER...
I MEAN, NOT ON PURPOSE.
PETER, YOU FORGET THAT WHEN I WAS YOUR AGE, HEROIN WAS LEGAL.
REMIND ME TO TELL YOU ABOUT MADRAS SOME TIME.
The Daily
Royal wedding

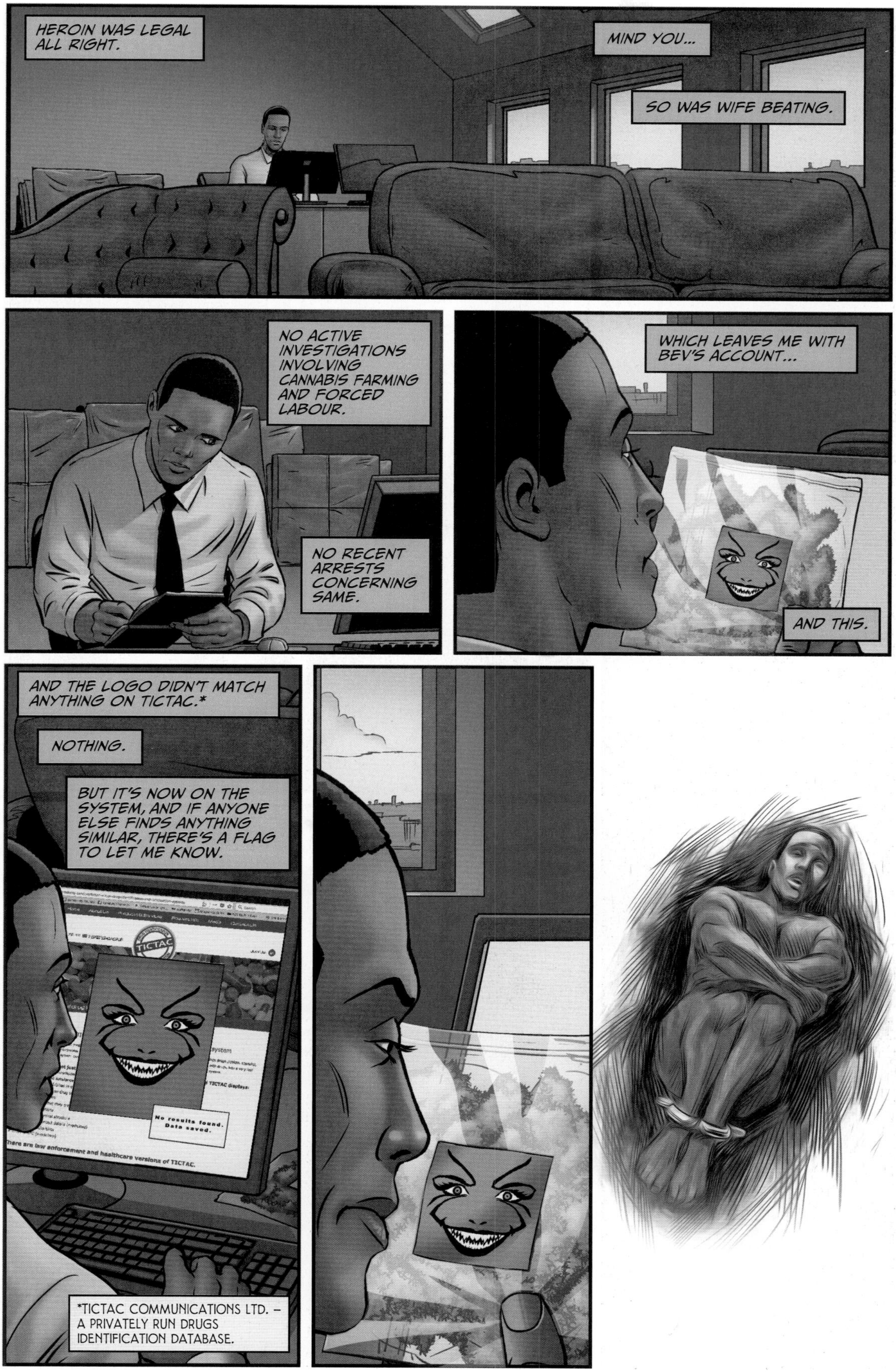
HEROIN WAS LEGAL ALL RIGHT.
MIND YOU...
SO WAS WIFE BEATING.
NO ACTIVE INVESTIGATIONS INVOLVING CANNABIS FARMING AND FORCED LABOUR.
NO RECENT ARRESTS CONCERNING SAME.
WHICH LEAVES ME WITH BEV'S ACCOUNT...
AND THIS.
AND THE LOGO DIDN'T MATCH ANYTHING ON TICTAC.*
NOTHING.
BUT IT'S NOW ON THE SYSTEM, AND IF ANYONE ELSE FINDS ANYTHING SIMILAR, THERE'S A FLAG TO LET ME KNOW.
TICTAC
No results found. Data saved.
There are law enforcement and healthcare versions of TICTAC.
*TICTAC COMMUNICATIONS LTD. – A PRIVATELY RUN DRUGS IDENTIFICATION DATABASE.

ALL THAT LEAVES ME WITH TWO LINES OF ENQUIRY...

SOME KIND OF ANALYSIS OF THE WEED ITSELF.

IF I CAN FIND AN EXPERT WHO CAN TELL ME SOMETHING USEFUL...

ABOUT THIS STRAIN AND WHERE IT CAME FROM.

MAYBE SOMEONE AT KEW GARDENS?

AND THEN THERE'S THE GIRL AT THE PARTY.

I DIDN'T GET HER NAME.

I HAVE NO IDEA WHO SHE IS, OR WHERE I CAN FIND HER.

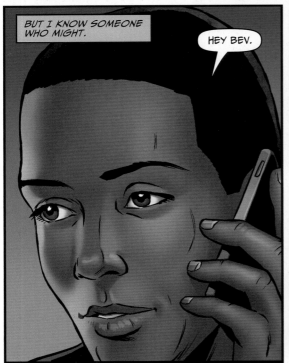

BUT I KNOW SOMEONE WHO MIGHT.

HEY BEV.

I'M GLAD YOU CALLED.

I WANTED TO MAKE UP FOR LAST NIGHT.

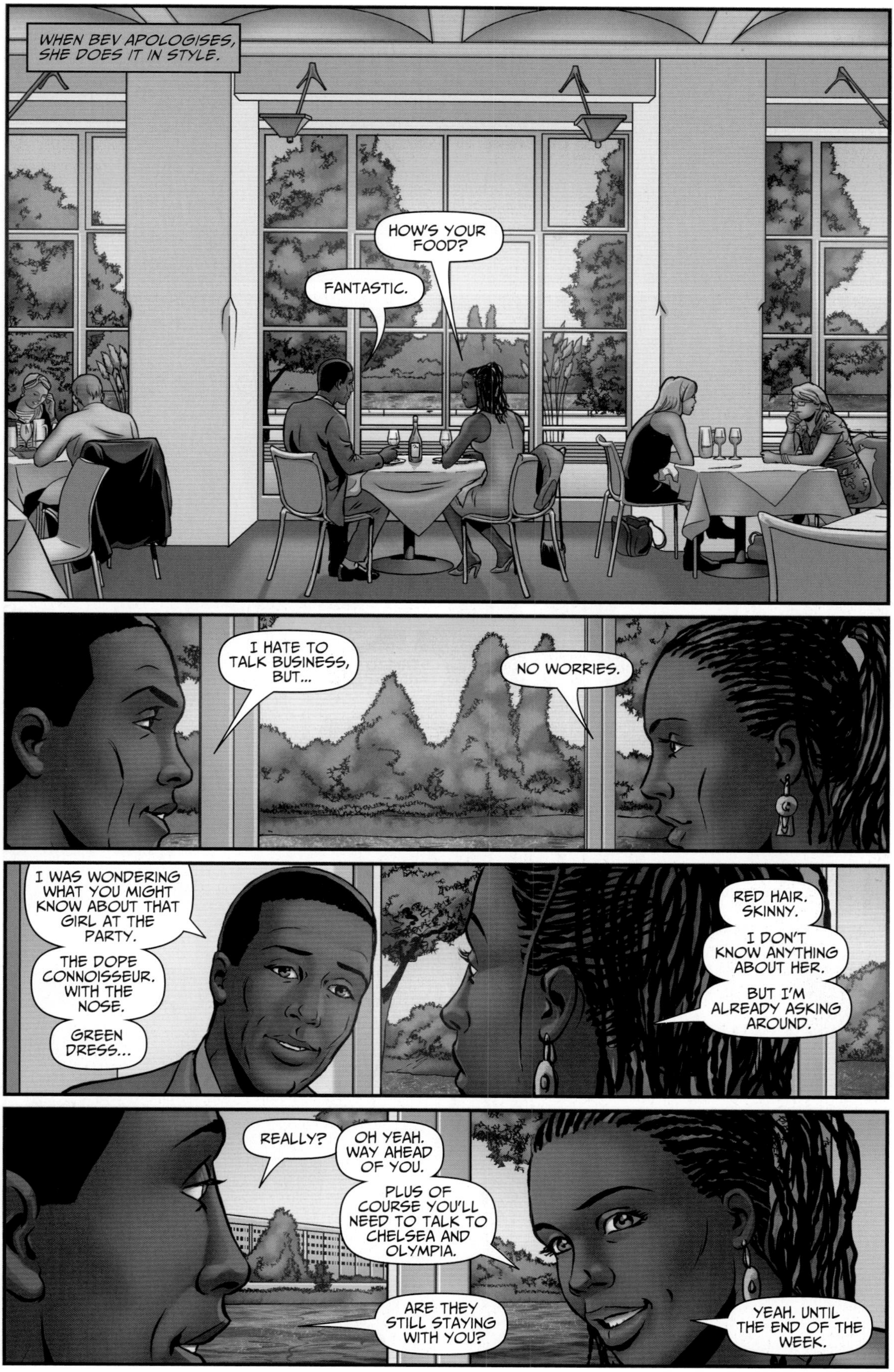
WHEN BEV APOLOGISES, SHE DOES IT IN STYLE.
HOW'S YOUR FOOD?
FANTASTIC.
I HATE TO TALK BUSINESS, BUT...
NO WORRIES.
I WAS WONDERING WHAT YOU MIGHT KNOW ABOUT THAT GIRL AT THE PARTY.
THE DOPE CONNOISSEUR. WITH THE NOSE.
GREEN DRESS...
RED HAIR. SKINNY.
I DON'T KNOW ANYTHING ABOUT HER.
BUT I'M ALREADY ASKING AROUND.
REALLY?
OH YEAH. WAY AHEAD OF YOU.
PLUS OF COURSE YOU'LL NEED TO TALK TO CHELSEA AND OLYMPIA.
ARE THEY STILL STAYING WITH YOU?
YEAH. UNTIL THE END OF THE WEEK.

"I HOPE THEY'RE ALL RIGHT."

YOU DON'T THINK THIS IS A BIT CONSPICUOUS?

YOU SAID TO NICK A CAR.

YEAH, BUT DID YOU HAVE TO NICK THIS ONE?

IF YOU WANT TO MAKE YOURSELF USEFUL, CHECK THE BAG.

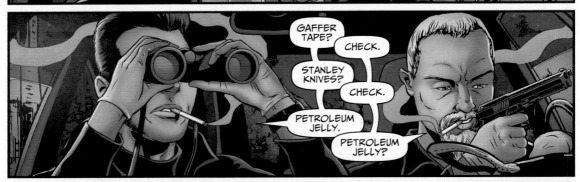

GAFFER TAPE?

CHECK.

STANLEY KNIVES?

CHECK.

PETROLEUM JELLY.

PETROLEUM JELLY?

"THE CLIENT SAID WE COULD DO ANYTHING WE LIKED WITH THOSE TWO.

"SO LONG AS WE PUT THE FEAR OF GOD INTO THEM."

AND THAT'S NOT ALL I'M GOING TO PUT INTO THEM.

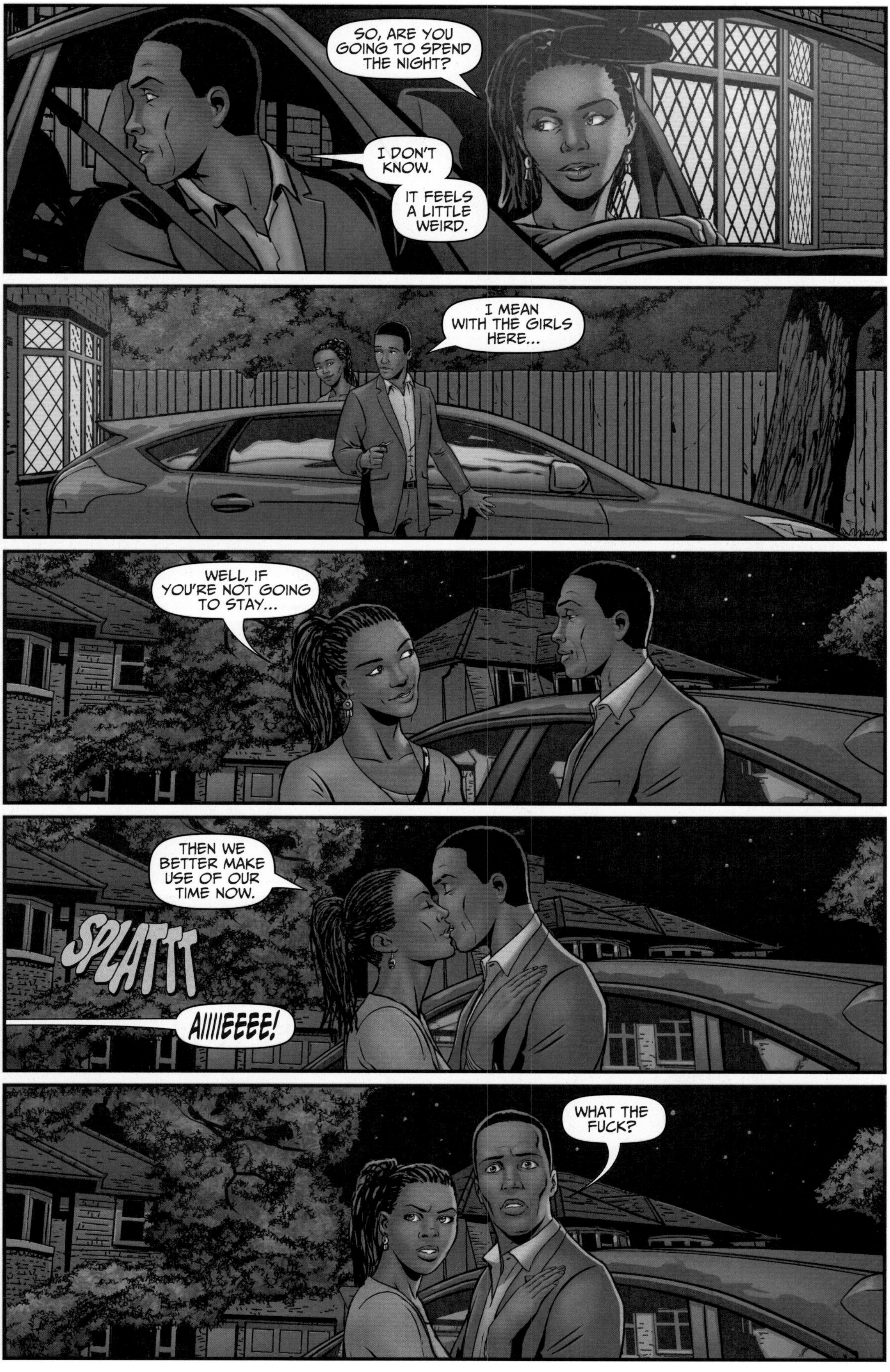
SO, ARE YOU GOING TO SPEND THE NIGHT?
I DON'T KNOW.
IT FEELS A LITTLE WEIRD.
I MEAN WITH THE GIRLS HERE...
WELL, IF YOU'RE NOT GOING TO STAY...
THEN WE BETTER MAKE USE OF OUR TIME NOW.
SPLATTT
AIIIIEEEE!
WHAT THE FUCK?

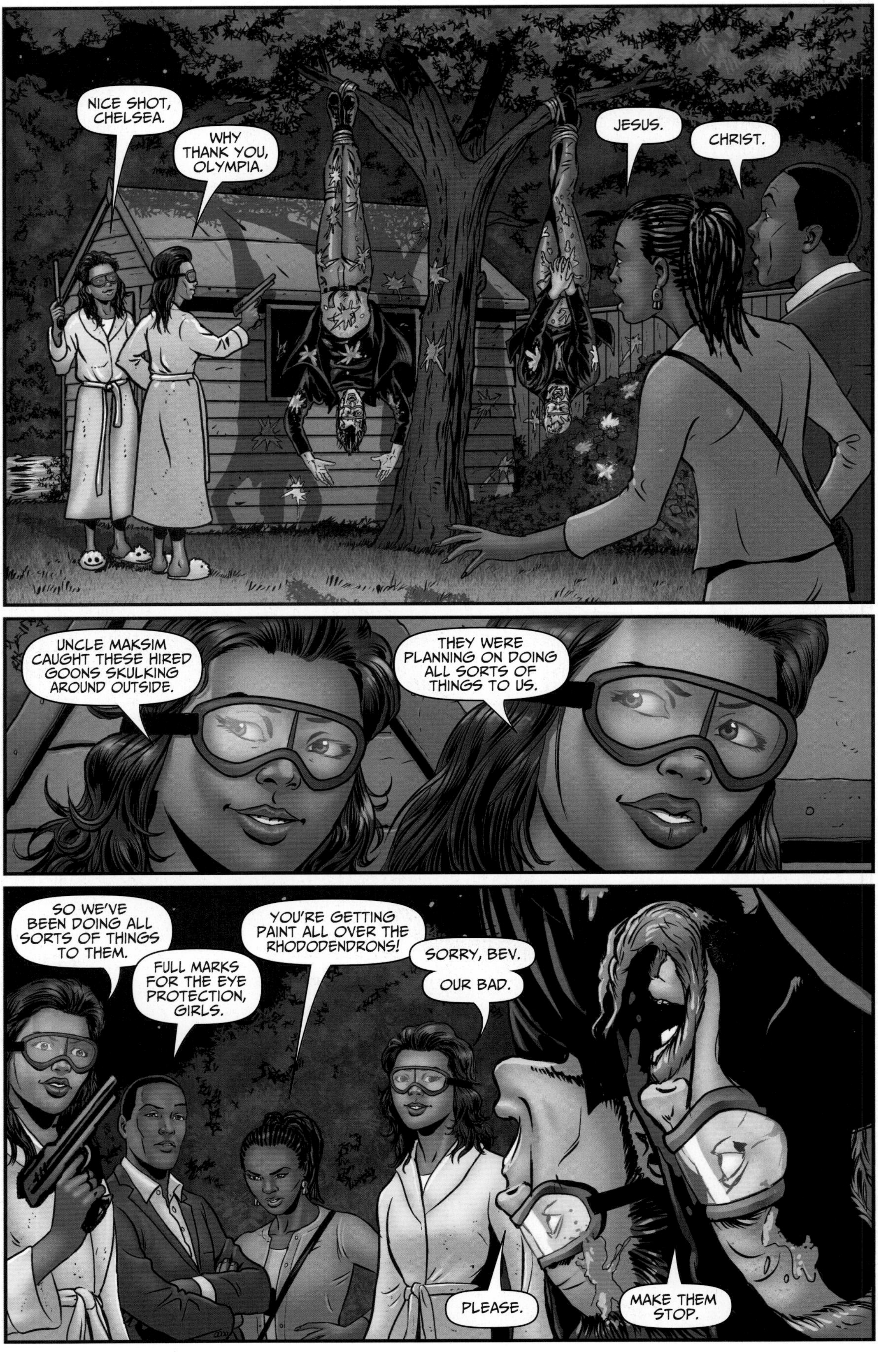
NICE SHOT, CHELSEA.
WHY THANK YOU, OLYMPIA.
JESUS.
CHRIST.
UNCLE MAKSIM CAUGHT THESE HIRED GOONS SKULKING AROUND OUTSIDE.
THEY WERE PLANNING ON DOING ALL SORTS OF THINGS TO US.
SO WE'VE BEEN DOING ALL SORTS OF THINGS TO THEM.
FULL MARKS FOR THE EYE PROTECTION, GIRLS.
YOU'RE GETTING PAINT ALL OVER THE RHODODENDRONS!
SORRY, BEV.
OUR BAD.
PLEASE.
MAKE THEM STOP.

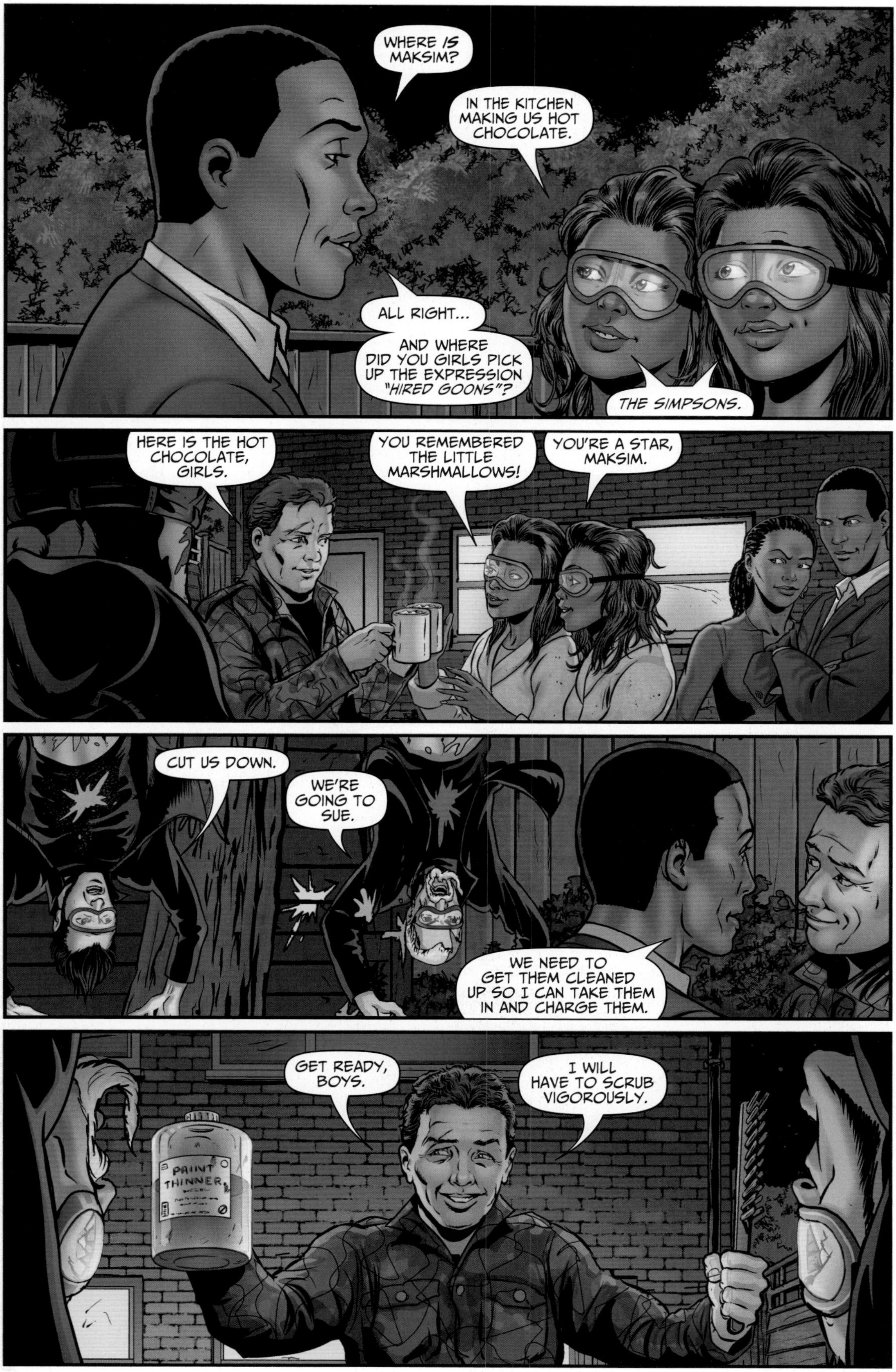
WHERE *IS* MAKSIM?
IN THE KITCHEN MAKING US HOT CHOCOLATE.
ALL RIGHT...
AND WHERE DID YOU GIRLS PICK UP THE EXPRESSION *"HIRED GOONS"*?
THE SIMPSONS.
HERE IS THE HOT CHOCOLATE, GIRLS.
YOU REMEMBERED THE LITTLE MARSHMALLOWS!
YOU'RE A STAR, MAKSIM.
CUT US DOWN.
WE'RE GOING TO SUE.
WE NEED TO GET THEM CLEANED UP SO I CAN TAKE THEM IN AND CHARGE THEM.
GET READY, BOYS.
I WILL HAVE TO SCRUB VIGOROUSLY.
PAINT THINNER

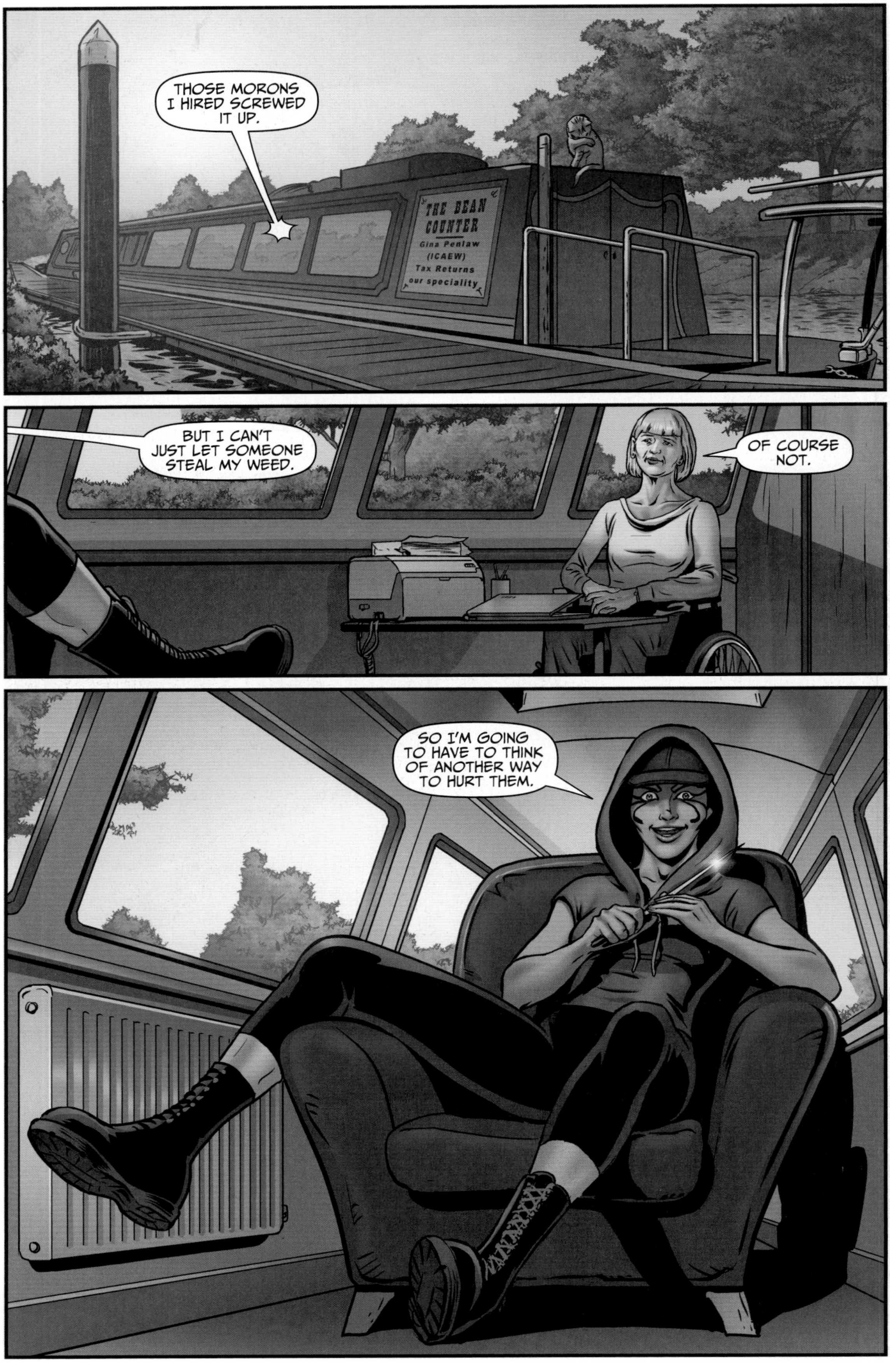
THOSE MORONS I HIRED SCREWED IT UP.
THE BEAN COUNTER
Gina Penlaw (ICAEW)
Tax Returns our speciality
BUT I CAN'T JUST LET SOMEONE STEAL MY WEED.
OF COURSE NOT.
SO I'M GOING TO HAVE TO THINK OF ANOTHER WAY TO HURT THEM.

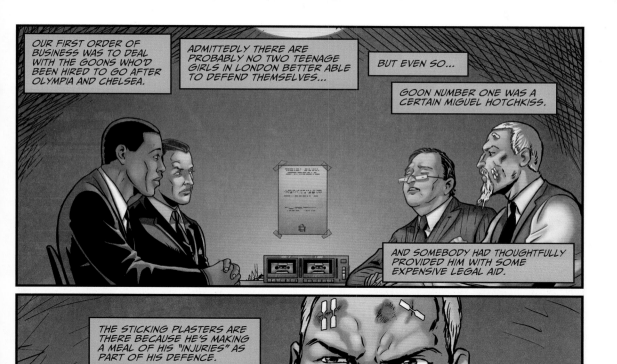

OUR FIRST ORDER OF BUSINESS WAS TO DEAL WITH THE GOONS WHO'D BEEN HIRED TO GO AFTER OLYMPIA AND CHELSEA.

ADMITTEDLY THERE ARE PROBABLY NO TWO TEENAGE GIRLS IN LONDON BETTER ABLE TO DEFEND THEMSELVES...

BUT EVEN SO...

GOON NUMBER ONE WAS A CERTAIN MIGUEL HOTCHKISS.

AND SOMEBODY HAD THOUGHTFULLY PROVIDED HIM WITH SOME EXPENSIVE LEGAL AID.

THE STICKING PLASTERS ARE THERE BECAUSE HE'S MAKING A MEAL OF HIS "INJURIES" AS PART OF HIS DEFENCE.

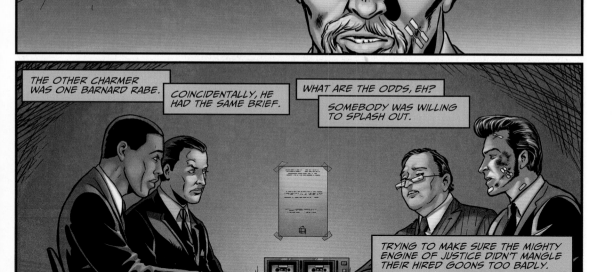

THE OTHER CHARMER WAS ONE BARNARD RABE.

COINCIDENTALLY, HE HAD THE SAME BRIEF.

WHAT ARE THE ODDS, EH?

SOMEBODY WAS WILLING TO SPLASH OUT.

TRYING TO MAKE SURE THE MIGHTY ENGINE OF JUSTICE DIDN'T MANGLE THEIR HIRED GOONS TOO BADLY.

THEIR DEFENCE WAS ESSENTIALLY AS FOLLOWS...

THEY'D TAKEN THE NOTION TO GO OUT FOR A PLEASANT MOONLIGHT STROLL.

THE WAY YOU DO.

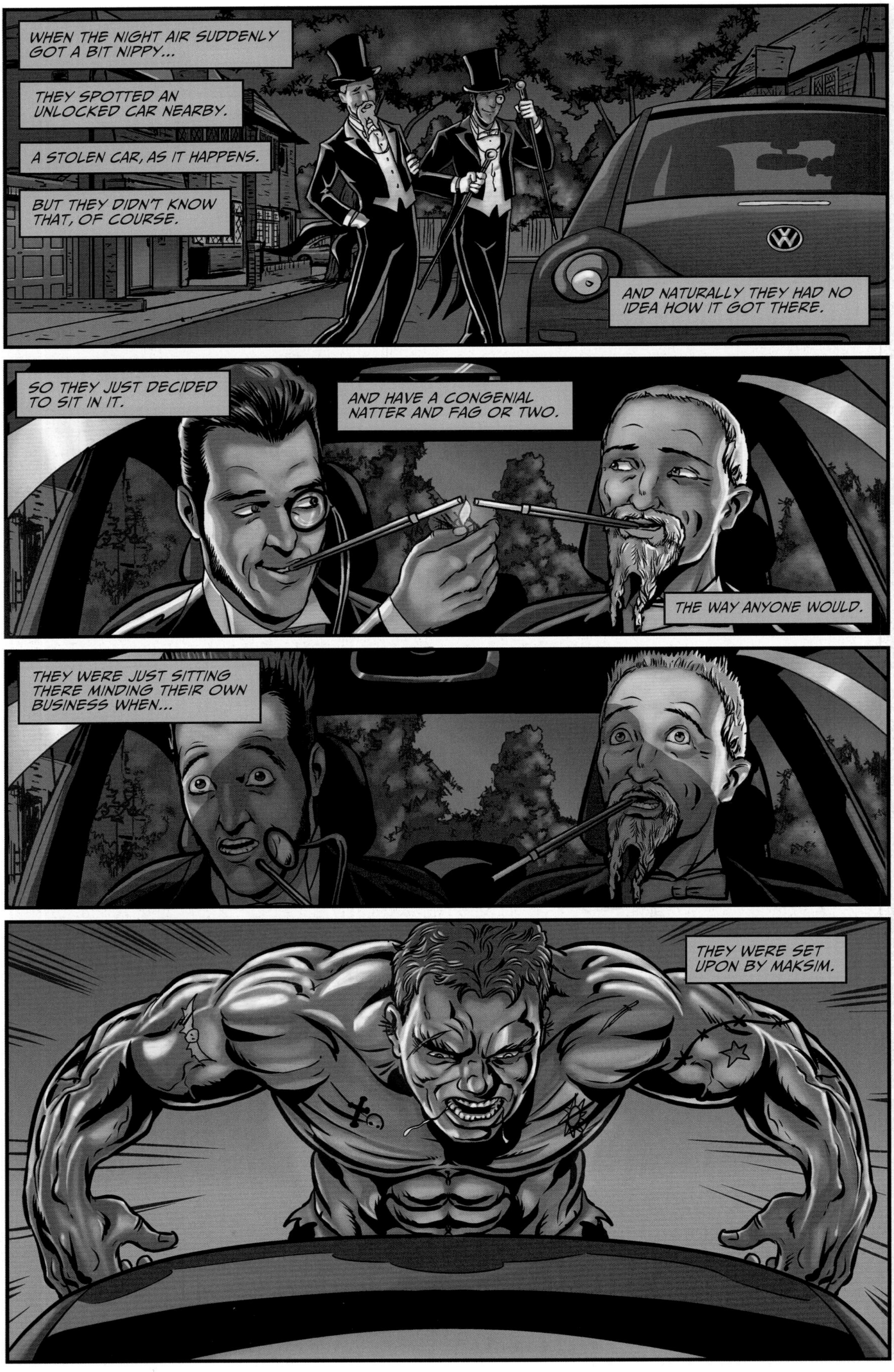
WHEN THE NIGHT AIR SUDDENLY GOT A BIT NIPPY...
THEY SPOTTED AN UNLOCKED CAR NEARBY.
A STOLEN CAR, AS IT HAPPENS.
BUT THEY DIDN'T KNOW THAT, OF COURSE.
AND NATURALLY THEY HAD NO IDEA HOW IT GOT THERE.
SO THEY JUST DECIDED TO SIT IN IT.
AND HAVE A CONGENIAL NATTER AND FAG OR TWO.
THE WAY ANYONE WOULD.
THEY WERE JUST SITTING THERE MINDING THEIR OWN BUSINESS WHEN...
THEY WERE SET UPON BY MAKSIM.

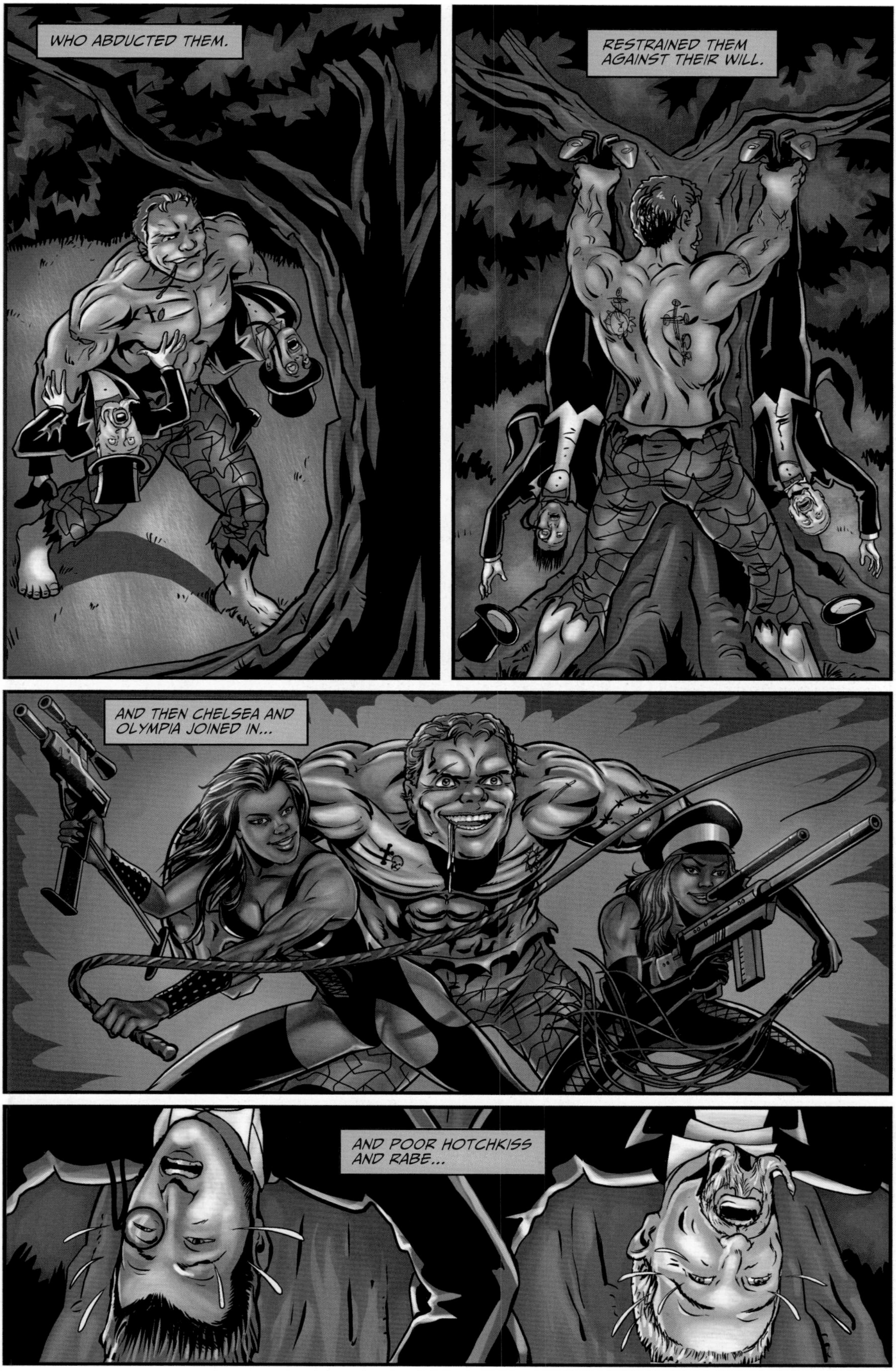
WHO ABDUCTED THEM.
RESTRAINED THEM AGAINST THEIR WILL.
AND THEN CHELSEA AND OLYMPIA JOINED IN...
AND POOR HOTCHKISS AND RABE...

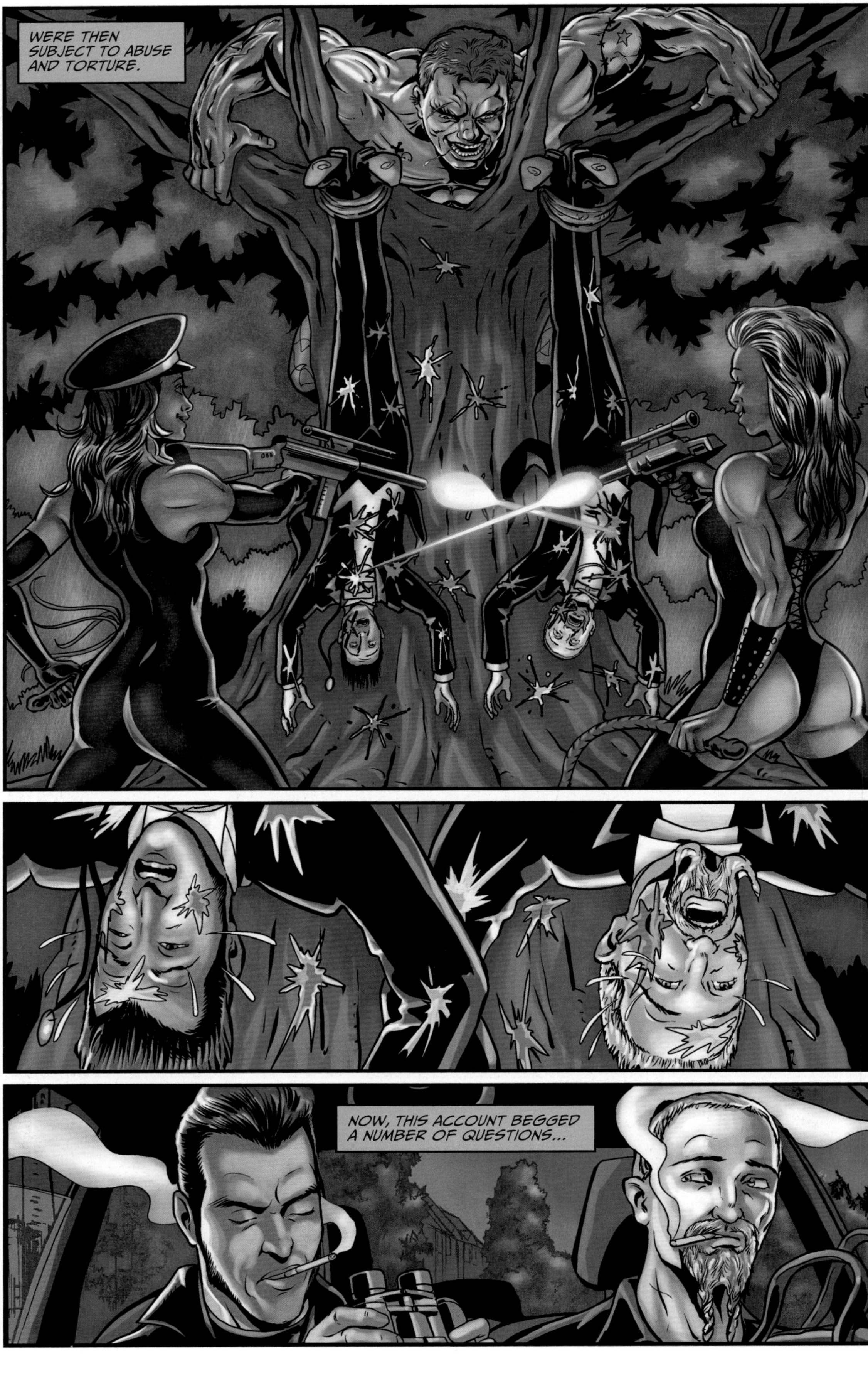
WERE THEN SUBJECT TO ABUSE AND TORTURE.
NOW, THIS ACCOUNT BEGGED A NUMBER OF QUESTIONS...

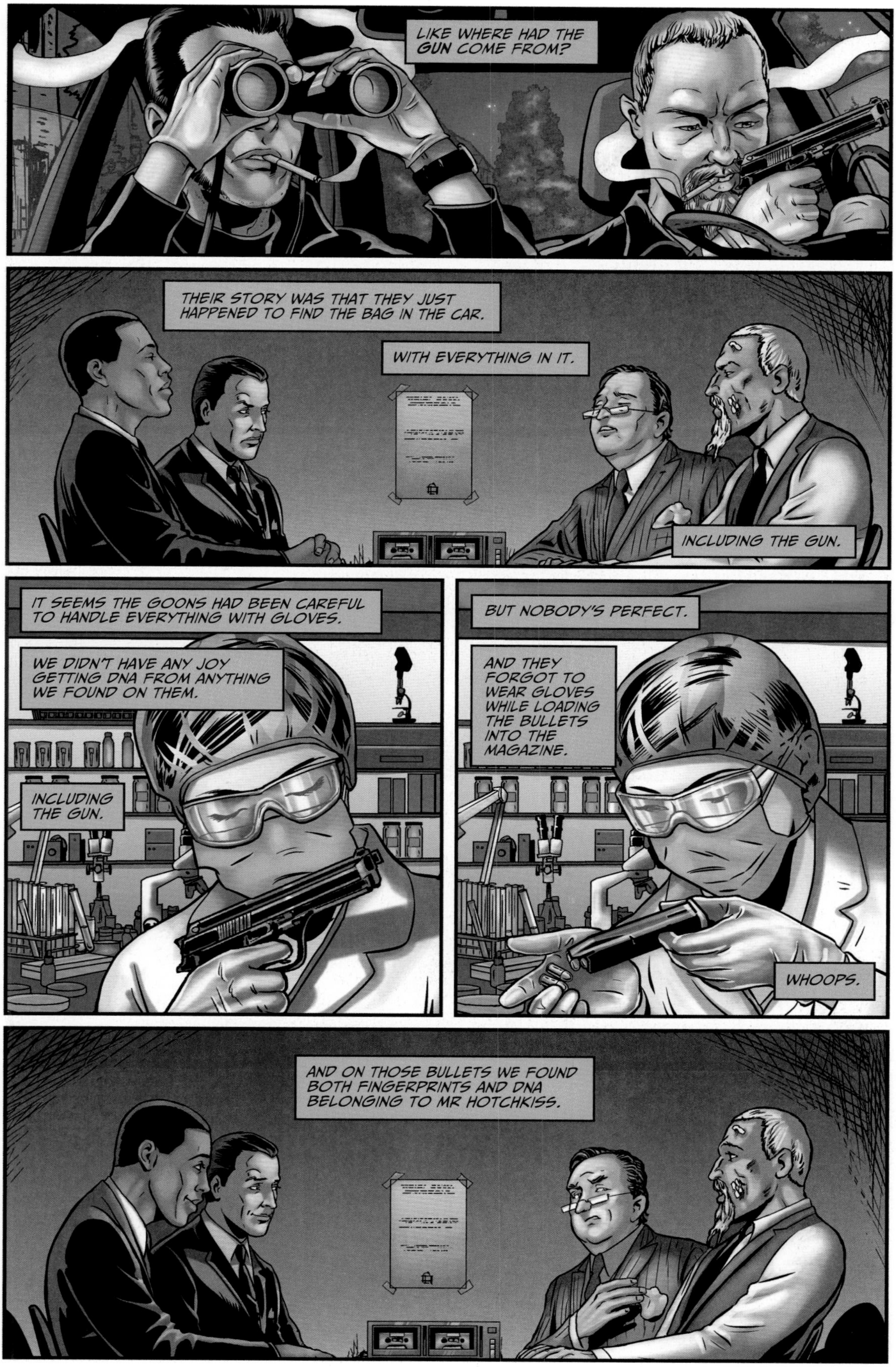
LIKE WHERE HAD THE GUN COME FROM?
THEIR STORY WAS THAT THEY JUST HAPPENED TO FIND THE BAG IN THE CAR.
WITH EVERYTHING IN IT.
INCLUDING THE GUN.
IT SEEMS THE GOONS HAD BEEN CAREFUL TO HANDLE EVERYTHING WITH GLOVES.
WE DIDN'T HAVE ANY JOY GETTING DNA FROM ANYTHING WE FOUND ON THEM.
INCLUDING THE GUN.
BUT NOBODY'S PERFECT.
AND THEY FORGOT TO WEAR GLOVES WHILE LOADING THE BULLETS INTO THE MAGAZINE.
WHOOPS.
AND ON THOSE BULLETS WE FOUND BOTH FINGERPRINTS AND DNA BELONGING TO MR HOTCHKISS.

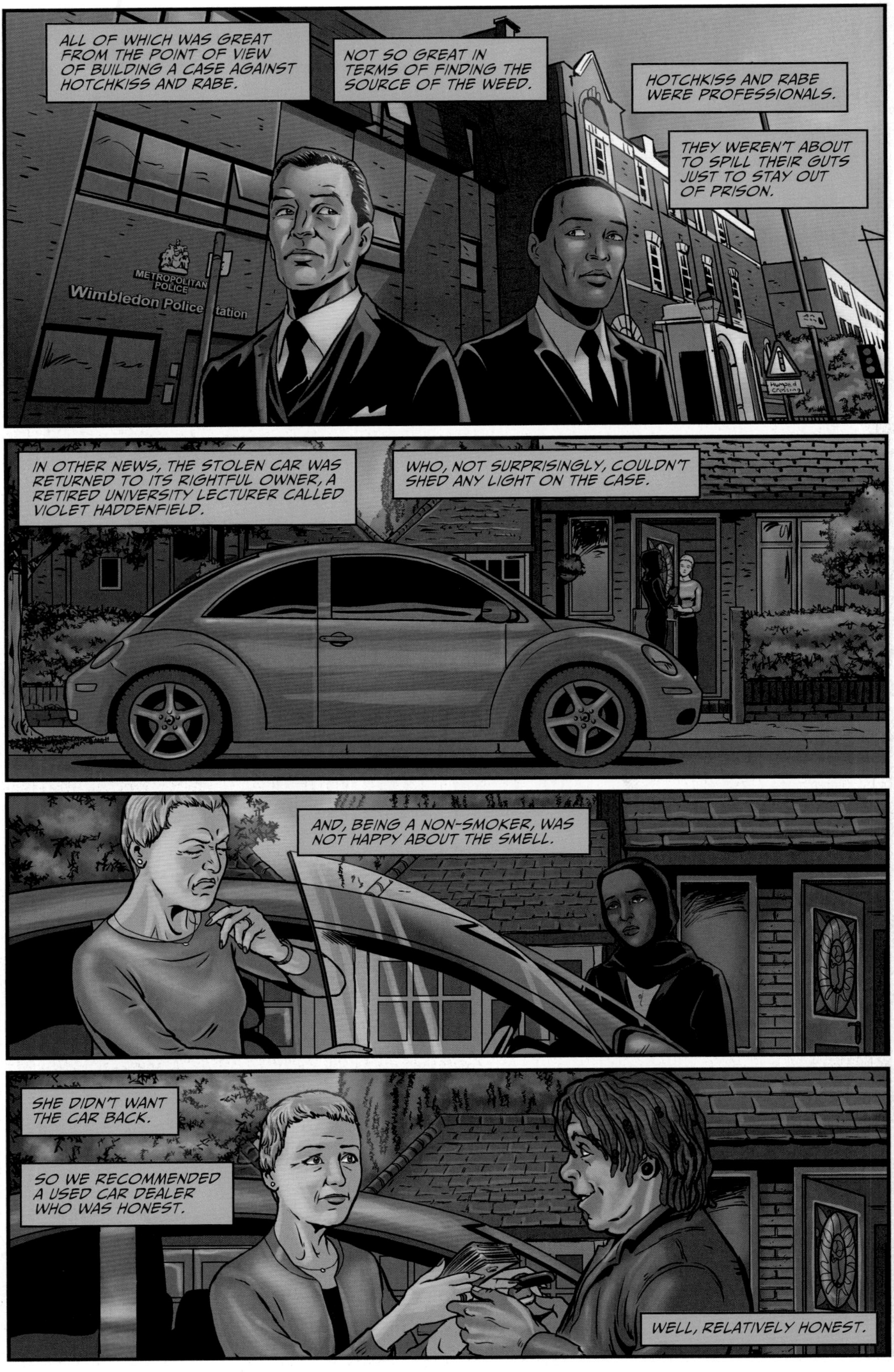
ALL OF WHICH WAS GREAT FROM THE POINT OF VIEW OF BUILDING A CASE AGAINST HOTCHKISS AND RABE.
NOT SO GREAT IN TERMS OF FINDING THE SOURCE OF THE WEED.
HOTCHKISS AND RABE WERE PROFESSIONALS.
THEY WEREN'T ABOUT TO SPILL THEIR GUTS JUST TO STAY OUT OF PRISON.
METROPOLITAN POLICE
Wimbledon Police Station
IN OTHER NEWS, THE STOLEN CAR WAS RETURNED TO ITS RIGHTFUL OWNER, A RETIRED UNIVERSITY LECTURER CALLED VIOLET HADDENFIELD.
WHO, NOT SURPRISINGLY, COULDN'T SHED ANY LIGHT ON THE CASE.
AND, BEING A NON-SMOKER, WAS NOT HAPPY ABOUT THE SMELL.
SHE DIDN'T WANT THE CAR BACK.
SO WE RECOMMENDED A USED CAR DEALER WHO WAS HONEST.
WELL, RELATIVELY HONEST.

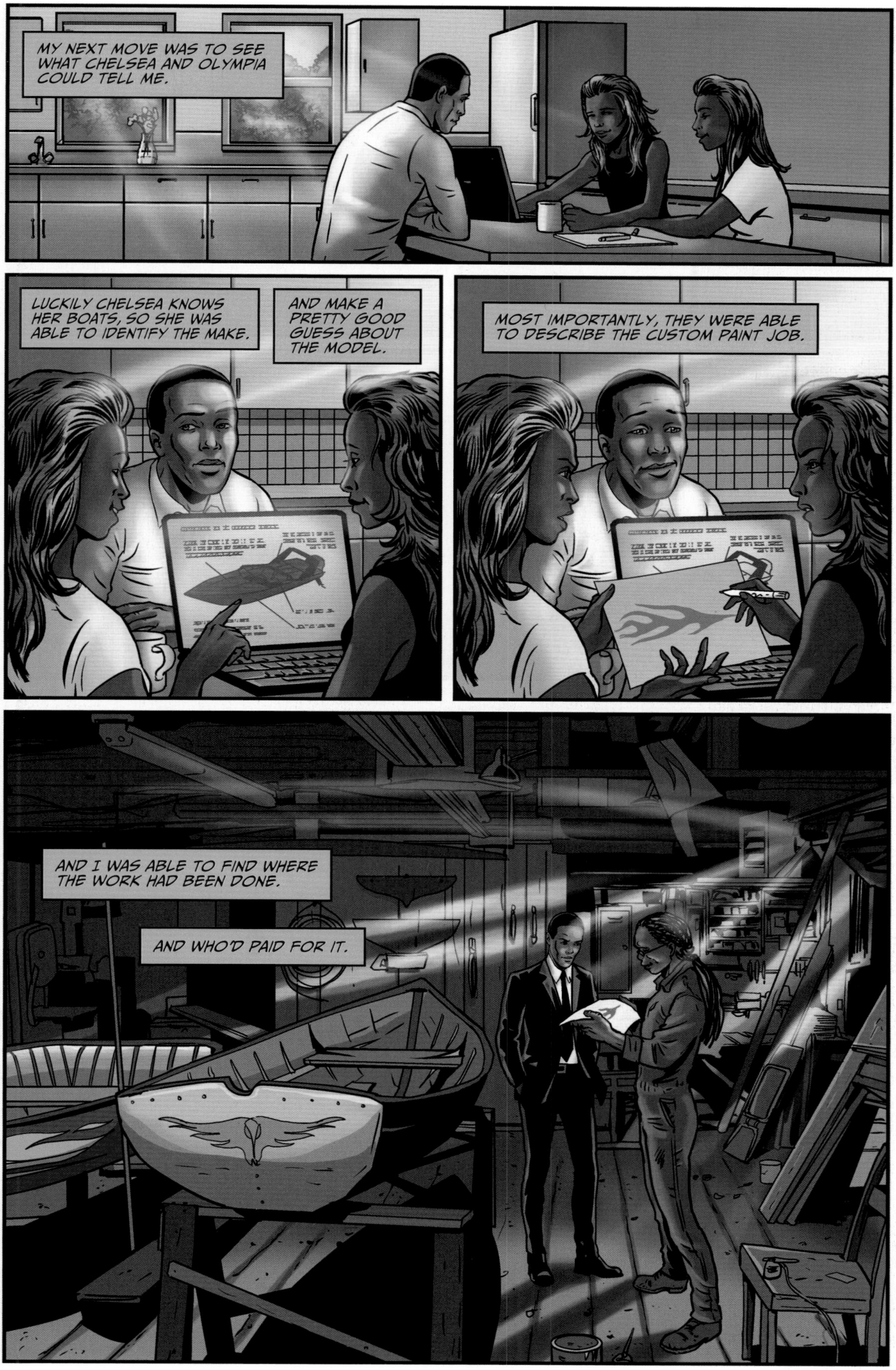
MY NEXT MOVE WAS TO SEE WHAT CHELSEA AND OLYMPIA COULD TELL ME.
LUCKILY CHELSEA KNOWS HER BOATS, SO SHE WAS ABLE TO IDENTIFY THE MAKE.
AND MAKE A PRETTY GOOD GUESS ABOUT THE MODEL.
MOST IMPORTANTLY, THEY WERE ABLE TO DESCRIBE THE CUSTOM PAINT JOB.
AND I WAS ABLE TO FIND WHERE THE WORK HAD BEEN DONE.
AND WHO'D PAID FOR IT.

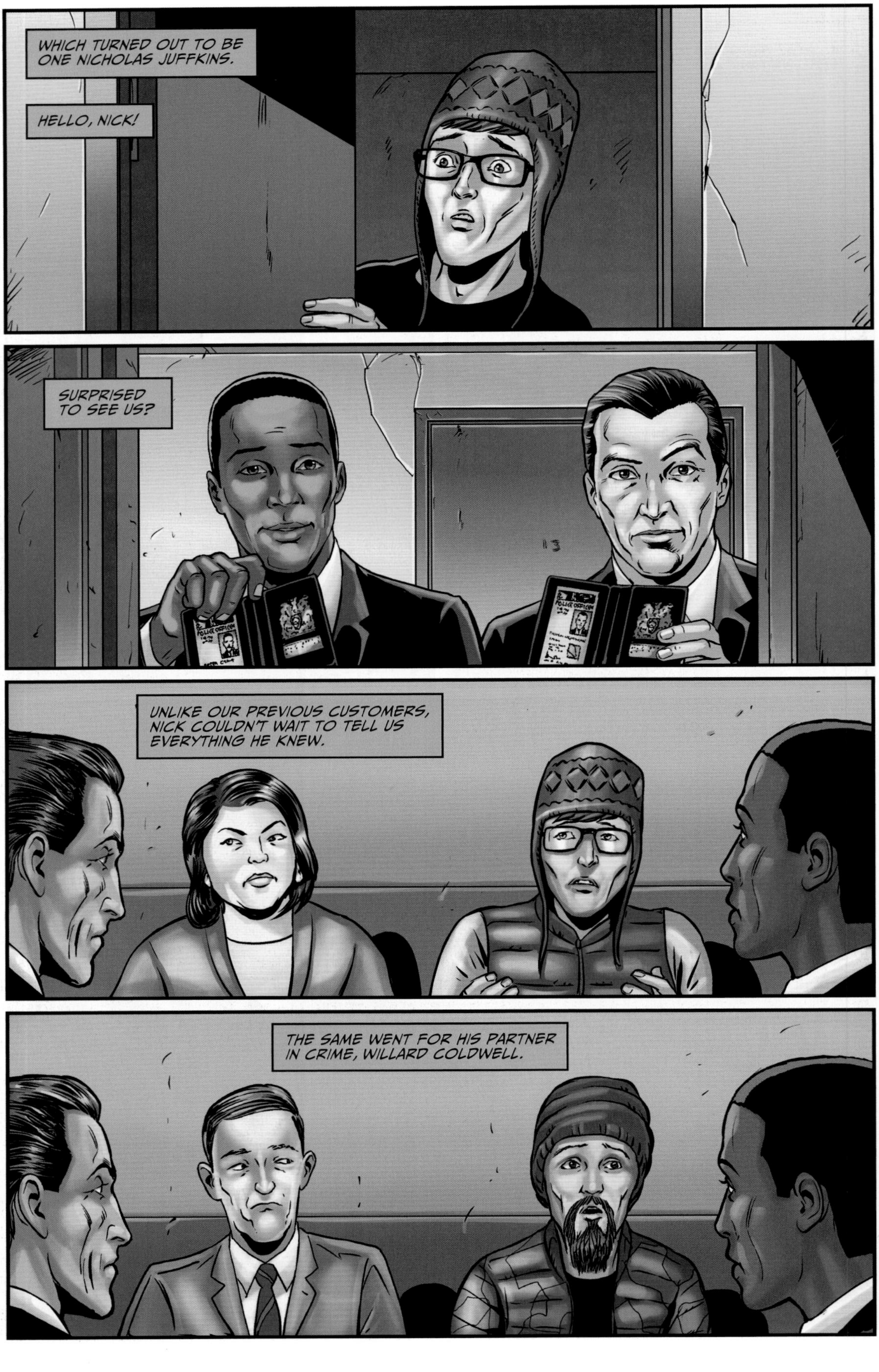
WHICH TURNED OUT TO BE ONE NICHOLAS JUFFKINS.
HELLO, NICK!
SURPRISED TO SEE US?
UNLIKE OUR PREVIOUS CUSTOMERS, NICK COULDN'T WAIT TO TELL US EVERYTHING HE KNEW.
THE SAME WENT FOR HIS PARTNER IN CRIME, WILLARD COLDWELL.

UNFORTUNATELY, EVERYTHING THEY KNEW PROVED TO BE NOT VERY MUCH.

EVERY SO OFTEN NICK WOULD RECEIVE A MOBILE PHONE IN THE POST.

HE WOULD CARRY IT EVERYWHERE WITH HIM UNTIL HE RECEIVED A TEXT.

THE TEXT SPECIFIED A SERIES OF TIMES AND PLACES.

THEN NICK WOULD CALL BILLY.

ALL THE PLACES WERE LOCATIONS ALONG THE RIVER.

Hot Stuff

THE FIRST ONE WAS A PICK UP, WHERE THEY COLLECTED THE WEED.

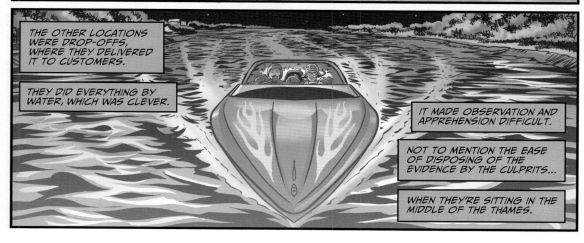

THE OTHER LOCATIONS WERE DROP-OFFS, WHERE THEY DELIVERED IT TO CUSTOMERS.

THEY DID EVERYTHING BY WATER, WHICH WAS CLEVER.

IT MADE OBSERVATION AND APPREHENSION DIFFICULT.

NOT TO MENTION THE EASE OF DISPOSING OF THE EVIDENCE BY THE CULPRITS...

WHEN THEY'RE SITTING IN THE MIDDLE OF THE THAMES.

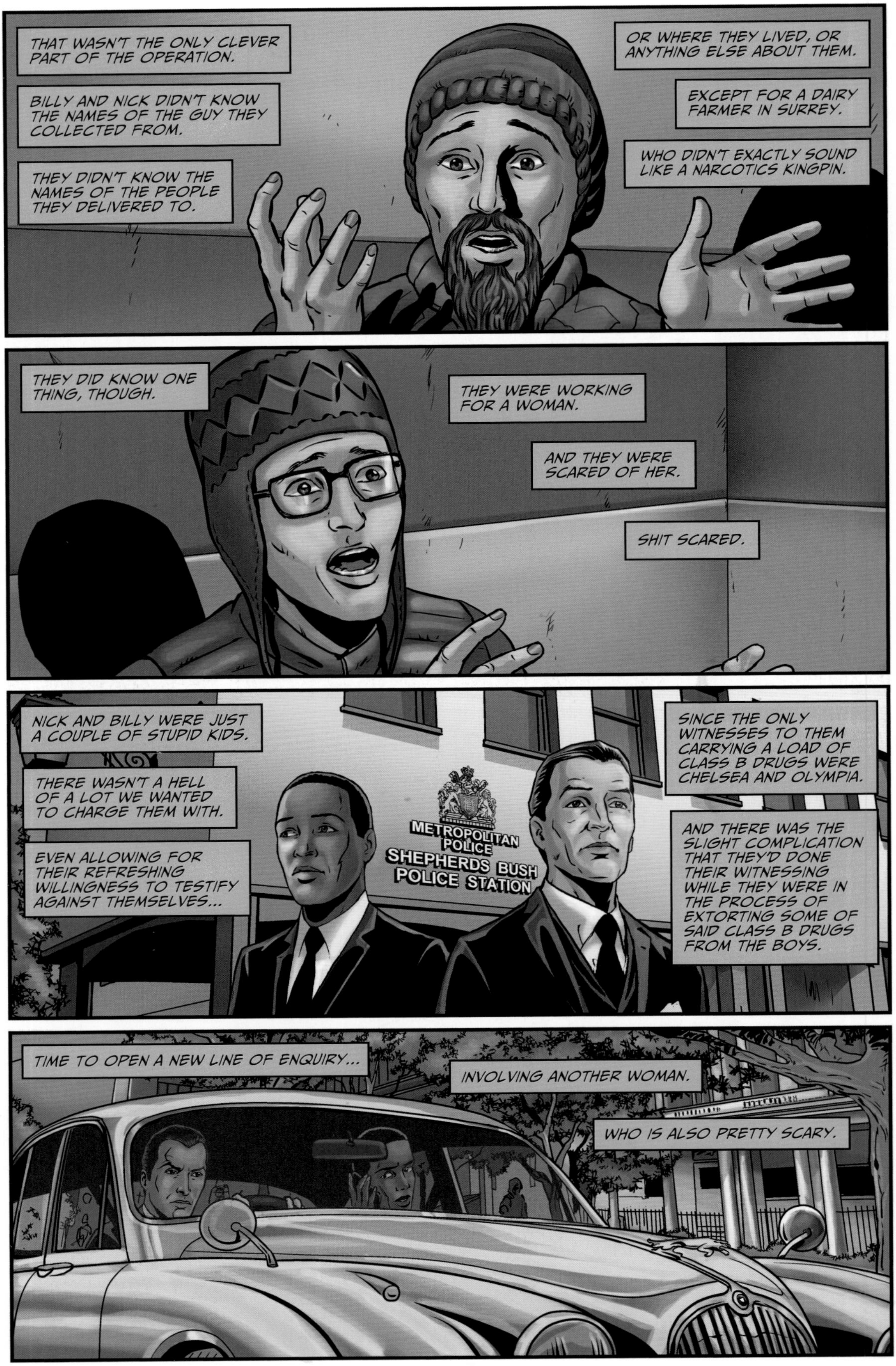
THAT WASN'T THE ONLY CLEVER PART OF THE OPERATION.
BILLY AND NICK DIDN'T KNOW THE NAMES OF THE GUY THEY COLLECTED FROM.
THEY DIDN'T KNOW THE NAMES OF THE PEOPLE THEY DELIVERED TO.
OR WHERE THEY LIVED, OR ANYTHING ELSE ABOUT THEM.
EXCEPT FOR A DAIRY FARMER IN SURREY.
WHO DIDN'T EXACTLY SOUND LIKE A NARCOTICS KINGPIN.
THEY DID KNOW ONE THING, THOUGH.
THEY WERE WORKING FOR A WOMAN.
AND THEY WERE SCARED OF HER.
SHIT SCARED.
NICK AND BILLY WERE JUST A COUPLE OF STUPID KIDS.
THERE WASN'T A HELL OF A LOT WE WANTED TO CHARGE THEM WITH.
EVEN ALLOWING FOR THEIR REFRESHING WILLINGNESS TO TESTIFY AGAINST THEMSELVES...
METROPOLITAN POLICE
SHEPHERDS BUSH POLICE STATION
SINCE THE ONLY WITNESSES TO THEM CARRYING A LOAD OF CLASS B DRUGS WERE CHELSEA AND OLYMPIA.
AND THERE WAS THE SLIGHT COMPLICATION THAT THEY'D DONE THEIR WITNESSING WHILE THEY WERE IN THE PROCESS OF EXTORTING SOME OF SAID CLASS B DRUGS FROM THE BOYS.
TIME TO OPEN A NEW LINE OF ENQUIRY...
INVOLVING ANOTHER WOMAN.
WHO IS ALSO PRETTY SCARY.

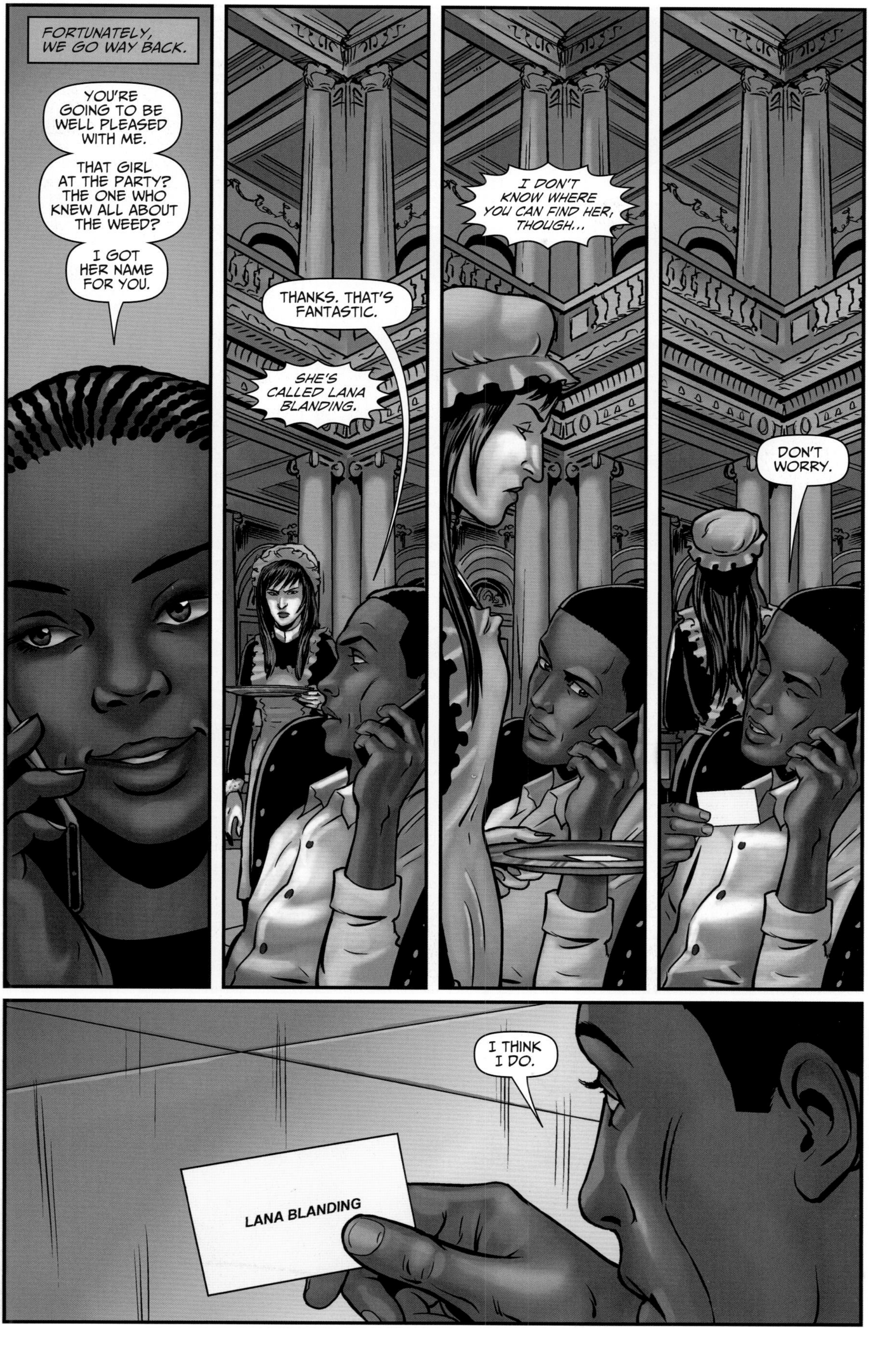
FORTUNATELY, WE GO WAY BACK.
YOU'RE GOING TO BE WELL PLEASED WITH ME.
THAT GIRL AT THE PARTY? THE ONE WHO KNEW ALL ABOUT THE WEED?
I GOT HER NAME FOR YOU.
THANKS. THAT'S FANTASTIC.
SHE'S CALLED LANA BLANDING.
I DON'T KNOW WHERE YOU CAN FIND HER, THOUGH...
DON'T WORRY.
I THINK I DO.
LANA BLANDING

MEET MISS BLANDING.

FULLY PAID UP MEMBER OF THE DEMI MONDE.

AND FRIENDLY NEIGHBOURHOOD GOBLIN GIRL.

THE CARD'S A NICE TOUCH.

YES, IT'S NOT OFTEN WE HAVE CALLERS FORMALLY ANNOUNCING THEMSELVES THESE DAYS.

WELL, I THOUGHT I'D POP BY AND HAVE A CHAT...

BECAUSE I CAN HELP YOU FIND THE PERSON WHO SELLS THAT WERELIGHT WEED.

WERELIGHT?

THAT CERTAINLY IS WELCOME NEWS, ISN'T IT, PETER?

YEAH. MOST WELCOME.

AND I DON'T MEAN ONE OF THE FOOT SOLDIERS.

NOT SOME LITTLE STREET LEVEL DEALER.

I CAN GIVE YOU THE BIG BOSS AT THE TOP OF THE FOOD CHAIN.

EXCELLENT.

THEN WHY DON'T YOU PROCEED TO DO SO?

I SENSED A MAJOR COMPLICATION COMING UP.

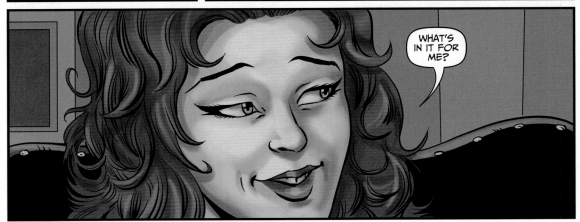

WHAT'S IN IT FOR ME?

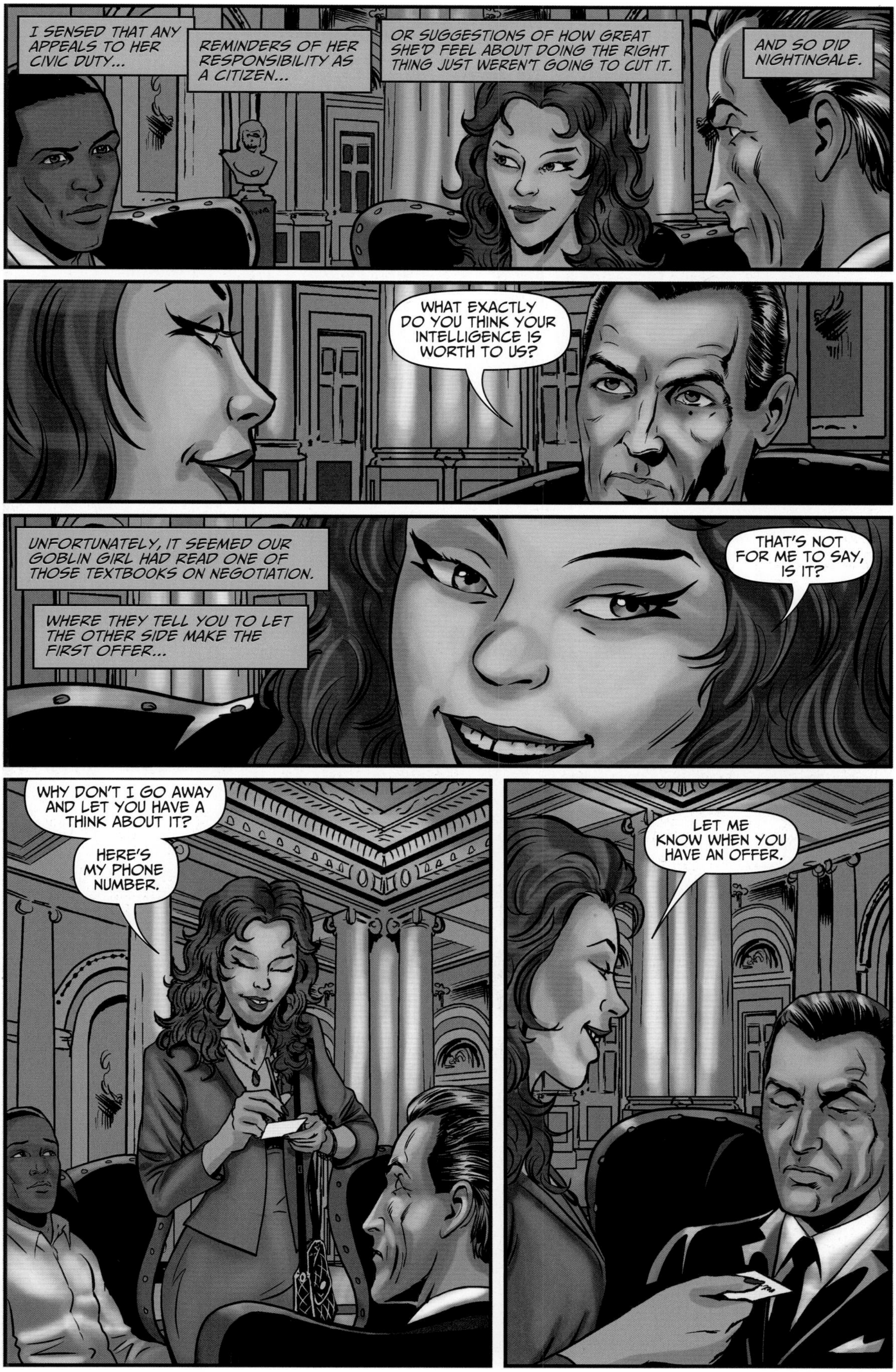
I SENSED THAT ANY APPEALS TO HER CIVIC DUTY...
REMINDERS OF HER RESPONSIBILITY AS A CITIZEN...
OR SUGGESTIONS OF HOW GREAT SHE'D FEEL ABOUT DOING THE RIGHT THING JUST WEREN'T GOING TO CUT IT.
AND SO DID NIGHTINGALE.
WHAT EXACTLY DO YOU THINK YOUR INTELLIGENCE IS WORTH TO US?
UNFORTUNATELY, IT SEEMED OUR GOBLIN GIRL HAD READ ONE OF THOSE TEXTBOOKS ON NEGOTIATION.
WHERE THEY TELL YOU TO LET THE OTHER SIDE MAKE THE FIRST OFFER...
THAT'S NOT FOR ME TO SAY, IS IT?
WHY DON'T I GO AWAY AND LET YOU HAVE A THINK ABOUT IT?
HERE'S MY PHONE NUMBER.
LET ME KNOW WHEN YOU HAVE AN OFFER.

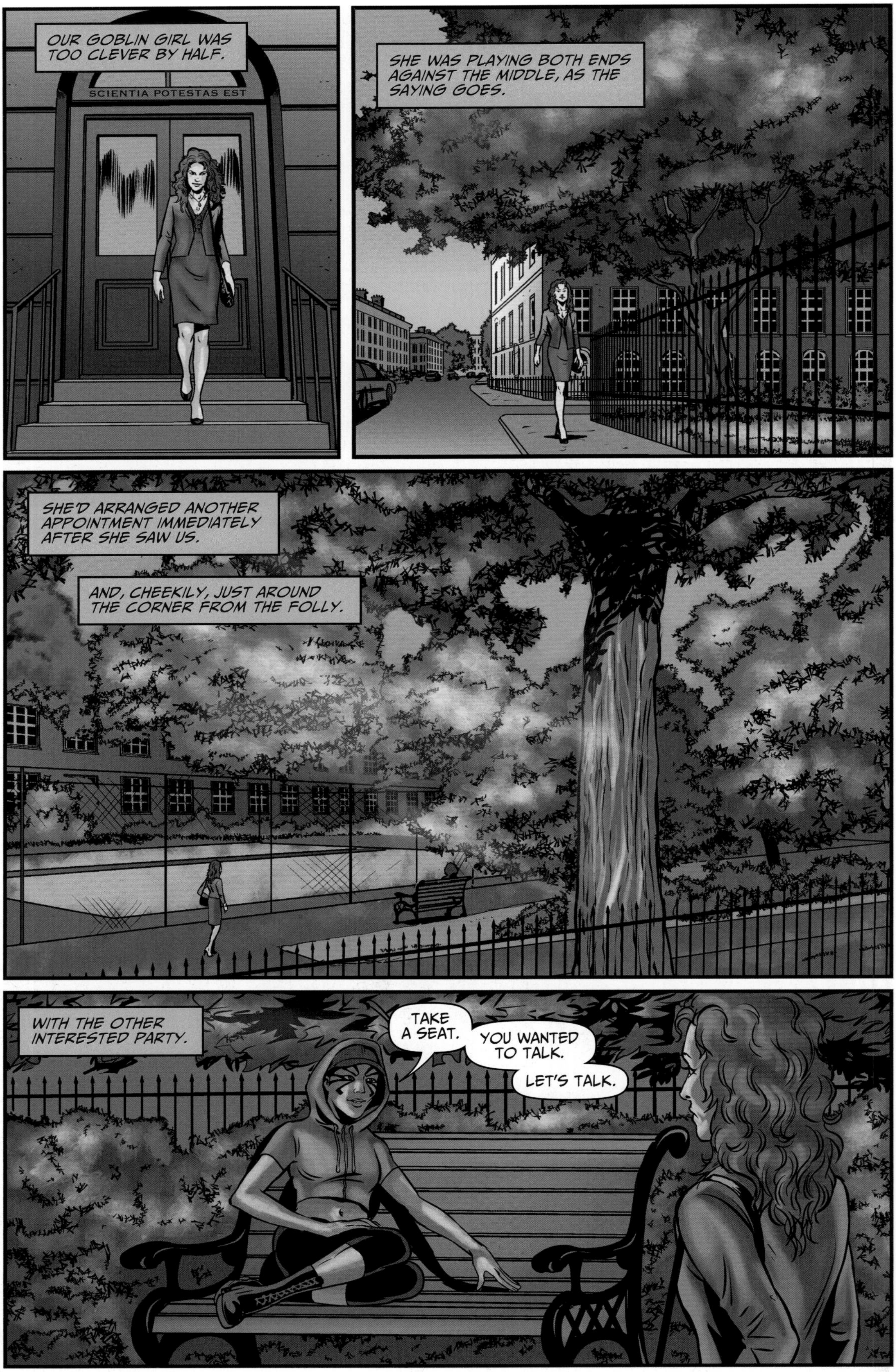
OUR GOBLIN GIRL WAS TOO CLEVER BY HALF.
SCIENTIA POTESTAS EST
SHE WAS PLAYING BOTH ENDS AGAINST THE MIDDLE, AS THE SAYING GOES.
SHE'D ARRANGED ANOTHER APPOINTMENT IMMEDIATELY AFTER SHE SAW US.
AND, CHEEKILY, JUST AROUND THE CORNER FROM THE FOLLY.
WITH THE OTHER INTERESTED PARTY.
TAKE A SEAT.
YOU WANTED TO TALK.
LET'S TALK.

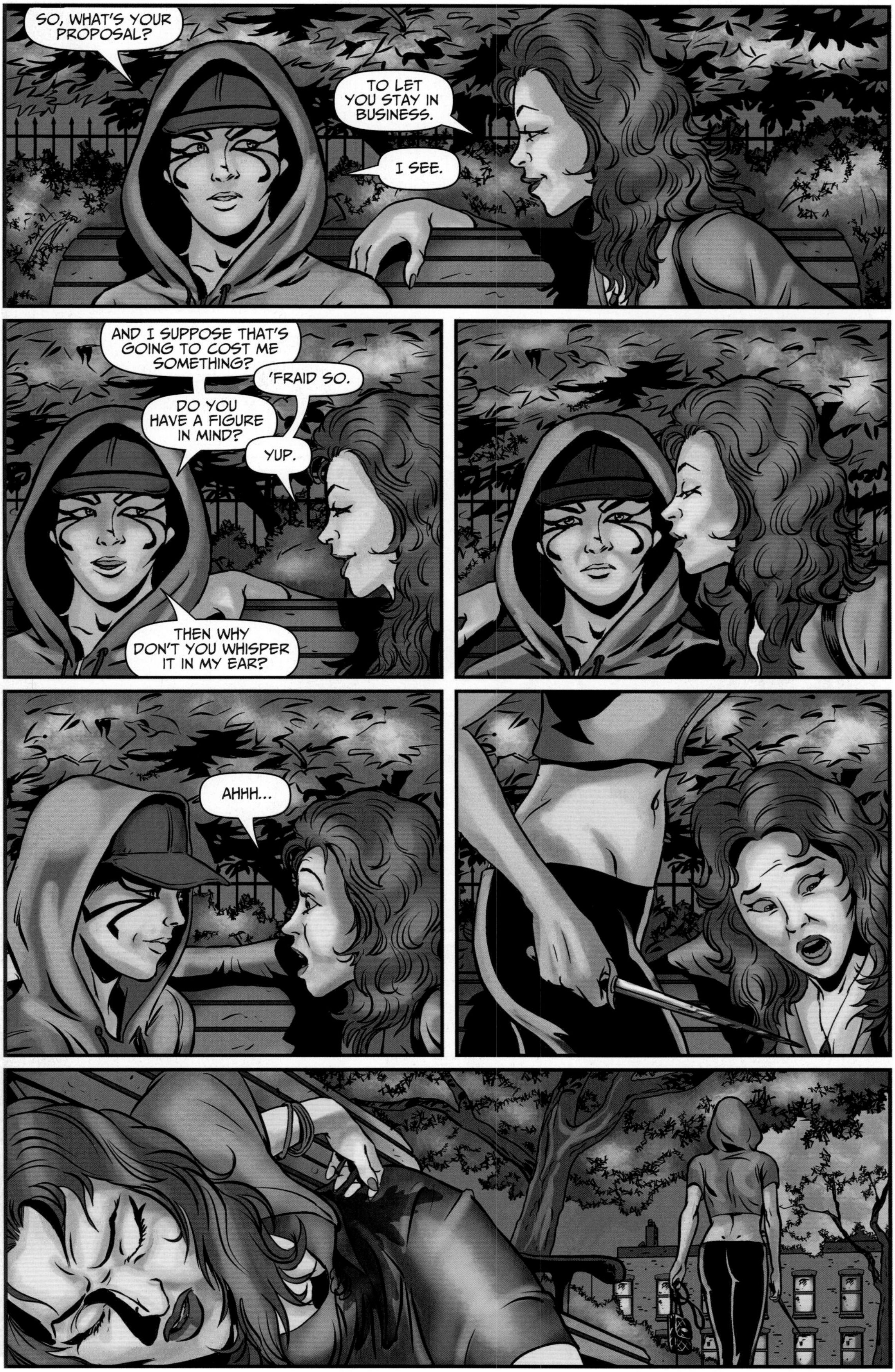
SO, WHAT'S YOUR PROPOSAL?
TO LET YOU STAY IN BUSINESS.
I SEE.
AND I SUPPOSE THAT'S GOING TO COST ME SOMETHING?
'FRAID SO.
DO YOU HAVE A FIGURE IN MIND?
YUP.
THEN WHY DON'T YOU WHISPER IT IN MY EAR?
AHHH...

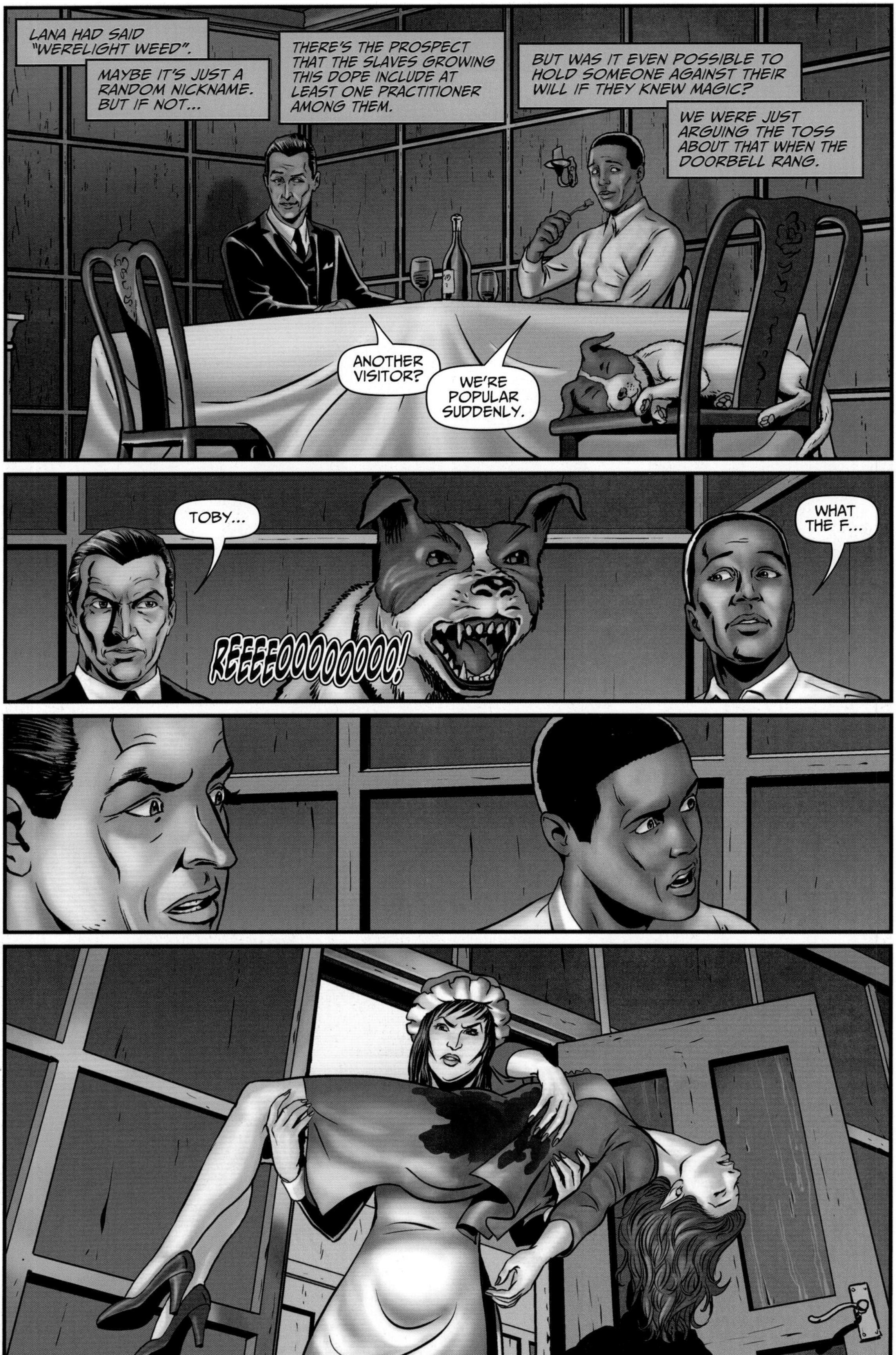
LANA HAD SAID "WERELIGHT WEED".
MAYBE IT'S JUST A RANDOM NICKNAME. BUT IF NOT...
THERE'S THE PROSPECT THAT THE SLAVES GROWING THIS DOPE INCLUDE AT LEAST ONE PRACTITIONER AMONG THEM.
BUT WAS IT EVEN POSSIBLE TO HOLD SOMEONE AGAINST THEIR WILL IF THEY KNEW MAGIC?
WE WERE JUST ARGUING THE TOSS ABOUT THAT WHEN THE DOORBELL RANG.
ANOTHER VISITOR?
WE'RE POPULAR SUDDENLY.
TOBY...
WHAT THE F...
REEEEOOOOOOOO!

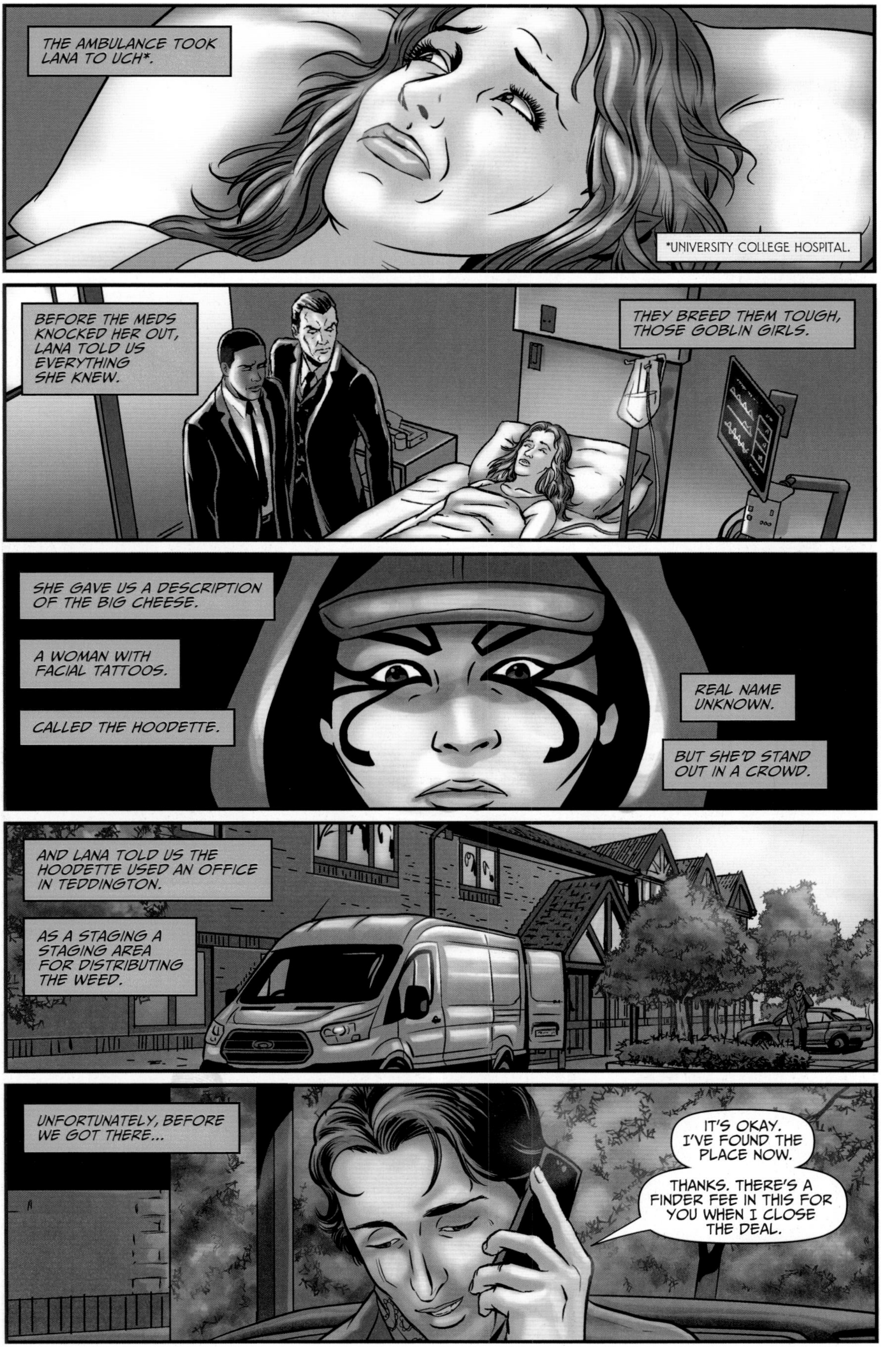
THE AMBULANCE TOOK LANA TO UCH*.
*UNIVERSITY COLLEGE HOSPITAL.
BEFORE THE MEDS KNOCKED HER OUT, LANA TOLD US EVERYTHING SHE KNEW.
THEY BREED THEM TOUGH, THOSE GOBLIN GIRLS.
SHE GAVE US A DESCRIPTION OF THE BIG CHEESE.
A WOMAN WITH FACIAL TATTOOS.
CALLED THE HOODETTE.
REAL NAME UNKNOWN.
BUT SHE'D STAND OUT IN A CROWD.
AND LANA TOLD US THE HOODETTE USED AN OFFICE IN TEDDINGTON.
AS A STAGING A STAGING AREA FOR DISTRIBUTING THE WEED.
UNFORTUNATELY, BEFORE WE GOT THERE...
IT'S OKAY. I'VE FOUND THE PLACE NOW.
THANKS. THERE'S A FINDER FEE IN THIS FOR YOU WHEN I CLOSE THE DEAL.

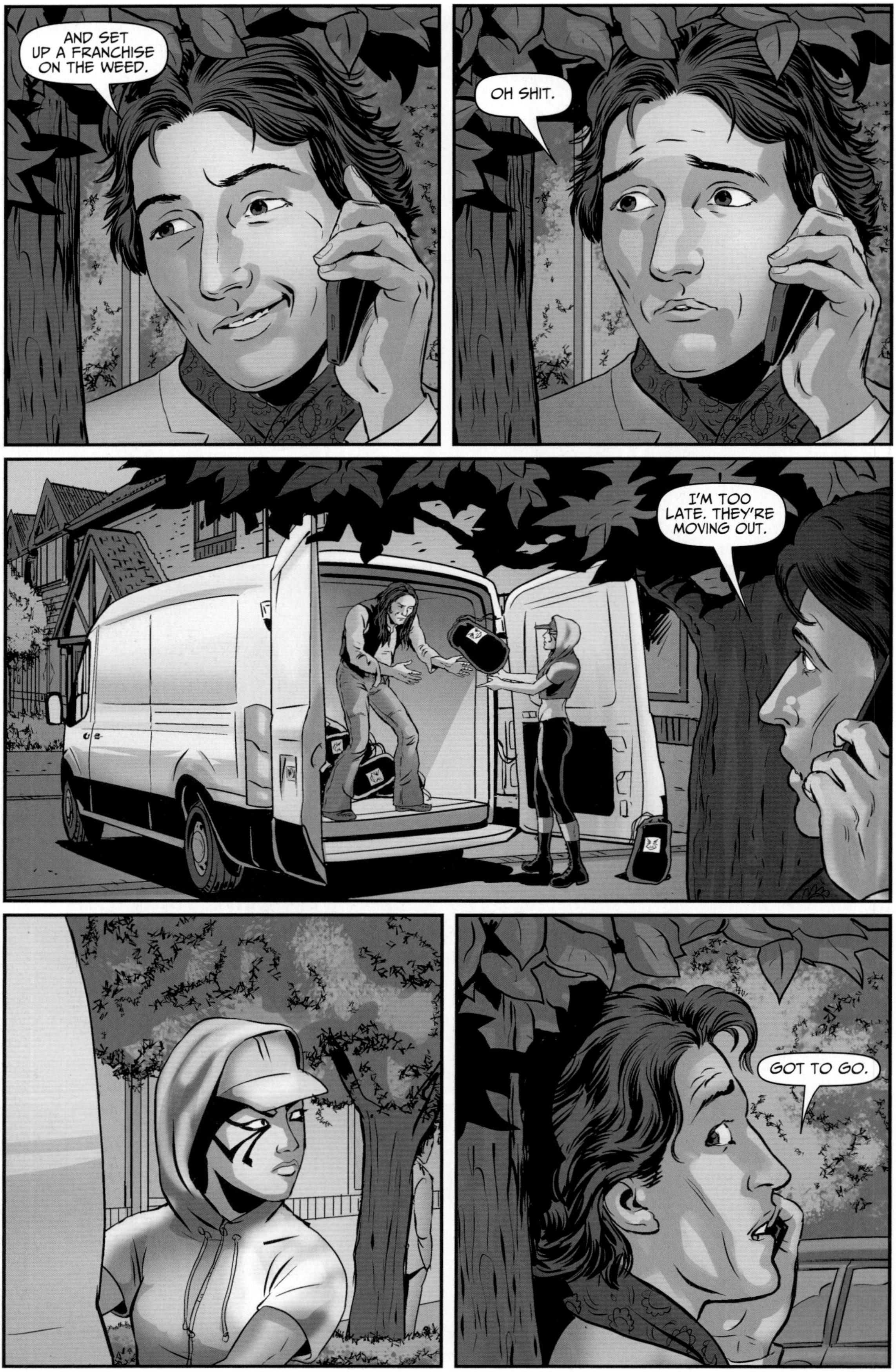
AND SET UP A FRANCHISE ON THE WEED.
OH SHIT.
I'M TOO LATE. THEY'RE MOVING OUT.
GOT TO GO.

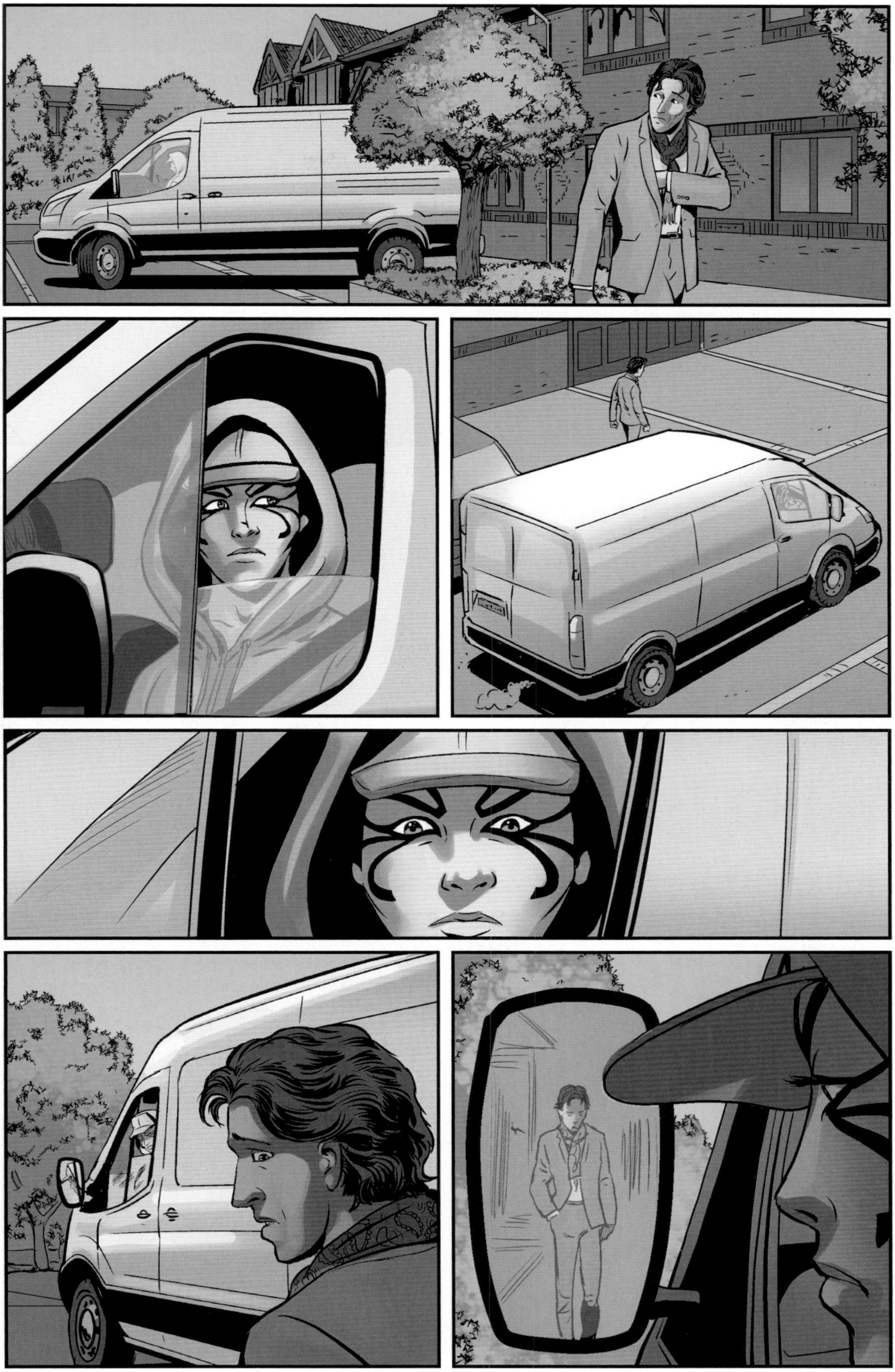

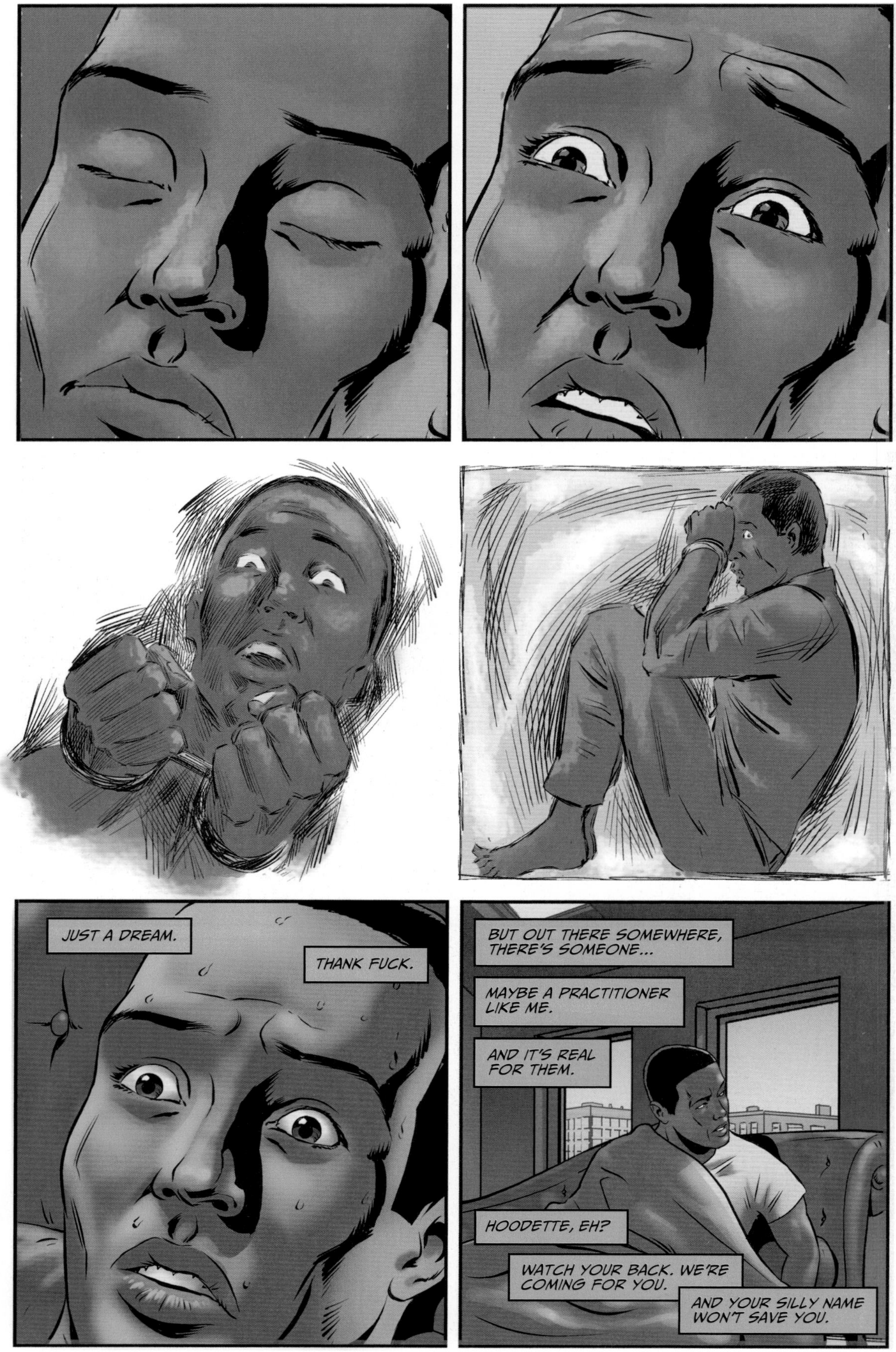
JUST A DREAM.
THANK FUCK.
BUT OUT THERE SOMEWHERE, THERE'S SOMEONE...
MAYBE A PRACTITIONER LIKE ME.
AND IT'S REAL FOR THEM.
HOODETTE, EH?
WATCH YOUR BACK. WE'RE COMING FOR YOU.
AND YOUR SILLY NAME WON'T SAVE YOU.

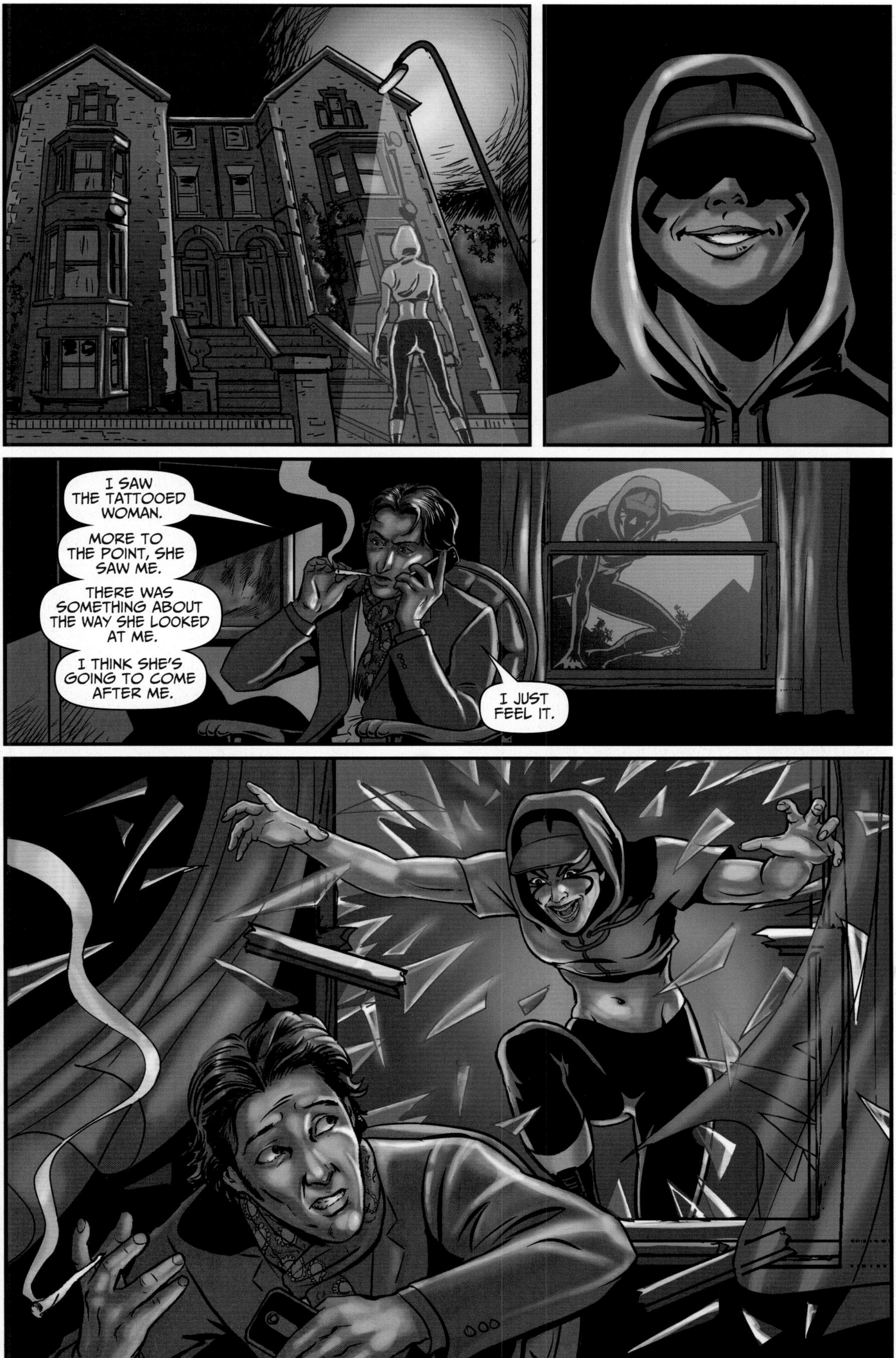
I SAW THE TATTOOED WOMAN.
MORE TO THE POINT, SHE SAW ME.
THERE WAS SOMETHING ABOUT THE WAY SHE LOOKED AT ME.
I THINK SHE'S GOING TO COME AFTER ME.
I JUST FEEL IT.

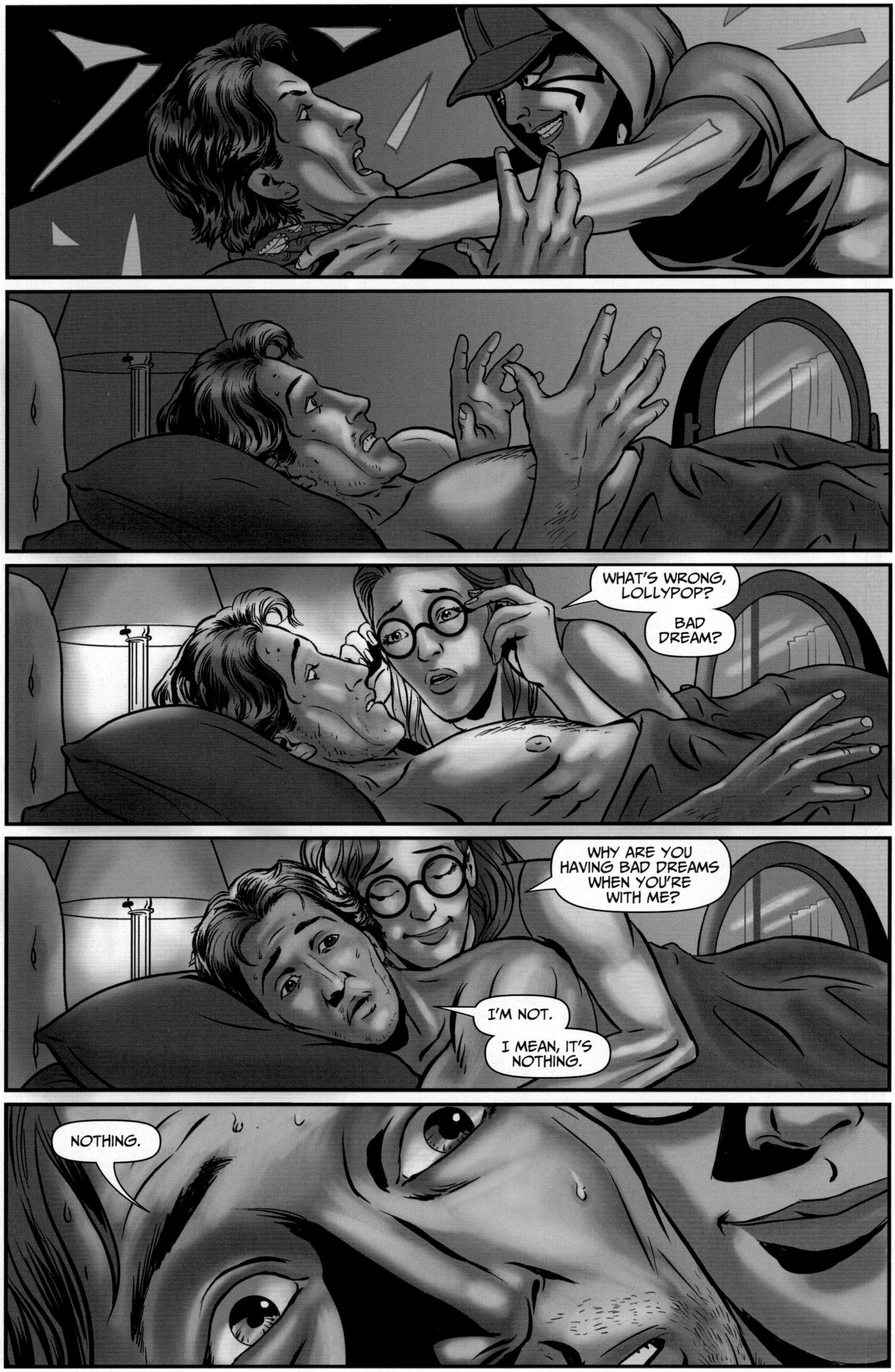
WHAT'S WRONG, LOLLYPOP?
BAD DREAM?
WHY ARE YOU HAVING BAD DREAMS WHEN YOU'RE WITH ME?
I'M NOT.
I MEAN, IT'S NOTHING.
NOTHING.

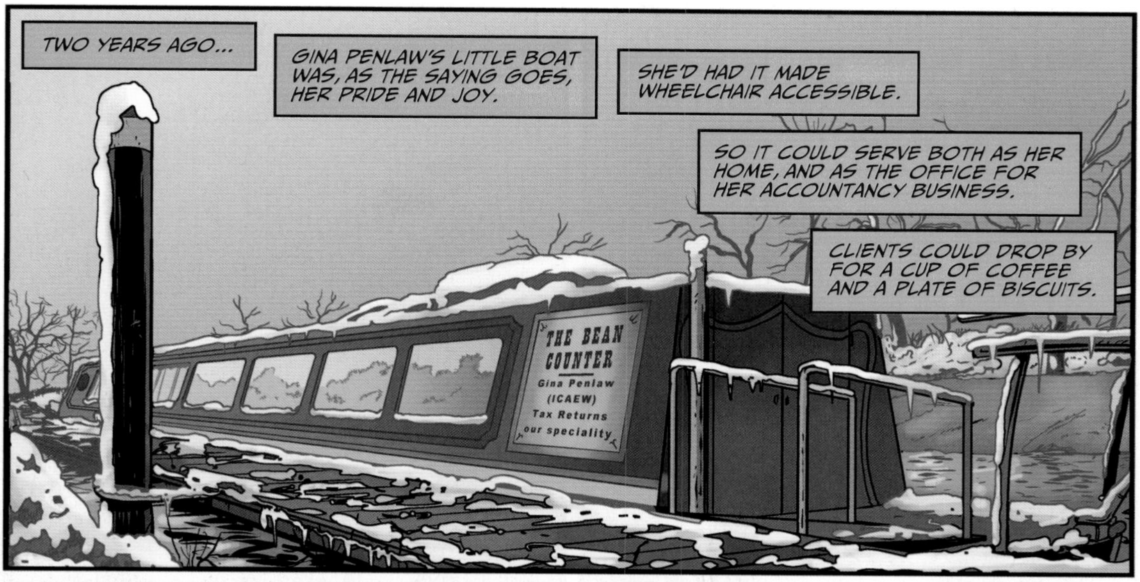
TWO YEARS AGO...
GINA PENLAW'S LITTLE BOAT WAS, AS THE SAYING GOES, HER PRIDE AND JOY.
SHE'D HAD IT MADE WHEELCHAIR ACCESSIBLE.
SO IT COULD SERVE BOTH AS HER HOME, AND AS THE OFFICE FOR HER ACCOUNTANCY BUSINESS.
CLIENTS COULD DROP BY FOR A CUP OF COFFEE AND A PLATE OF BISCUITS.
THE BEAN COUNTER
Gina Penlaw
(ICAEW)
Tax Returns
our speciality

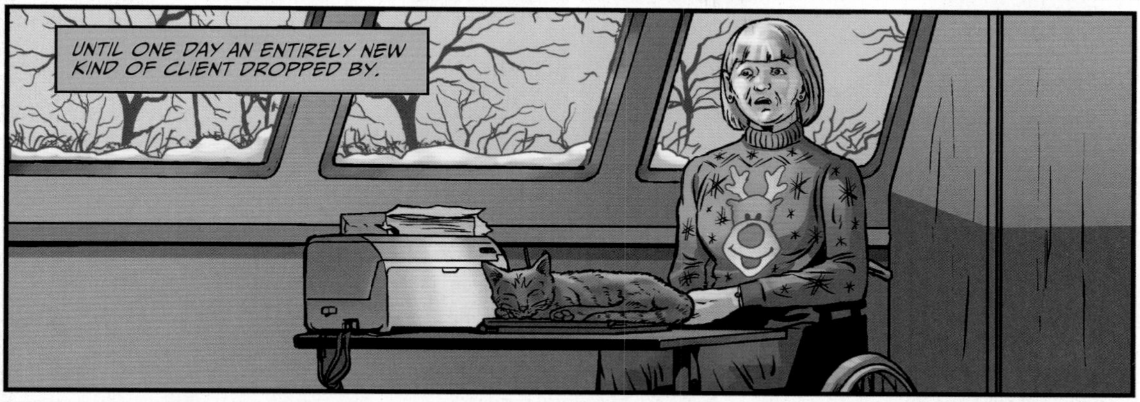
UNTIL ONE DAY AN ENTIRELY NEW KIND OF CLIENT DROPPED BY.

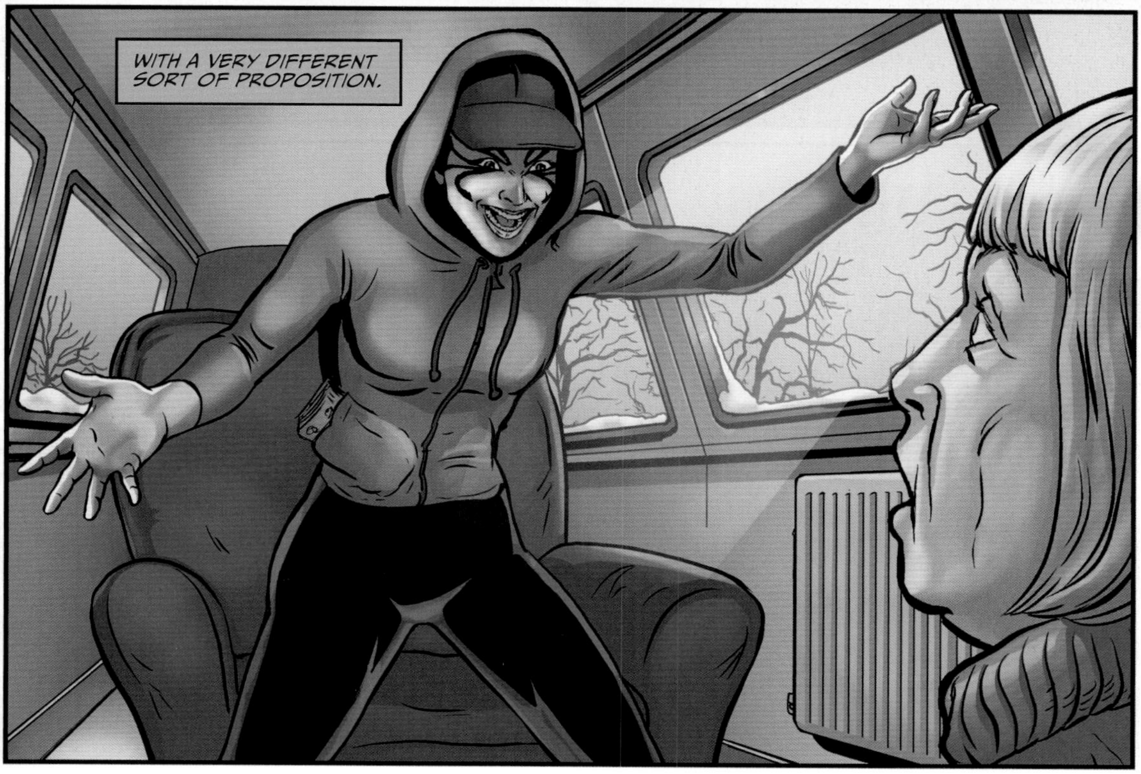
WITH A VERY DIFFERENT SORT OF PROPOSITION.

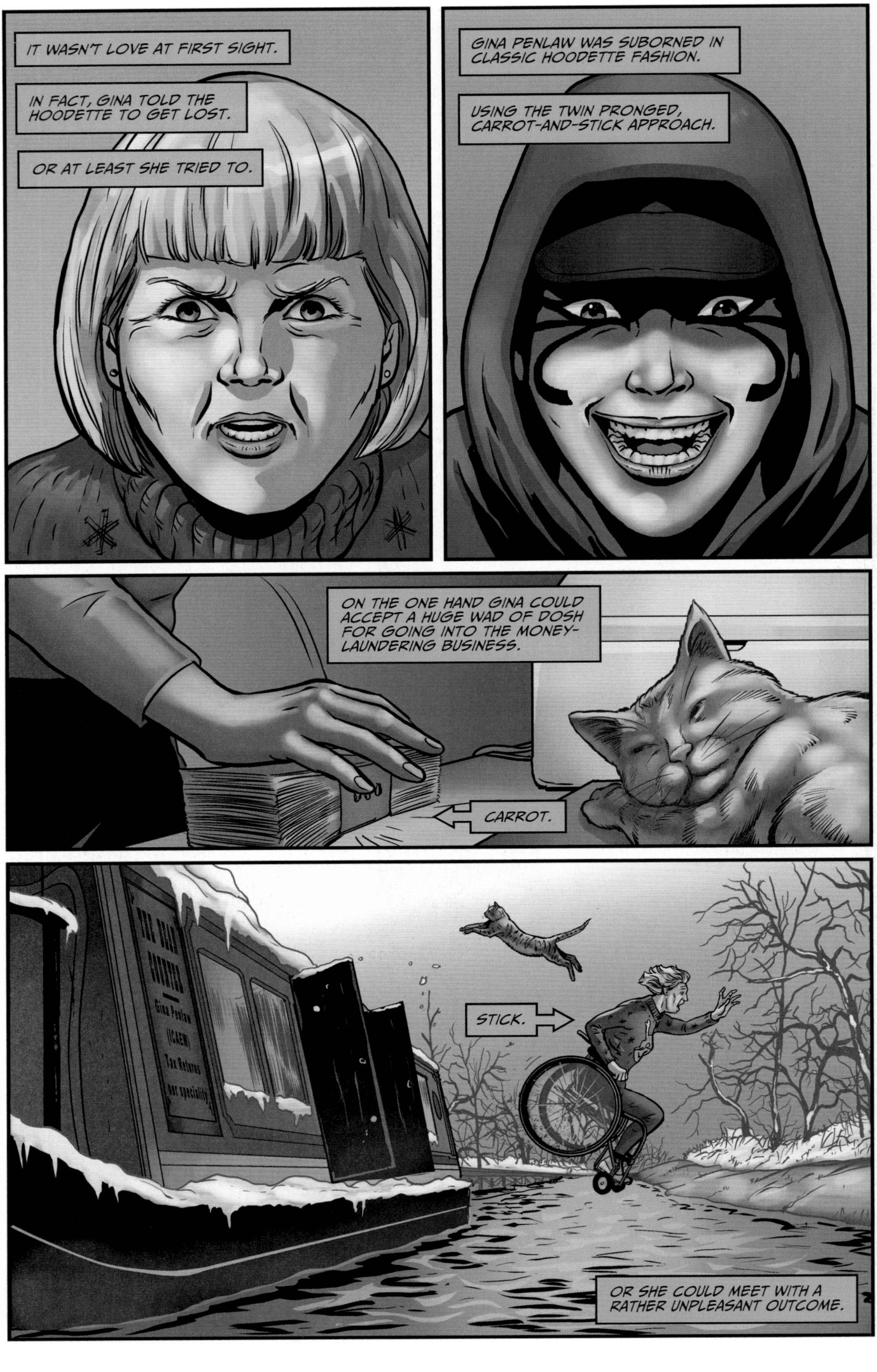
IT WASN'T LOVE AT FIRST SIGHT.
IN FACT, GINA TOLD THE HOODETTE TO GET LOST.
OR AT LEAST SHE TRIED TO.
GINA PENLAW WAS SUBORNED IN CLASSIC HOODETTE FASHION.
USING THE TWIN PRONGED, CARROT-AND-STICK APPROACH.
ON THE ONE HAND GINA COULD ACCEPT A HUGE WAD OF DOSH FOR GOING INTO THE MONEY-LAUNDERING BUSINESS.
CARROT.
Gina Penlaw
(ICAEW)
Tax Returns
our speciality
STICK.
OR SHE COULD MEET WITH A RATHER UNPLEASANT OUTCOME.

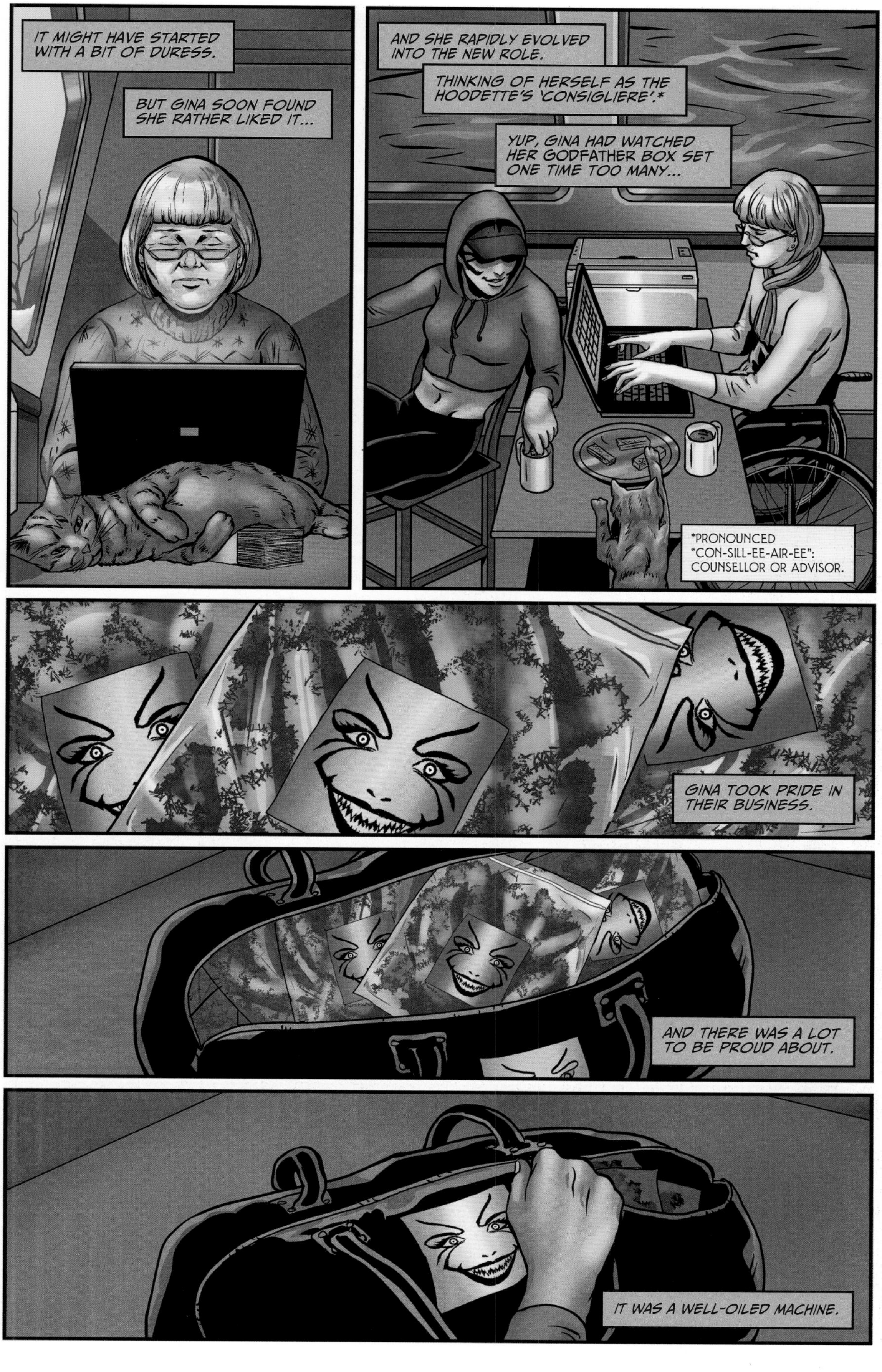

IT MIGHT HAVE STARTED WITH A BIT OF DURESS.
BUT GINA SOON FOUND SHE RATHER LIKED IT...
AND SHE RAPIDLY EVOLVED INTO THE NEW ROLE.
THINKING OF HERSELF AS THE HOODETTE'S 'CONSIGLIERE'.*
YUP, GINA HAD WATCHED HER GODFATHER BOX SET ONE TIME TOO MANY...
*PRONOUNCED "CON-SILL-EE-AIR-EE": COUNSELLOR OR ADVISOR.
GINA TOOK PRIDE IN THEIR BUSINESS.
AND THERE WAS A LOT TO BE PROUD ABOUT.
IT WAS A WELL-OILED MACHINE.

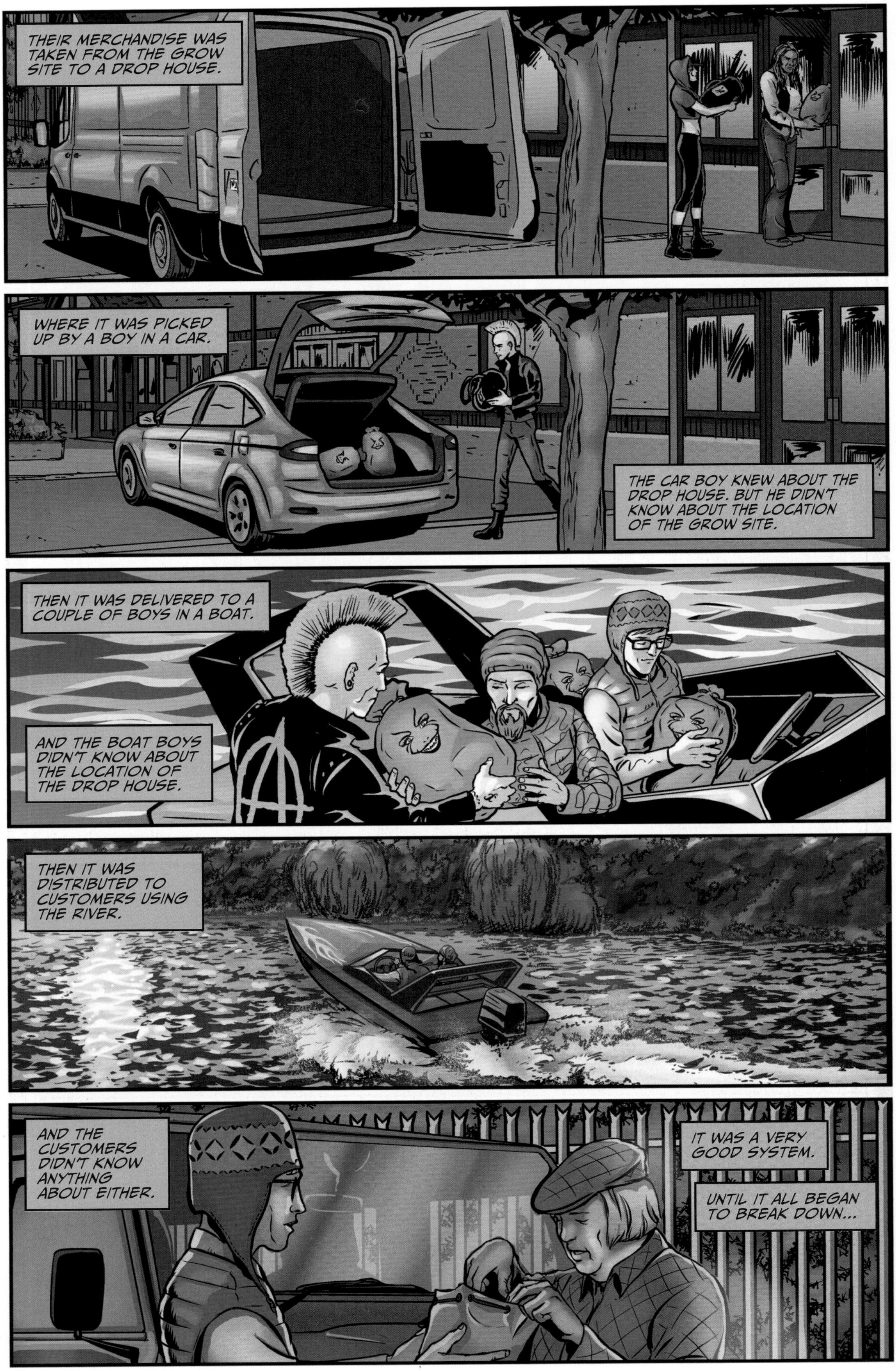
THEIR MERCHANDISE WAS TAKEN FROM THE GROW SITE TO A DROP HOUSE.
WHERE IT WAS PICKED UP BY A BOY IN A CAR.
THE CAR BOY KNEW ABOUT THE DROP HOUSE. BUT HE DIDN'T KNOW ABOUT THE LOCATION OF THE GROW SITE.
THEN IT WAS DELIVERED TO A COUPLE OF BOYS IN A BOAT.
AND THE BOAT BOYS DIDN'T KNOW ABOUT THE LOCATION OF THE DROP HOUSE.
THEN IT WAS DISTRIBUTED TO CUSTOMERS USING THE RIVER.
AND THE CUSTOMERS DIDN'T KNOW ANYTHING ABOUT EITHER.
IT WAS A VERY GOOD SYSTEM.
UNTIL IT ALL BEGAN TO BREAK DOWN...

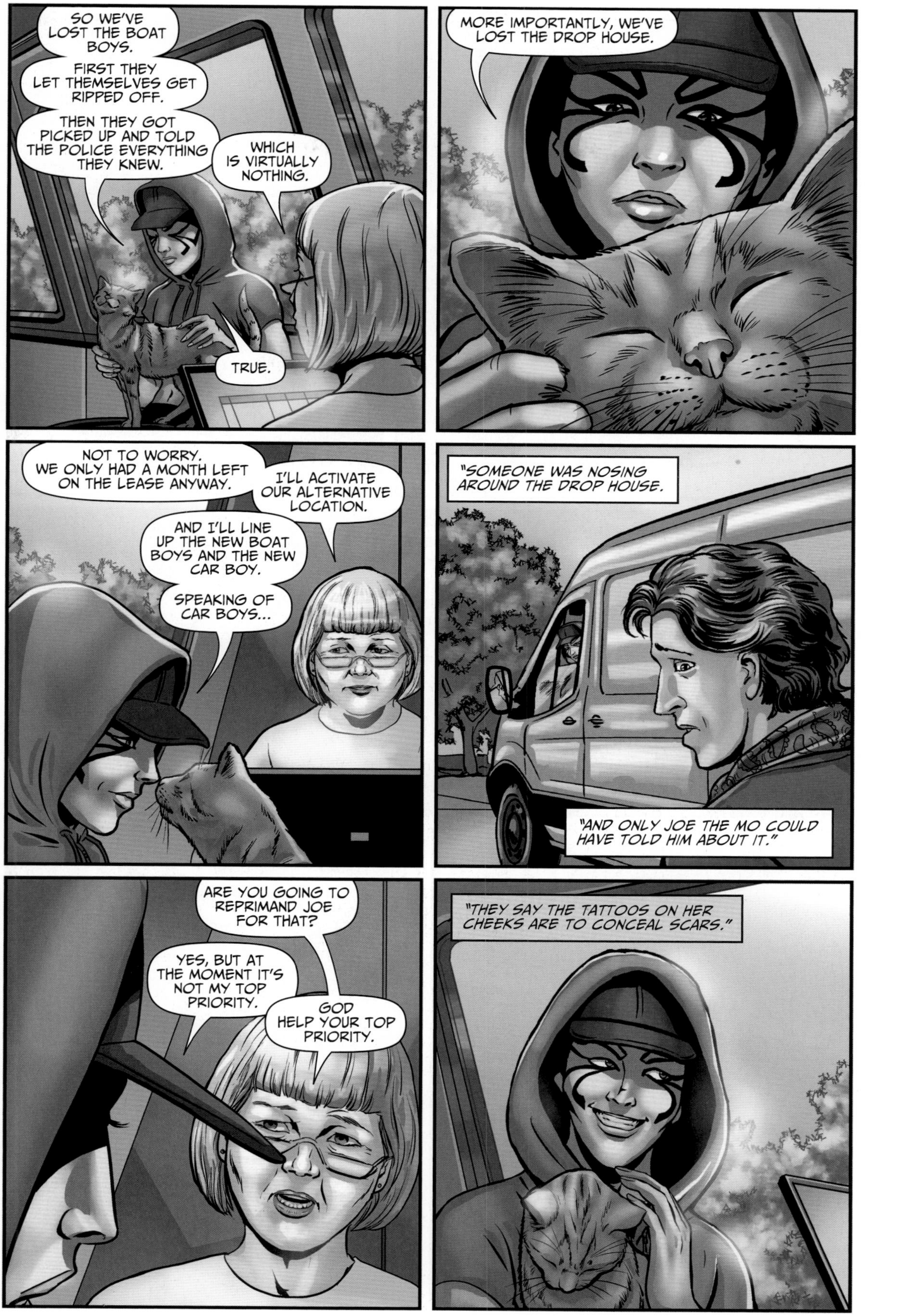
SO WE'VE LOST THE BOAT BOYS.
FIRST THEY LET THEMSELVES GET RIPPED OFF.
THEN THEY GOT PICKED UP AND TOLD THE POLICE EVERYTHING THEY KNEW.
WHICH IS VIRTUALLY NOTHING.
TRUE.
MORE IMPORTANTLY, WE'VE LOST THE DROP HOUSE.
NOT TO WORRY. WE ONLY HAD A MONTH LEFT ON THE LEASE ANYWAY.
I'LL ACTIVATE OUR ALTERNATIVE LOCATION.
AND I'LL LINE UP THE NEW BOAT BOYS AND THE NEW CAR BOY.
SPEAKING OF CAR BOYS...
"SOMEONE WAS NOSING AROUND THE DROP HOUSE.
"AND ONLY JOE THE MO COULD HAVE TOLD HIM ABOUT IT."
ARE YOU GOING TO REPRIMAND JOE FOR THAT?
YES, BUT AT THE MOMENT IT'S NOT MY TOP PRIORITY.
GOD HELP YOUR TOP PRIORITY.
"THEY SAY THE TATTOOS ON HER CHEEKS ARE TO CONCEAL SCARS."

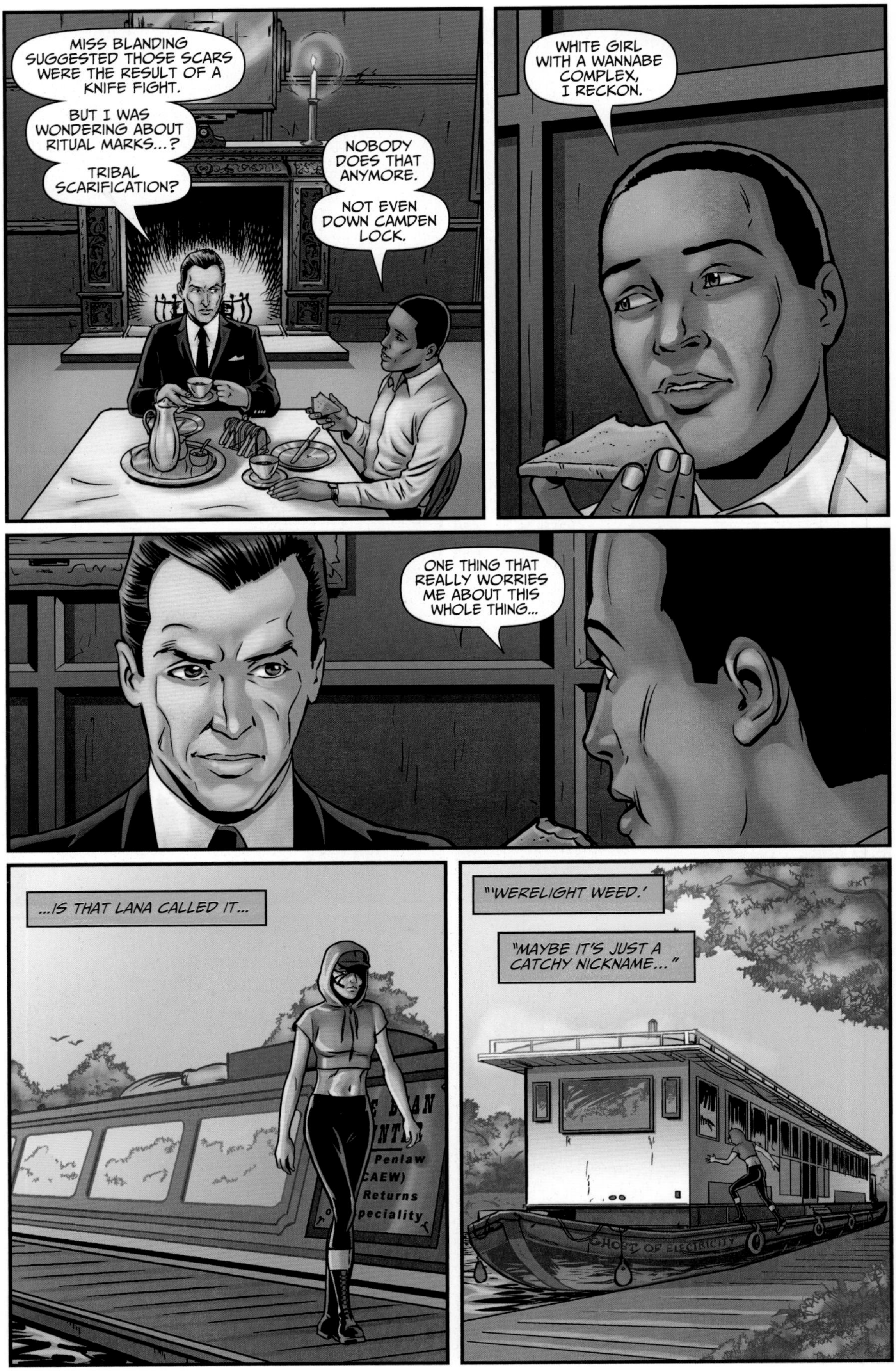
MISS BLANDING SUGGESTED THOSE SCARS WERE THE RESULT OF A KNIFE FIGHT.
BUT I WAS WONDERING ABOUT RITUAL MARKS...?
TRIBAL SCARIFICATION?
NOBODY DOES THAT ANYMORE.
NOT EVEN DOWN CAMDEN LOCK.
WHITE GIRL WITH A WANNABE COMPLEX, I RECKON.
ONE THING THAT REALLY WORRIES ME ABOUT THIS WHOLE THING...
...IS THAT LANA CALLED IT...
"'WERELIGHT WEED.'
"MAYBE IT'S JUST A CATCHY NICKNAME..."

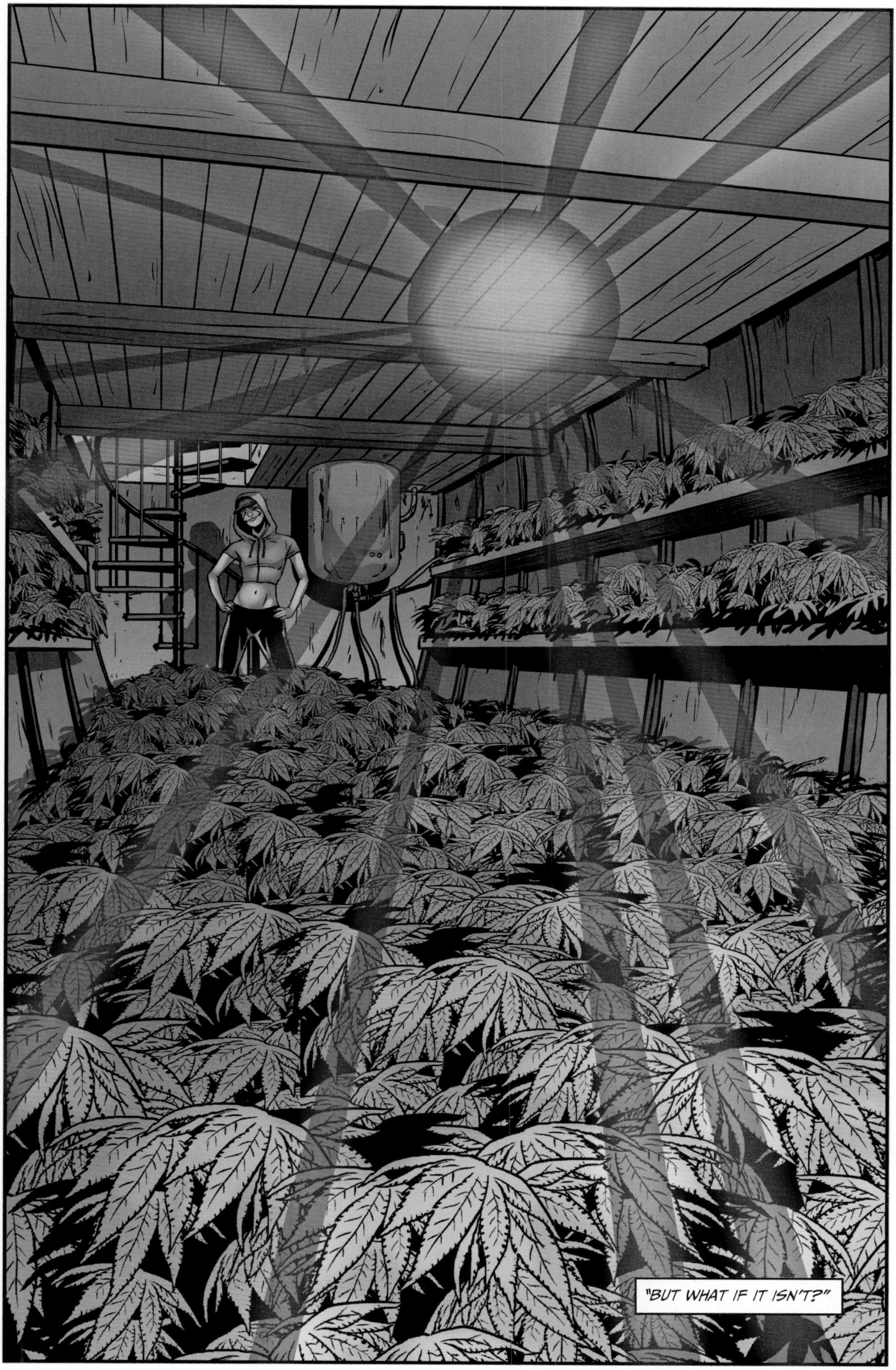
"BUT WHAT IF IT ISN'T?"

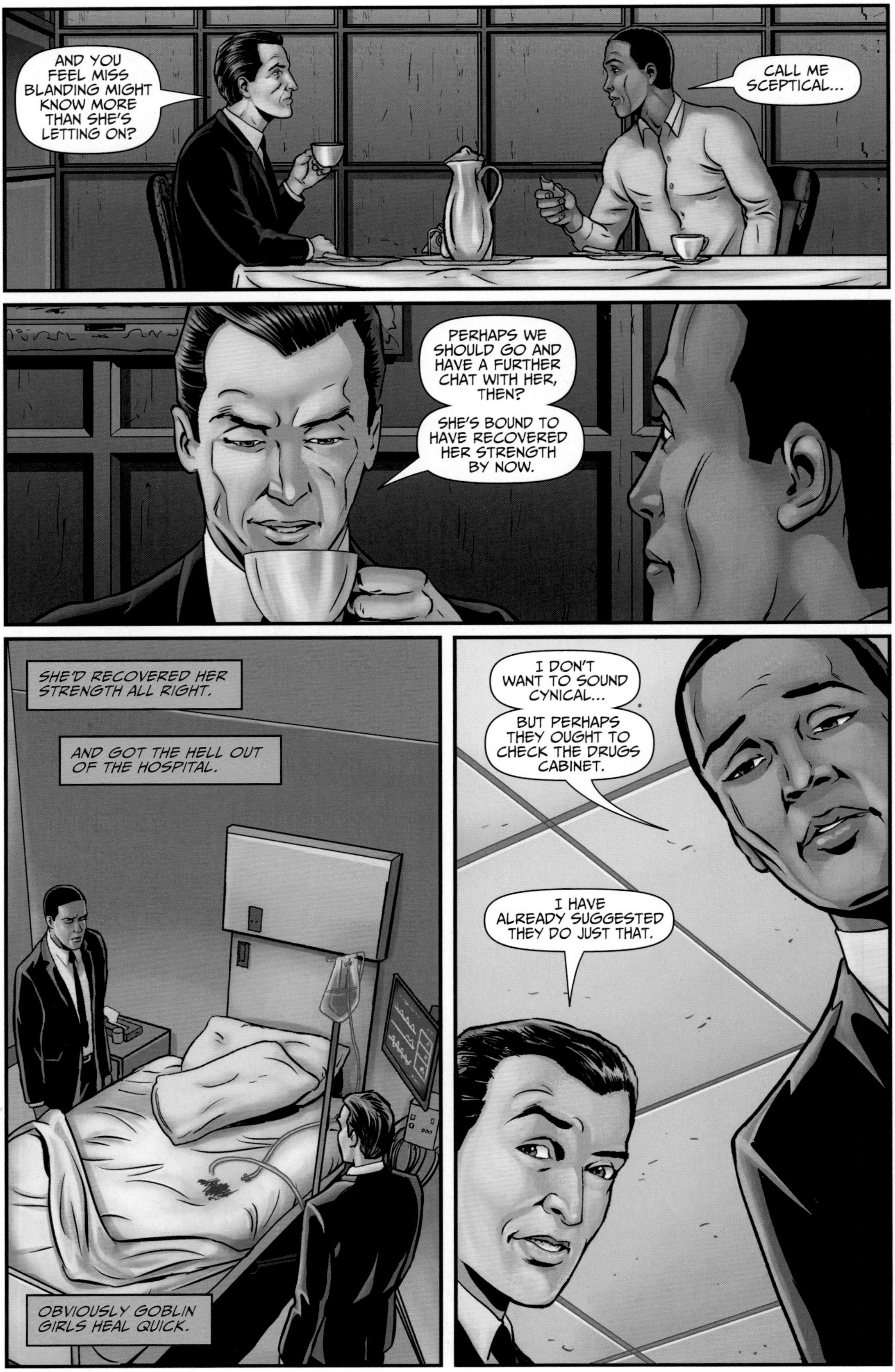
AND YOU FEEL MISS BLANDING MIGHT KNOW MORE THAN SHE'S LETTING ON?
CALL ME SCEPTICAL...
PERHAPS WE SHOULD GO AND HAVE A FURTHER CHAT WITH HER, THEN?
SHE'S BOUND TO HAVE RECOVERED HER STRENGTH BY NOW.
SHE'D RECOVERED HER STRENGTH ALL RIGHT.
AND GOT THE HELL OUT OF THE HOSPITAL.
OBVIOUSLY GOBLIN GIRLS HEAL QUICK.
I DON'T WANT TO SOUND CYNICAL...
BUT PERHAPS THEY OUGHT TO CHECK THE DRUGS CABINET.
I HAVE ALREADY SUGGESTED THEY DO JUST THAT.

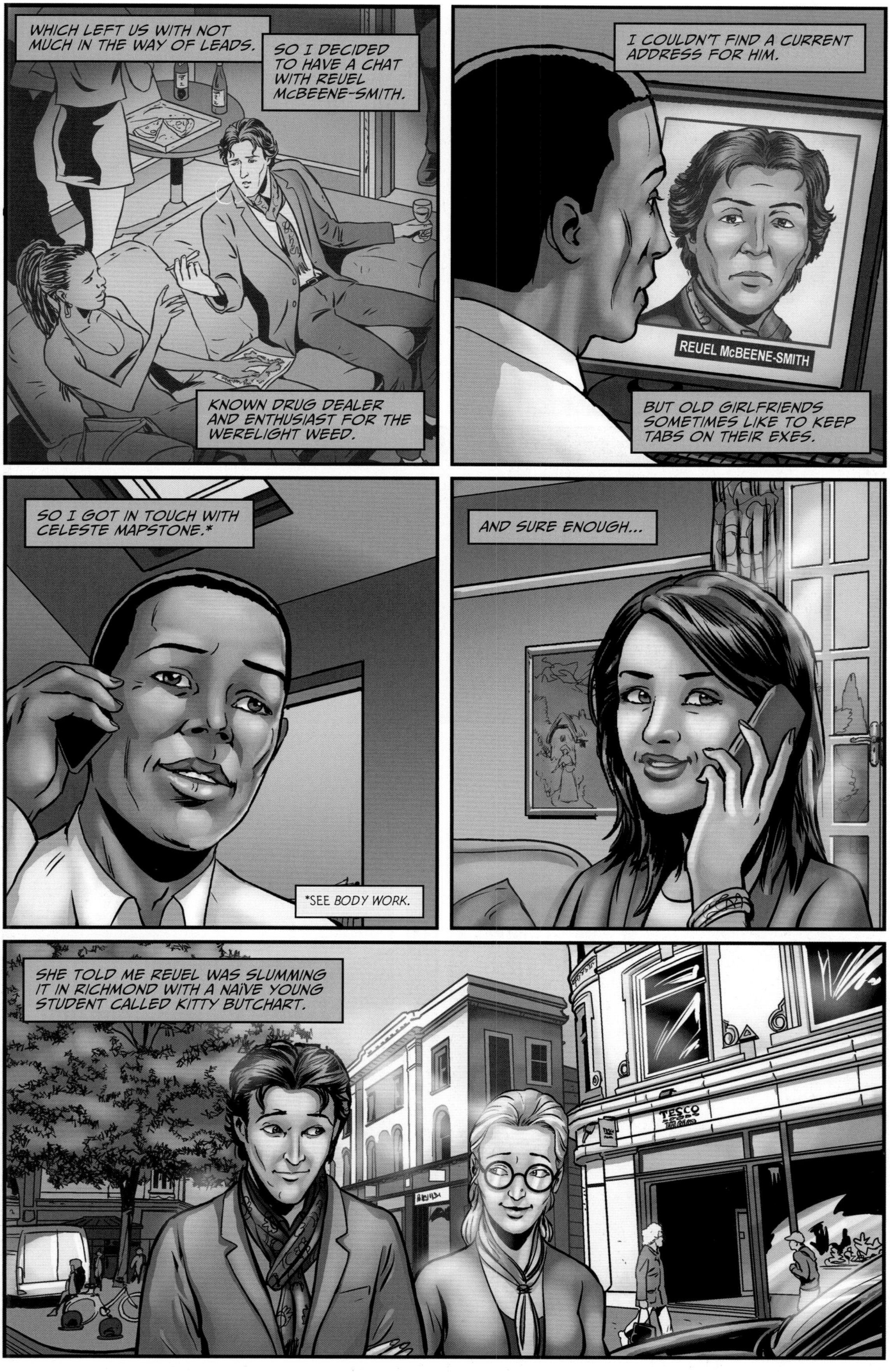
WHICH LEFT US WITH NOT MUCH IN THE WAY OF LEADS.
SO I DECIDED TO HAVE A CHAT WITH REUEL McBEENE-SMITH.
KNOWN DRUG DEALER AND ENTHUSIAST FOR THE WERELIGHT WEED.
I COULDN'T FIND A CURRENT ADDRESS FOR HIM.
REUEL McBEENE-SMITH
BUT OLD GIRLFRIENDS SOMETIMES LIKE TO KEEP TABS ON THEIR EXES.
SO I GOT IN TOUCH WITH CELESTE MAPSTONE.*
*SEE BODY WORK.
AND SURE ENOUGH...
SHE TOLD ME REUEL WAS SLUMMING IT IN RICHMOND WITH A NAÏVE YOUNG STUDENT CALLED KITTY BUTCHART.
TESCO

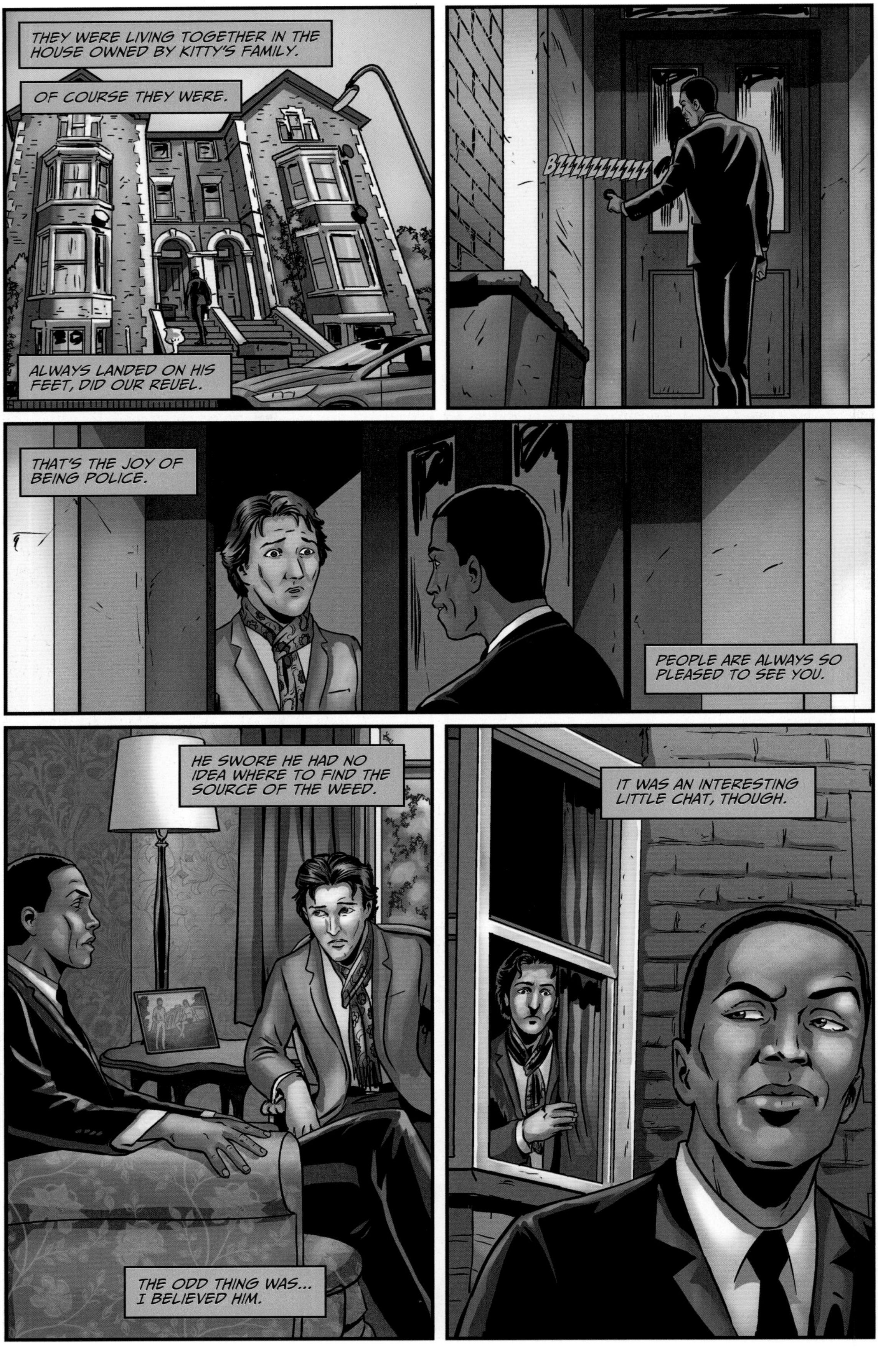
THEY WERE LIVING TOGETHER IN THE HOUSE OWNED BY KITTY'S FAMILY.
OF COURSE THEY WERE.
ALWAYS LANDED ON HIS FEET, DID OUR REUEL.
BZZZZZZZZZZZZ
THAT'S THE JOY OF BEING POLICE.
PEOPLE ARE ALWAYS SO PLEASED TO SEE YOU.
HE SWORE HE HAD NO IDEA WHERE TO FIND THE SOURCE OF THE WEED.
THE ODD THING WAS... I BELIEVED HIM.
IT WAS AN INTERESTING LITTLE CHAT, THOUGH.

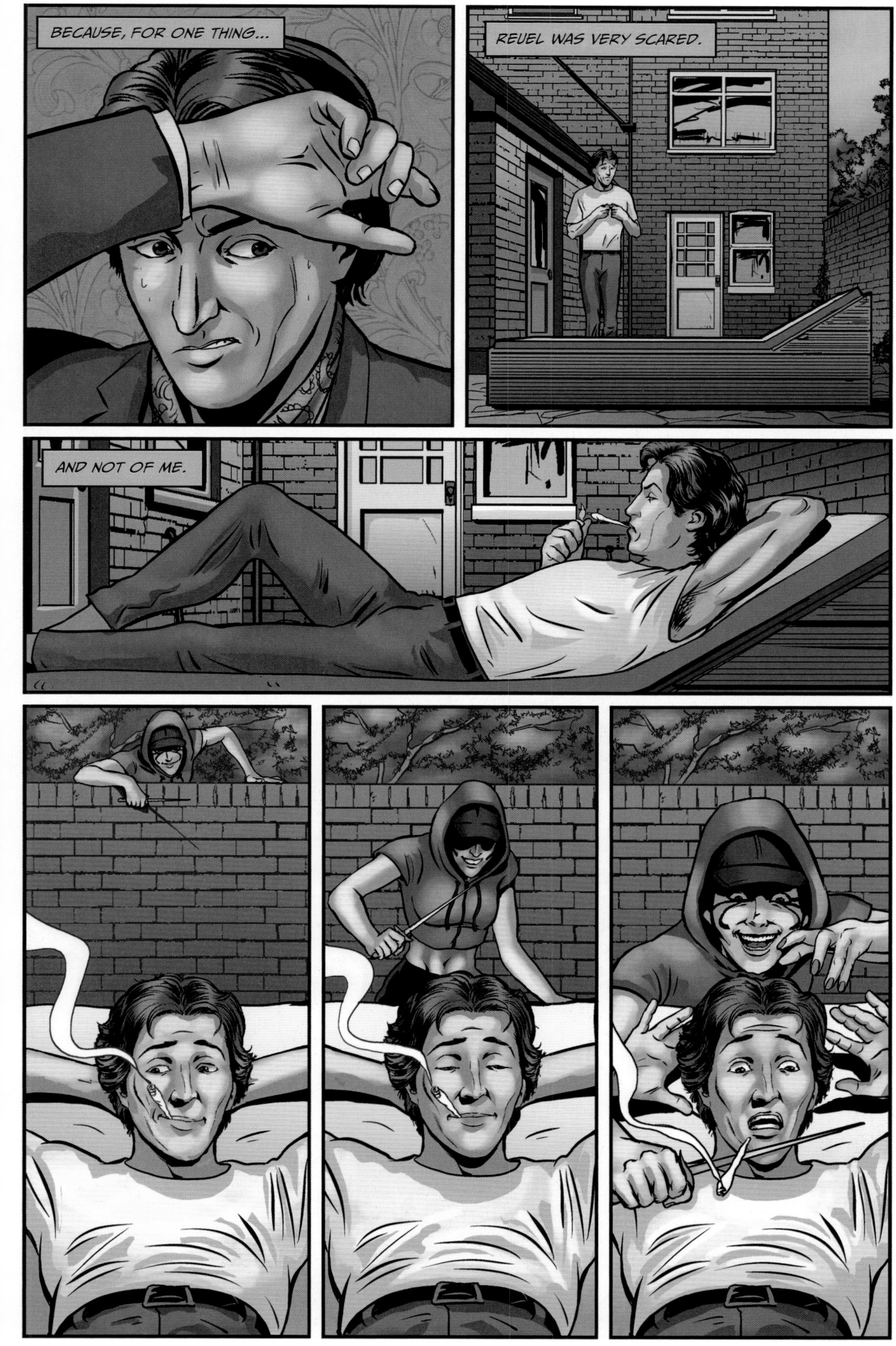
BECAUSE, FOR ONE THING...
REUEL WAS VERY SCARED.
AND NOT OF ME.

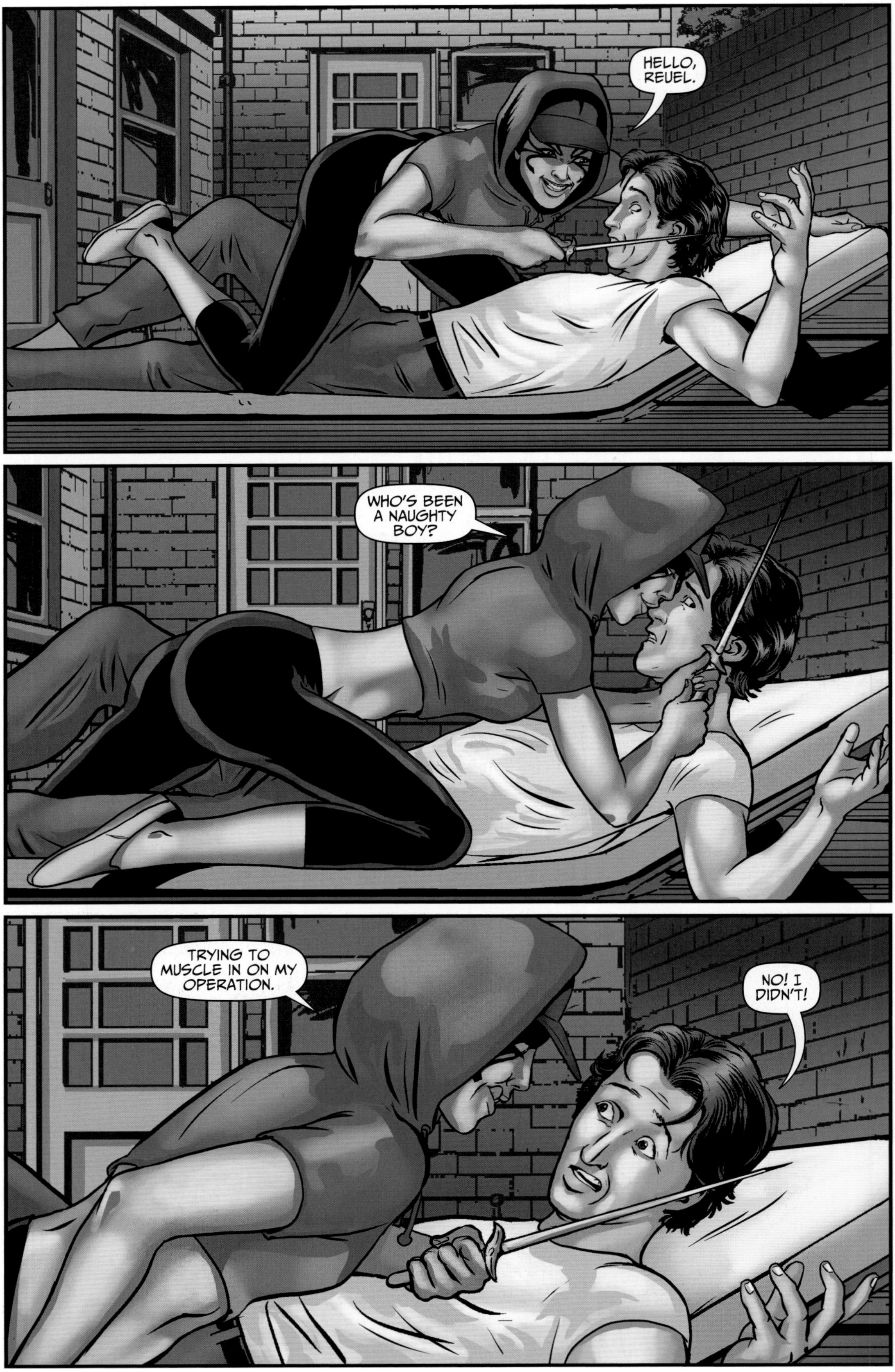
HELLO, REUEL.
WHO'S BEEN A NAUGHTY BOY?
TRYING TO MUSCLE IN ON MY OPERATION.
NO! I DIDN'T!

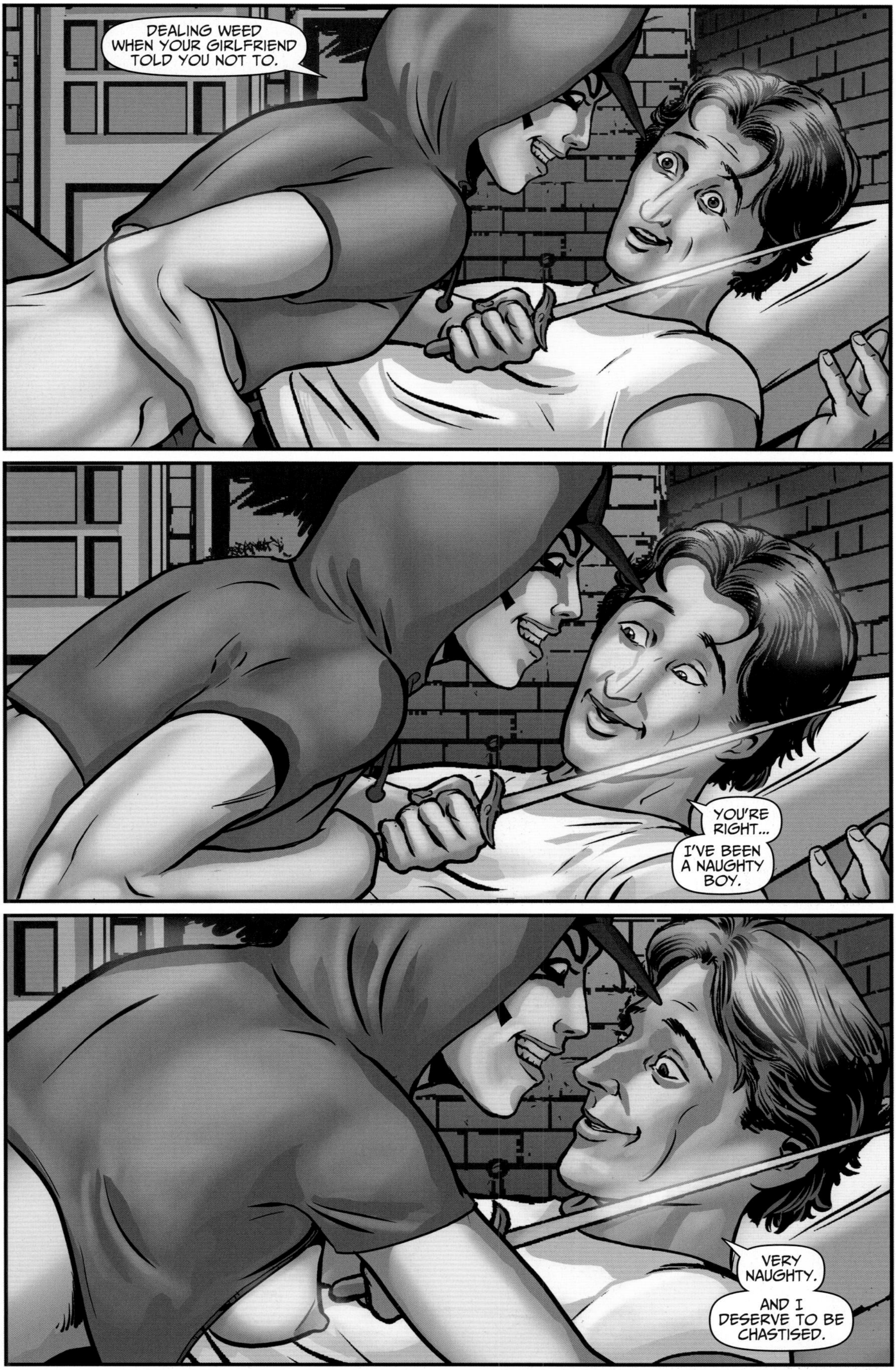
DEALING WEED WHEN YOUR GIRLFRIEND TOLD YOU NOT TO.
YOU'RE RIGHT...
I'VE BEEN A NAUGHTY BOY.
VERY NAUGHTY.
AND I DESERVE TO BE CHASTISED.

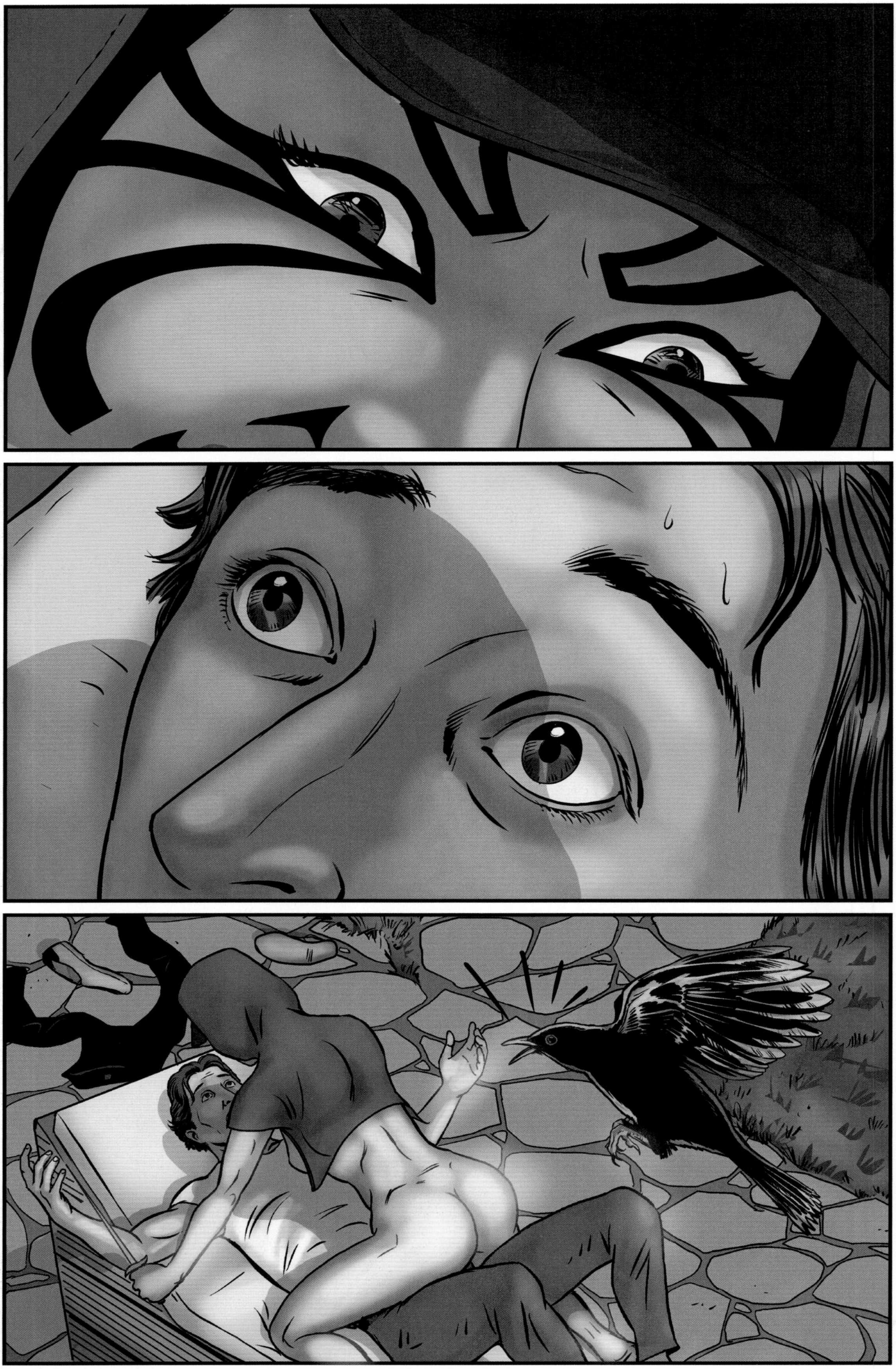

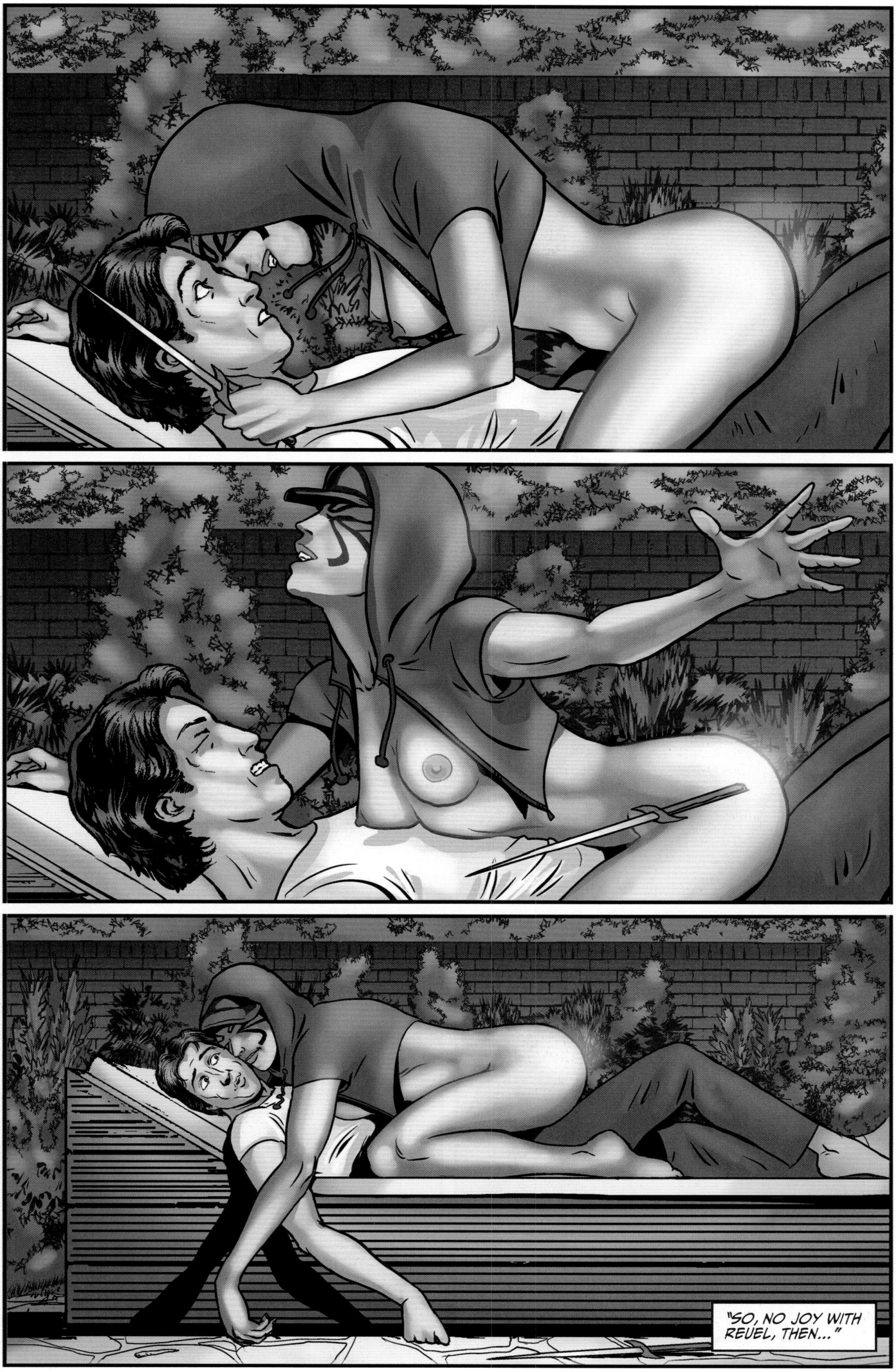
"SO, NO JOY WITH REUEL, THEN..."

AFRAID NOT.

HE DOESN'T KNOW ANYTHING, BUT HE'S DEFINITELY SCARED OF SOMETHING.

PROBABLY VERY SENSIBLE OF HIM.

HERE YOU ARE, BOY.

PINGGGG

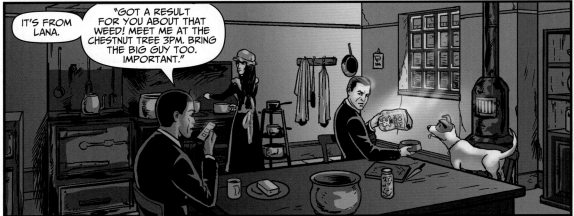

IT'S FROM LANA.

"GOT A RESULT FOR YOU ABOUT THAT WEED! MEET ME AT THE CHESTNUT TREE 3PM. BRING THE BIG GUY TOO. IMPORTANT."

THE BIG GUY?

APPARENTLY YOU'VE GOT A BIT OF REP.

CAN'T THINK WHY.

< Folly Feds (mobile)

Got a result for you about that weed! Meet me at the Chestnut Tree 3pm.

Bring the big guy too. Important.

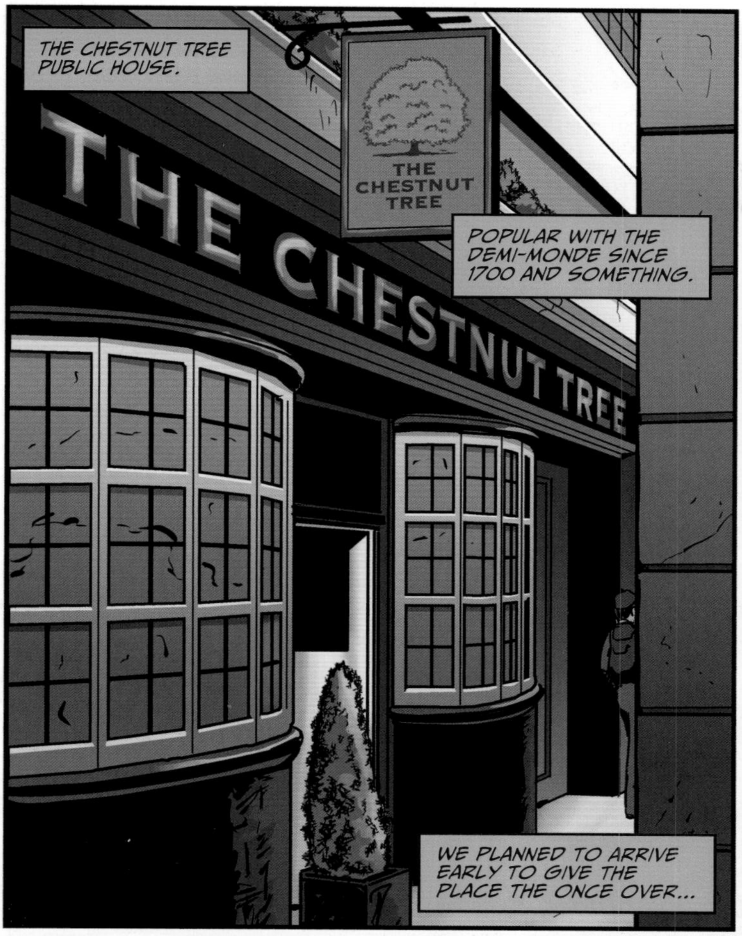
THE CHESTNUT TREE PUBLIC HOUSE.
THE CHESTNUT TREE
THE CHESTNUT TREE
POPULAR WITH THE DEMI-MONDE SINCE 1700 AND SOMETHING.
WE PLANNED TO ARRIVE EARLY TO GIVE THE PLACE THE ONCE OVER...

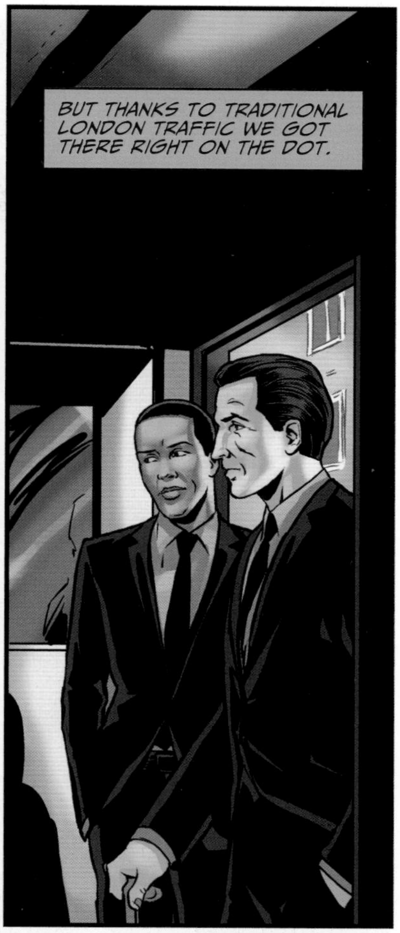
BUT THANKS TO TRADITIONAL LONDON TRAFFIC WE GOT THERE RIGHT ON THE DOT.

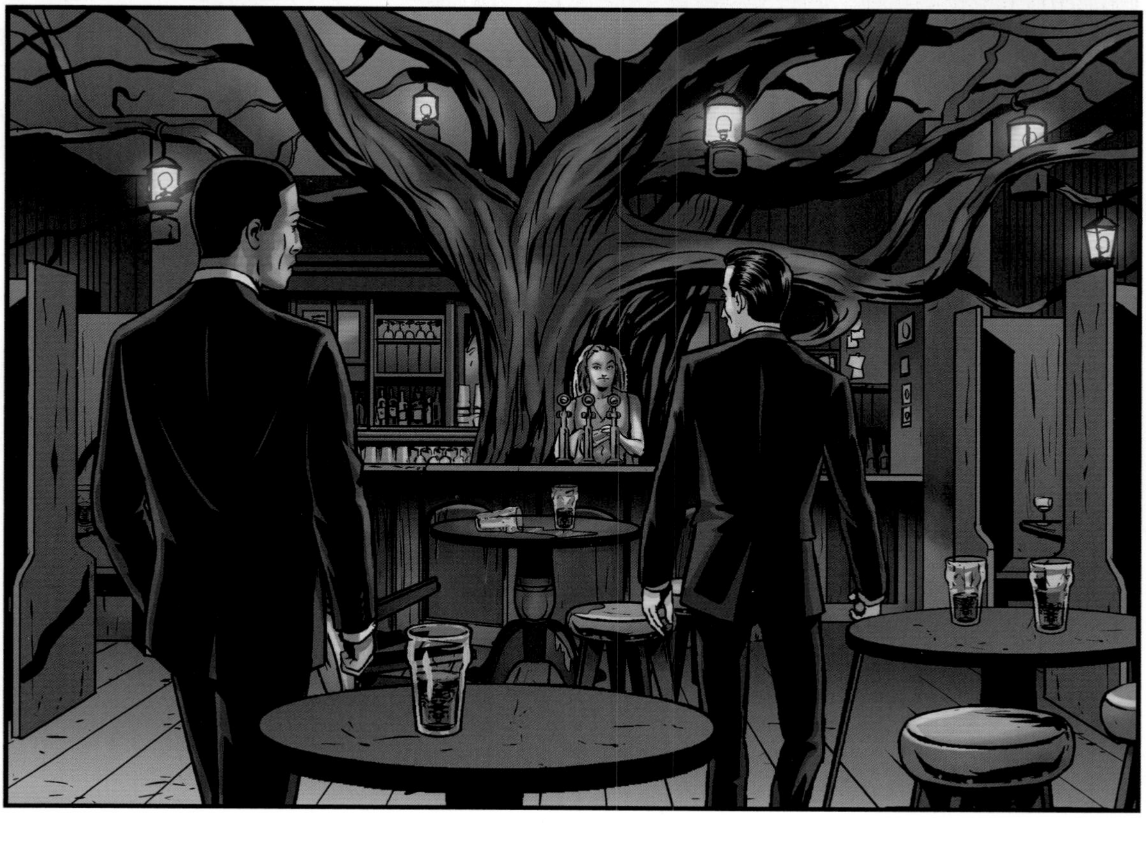

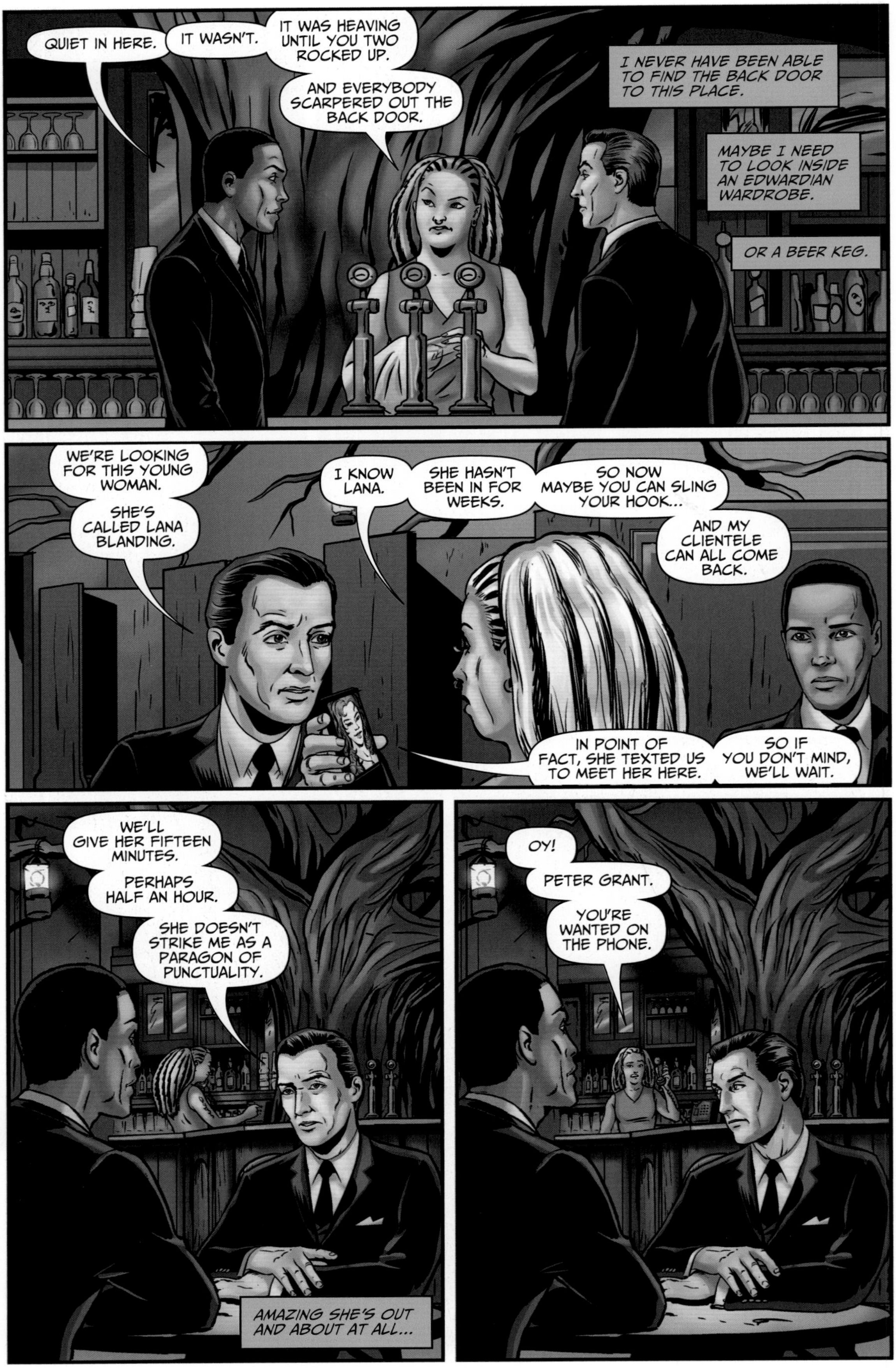
QUIET IN HERE.
IT WASN'T.
IT WAS HEAVING UNTIL YOU TWO ROCKED UP.
AND EVERYBODY SCARPERED OUT THE BACK DOOR.
I NEVER HAVE BEEN ABLE TO FIND THE BACK DOOR TO THIS PLACE.
MAYBE I NEED TO LOOK INSIDE AN EDWARDIAN WARDROBE.
OR A BEER KEG.
WE'RE LOOKING FOR THIS YOUNG WOMAN.
SHE'S CALLED LANA BLANDING.
I KNOW LANA.
SHE HASN'T BEEN IN FOR WEEKS.
SO NOW MAYBE YOU CAN SLING YOUR HOOK...
AND MY CLIENTELE CAN ALL COME BACK.
IN POINT OF FACT, SHE TEXTED US TO MEET HER HERE.
SO IF YOU DON'T MIND, WE'LL WAIT.
WE'LL GIVE HER FIFTEEN MINUTES.
PERHAPS HALF AN HOUR.
SHE DOESN'T STRIKE ME AS A PARAGON OF PUNCTUALITY.
AMAZING SHE'S OUT AND ABOUT AT ALL...
OY!
PETER GRANT.
YOU'RE WANTED ON THE PHONE.

WHEN YOU'RE FINISHED CHATTING YOU CAN CLEAR OFF WITH YOUR GOVERNOR.

BEFORE THIS PLACE GETS A REPUTATION...

HELLO?

I DIDN'T TEXT YOU.

I DON'T EVEN HAVE MY PHONE.

THE HOODETTE TOOK IT WHEN SHE...

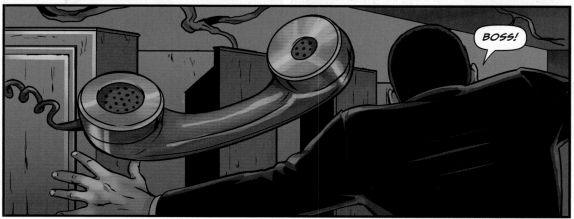

BOSS!

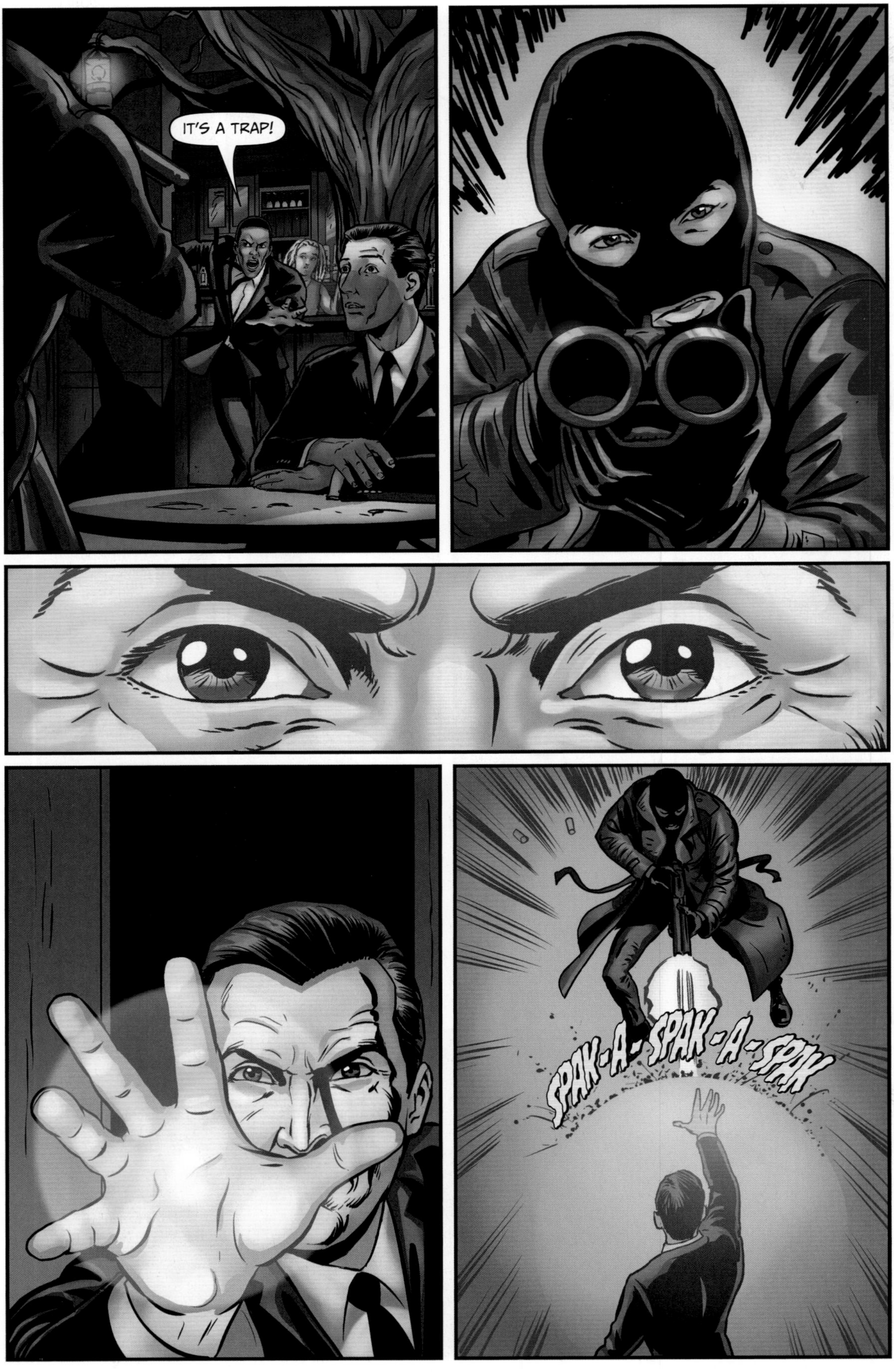
IT'S A TRAP!
SPAK-A-SPAK-A-SPAK

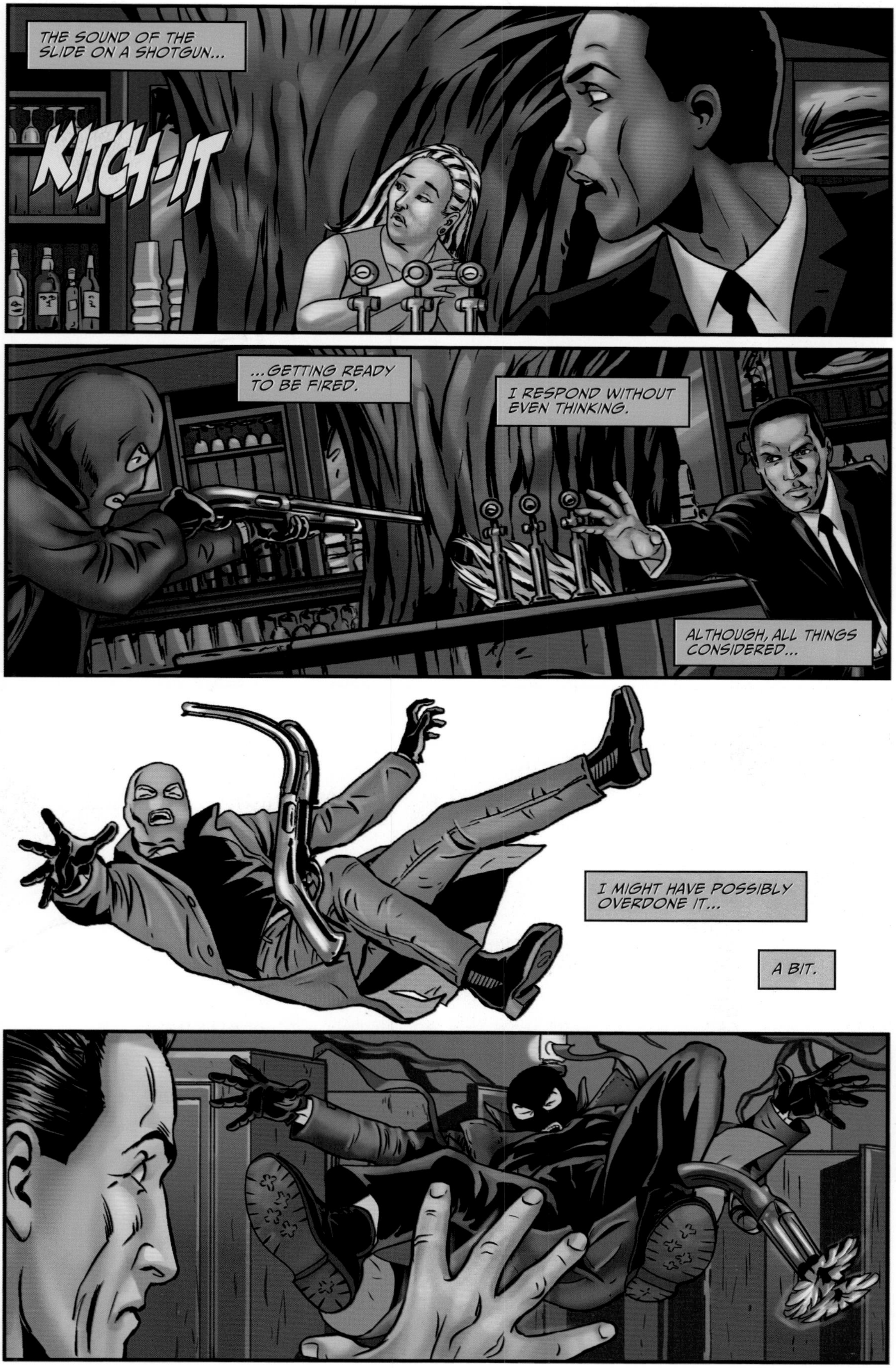
THE SOUND OF THE SLIDE ON A SHOTGUN...
KITCH-IT
...GETTING READY TO BE FIRED.
I RESPOND WITHOUT EVEN THINKING.
ALTHOUGH, ALL THINGS CONSIDERED...
I MIGHT HAVE POSSIBLY OVERDONE IT...
A BIT.

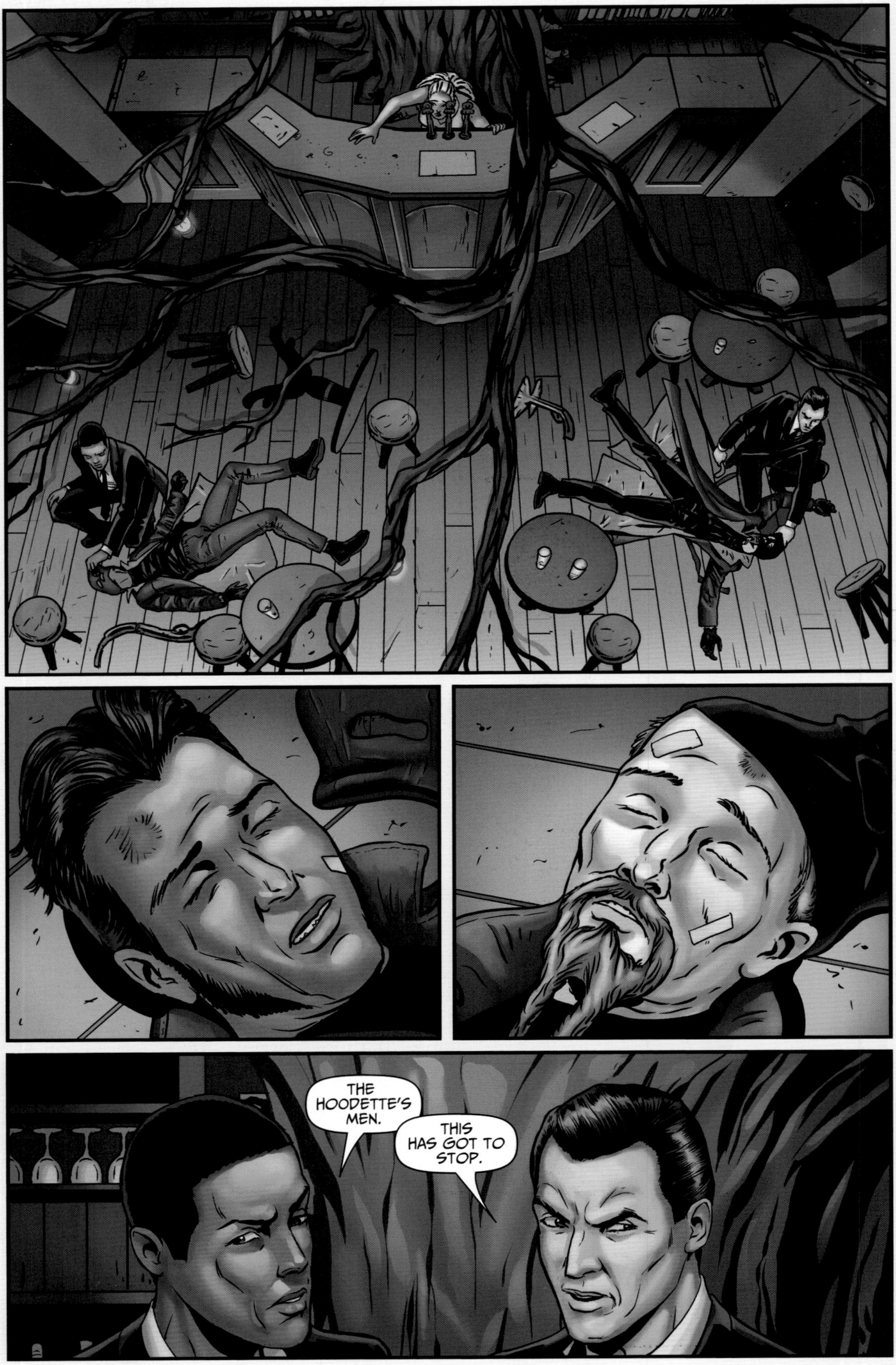
THE HOODETTE'S MEN.
THIS HAS GOT TO STOP.

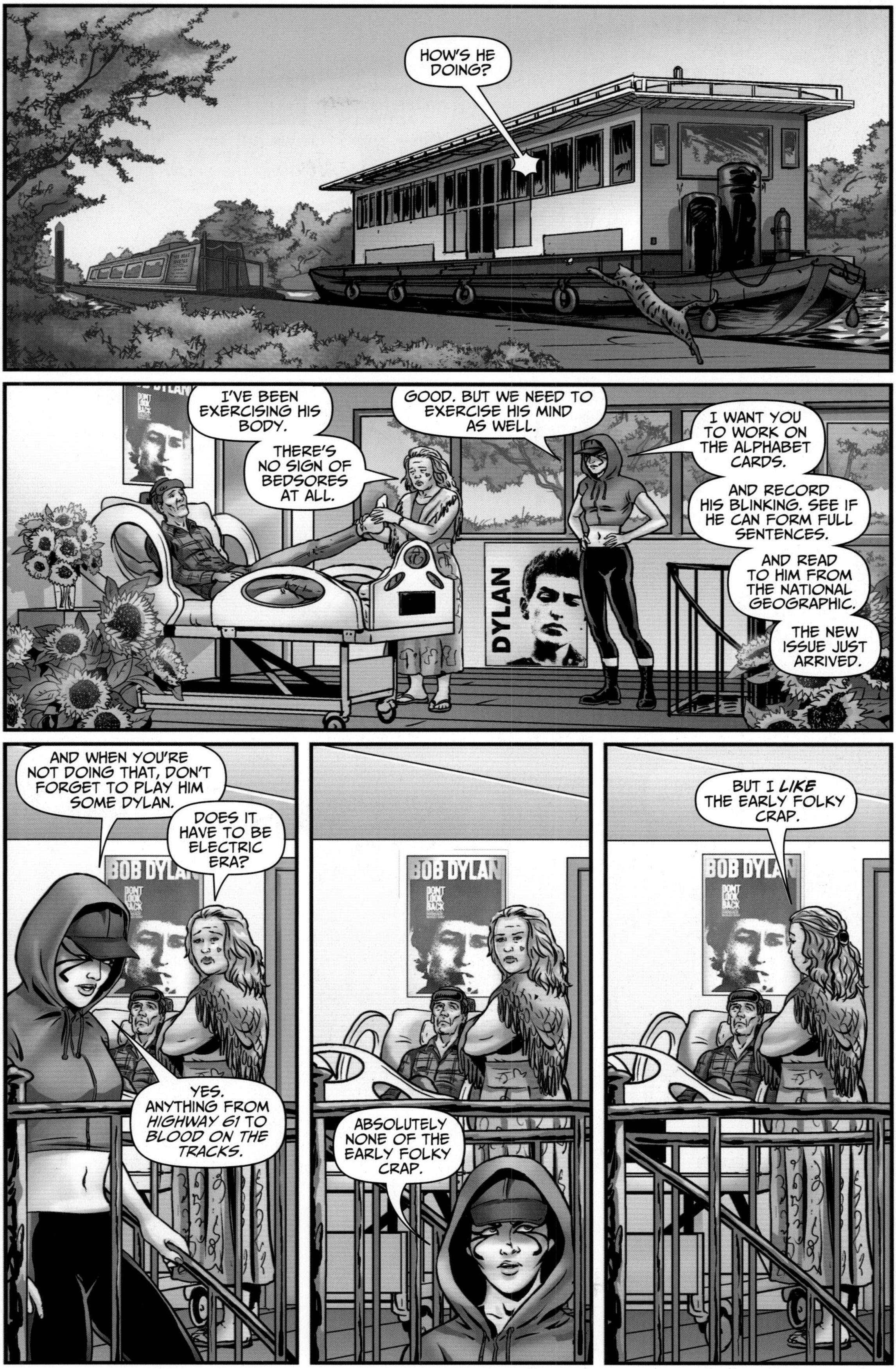
HOW'S HE DOING?
I'VE BEEN EXERCISING HIS BODY.
THERE'S NO SIGN OF BEDSORES AT ALL.
GOOD. BUT WE NEED TO EXERCISE HIS MIND AS WELL.
I WANT YOU TO WORK ON THE ALPHABET CARDS.
AND RECORD HIS BLINKING. SEE IF HE CAN FORM FULL SENTENCES.
AND READ TO HIM FROM THE NATIONAL GEOGRAPHIC.
THE NEW ISSUE JUST ARRIVED.
DYLAN
AND WHEN YOU'RE NOT DOING THAT, DON'T FORGET TO PLAY HIM SOME DYLAN.
DOES IT HAVE TO BE ELECTRIC ERA?
BOB DYLAN
DONT LOOK BACK
YES. ANYTHING FROM *HIGHWAY 61* TO *BLOOD ON THE TRACKS.*
BOB DYLAN
DONT LOOK BACK
ABSOLUTELY NONE OF THE EARLY FOLKY CRAP.
BUT I ***LIKE*** THE EARLY FOLKY CRAP.
BOB DYLAN
DONT LOOK BACK

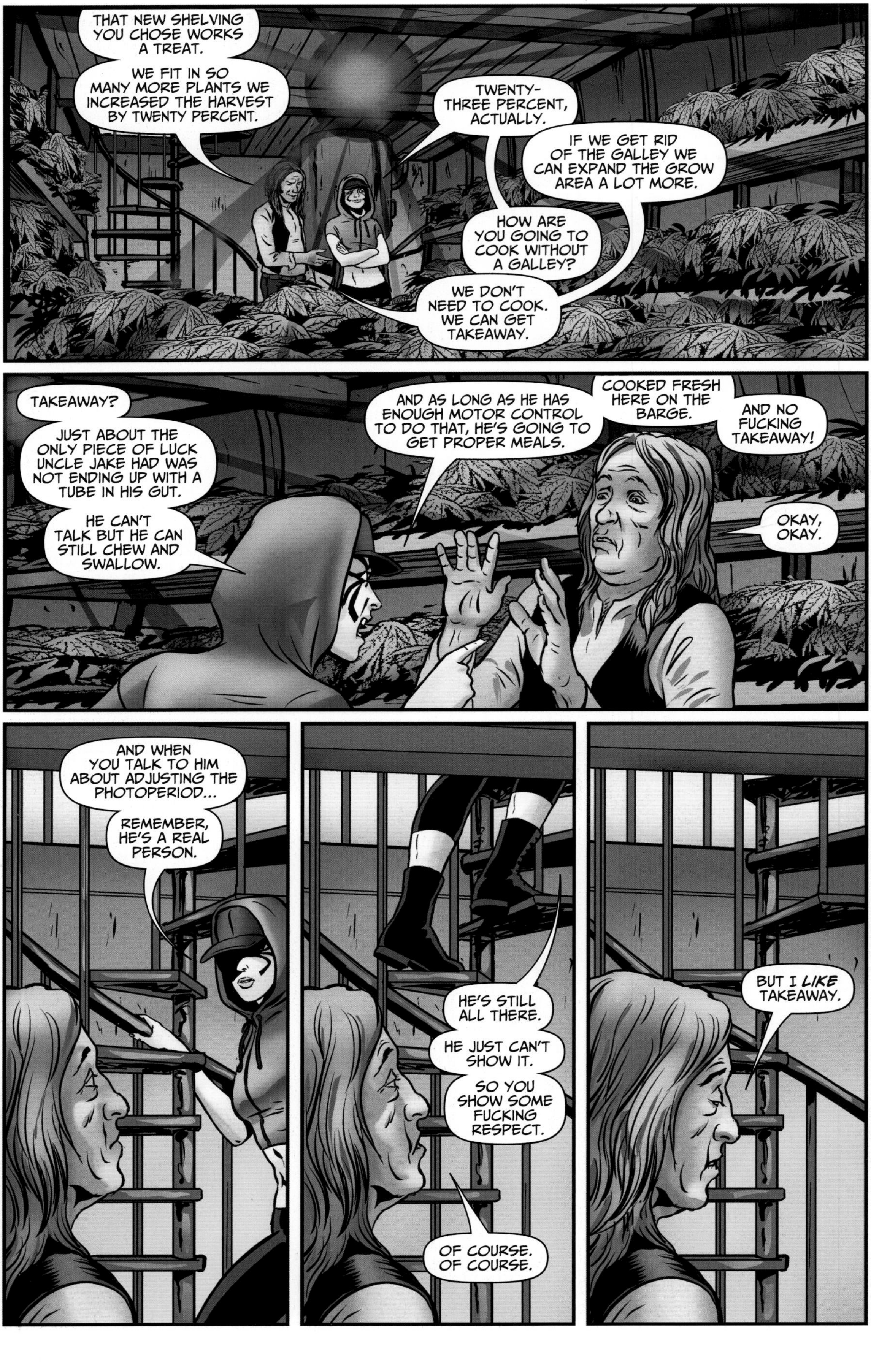
THAT NEW SHELVING YOU CHOSE WORKS A TREAT.
WE FIT IN SO MANY MORE PLANTS WE INCREASED THE HARVEST BY TWENTY PERCENT.
TWENTY-THREE PERCENT, ACTUALLY.
IF WE GET RID OF THE GALLEY WE CAN EXPAND THE GROW AREA A LOT MORE.
HOW ARE YOU GOING TO COOK WITHOUT A GALLEY?
WE DON'T NEED TO COOK. WE CAN GET TAKEAWAY.
TAKEAWAY?
JUST ABOUT THE ONLY PIECE OF LUCK UNCLE JAKE HAD WAS NOT ENDING UP WITH A TUBE IN HIS GUT.
HE CAN'T TALK BUT HE CAN STILL CHEW AND SWALLOW.
AND AS LONG AS HE HAS ENOUGH MOTOR CONTROL TO DO THAT, HE'S GOING TO GET PROPER MEALS.
COOKED FRESH HERE ON THE BARGE.
AND NO FUCKING TAKEAWAY!
OKAY, OKAY.
AND WHEN YOU TALK TO HIM ABOUT ADJUSTING THE PHOTOPERIOD...
REMEMBER, HE'S A REAL PERSON.
HE'S STILL ALL THERE.
HE JUST CAN'T SHOW IT.
SO YOU SHOW SOME FUCKING RESPECT.
OF COURSE. OF COURSE.
BUT I *LIKE* TAKEAWAY.

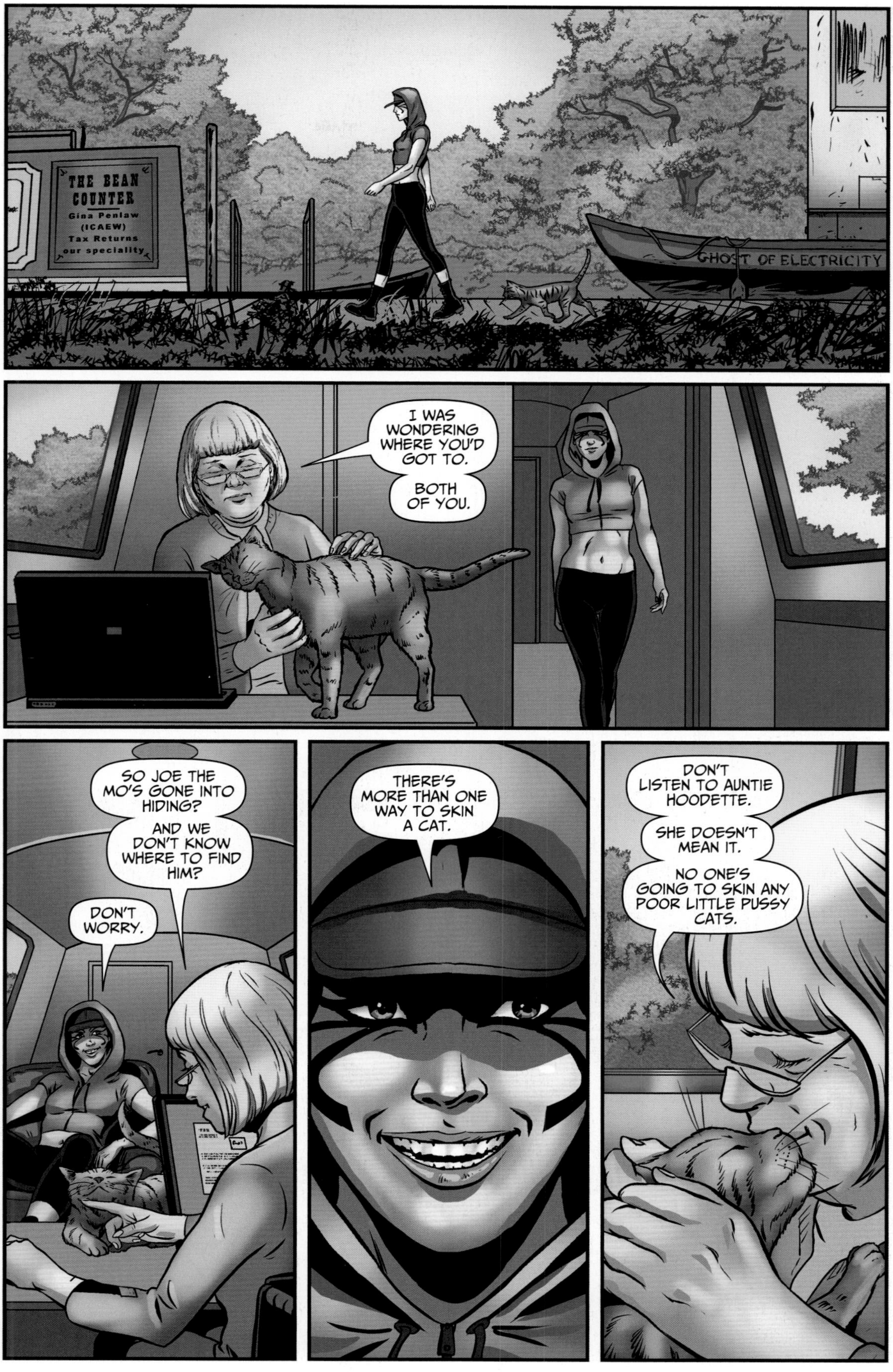
THE BEAN COUNTER
Gina Penlaw (ICAEW)
Tax Returns our speciality
GHOST OF ELECTRICITY
I WAS WONDERING WHERE YOU'D GOT TO.
BOTH OF YOU.
SO JOE THE MO'S GONE INTO HIDING?
AND WE DON'T KNOW WHERE TO FIND HIM?
DON'T WORRY.
THERE'S MORE THAN ONE WAY TO SKIN A CAT.
DON'T LISTEN TO AUNTIE HOODETTE.
SHE DOESN'T MEAN IT.
NO ONE'S GOING TO SKIN ANY POOR LITTLE PUSSY CATS.

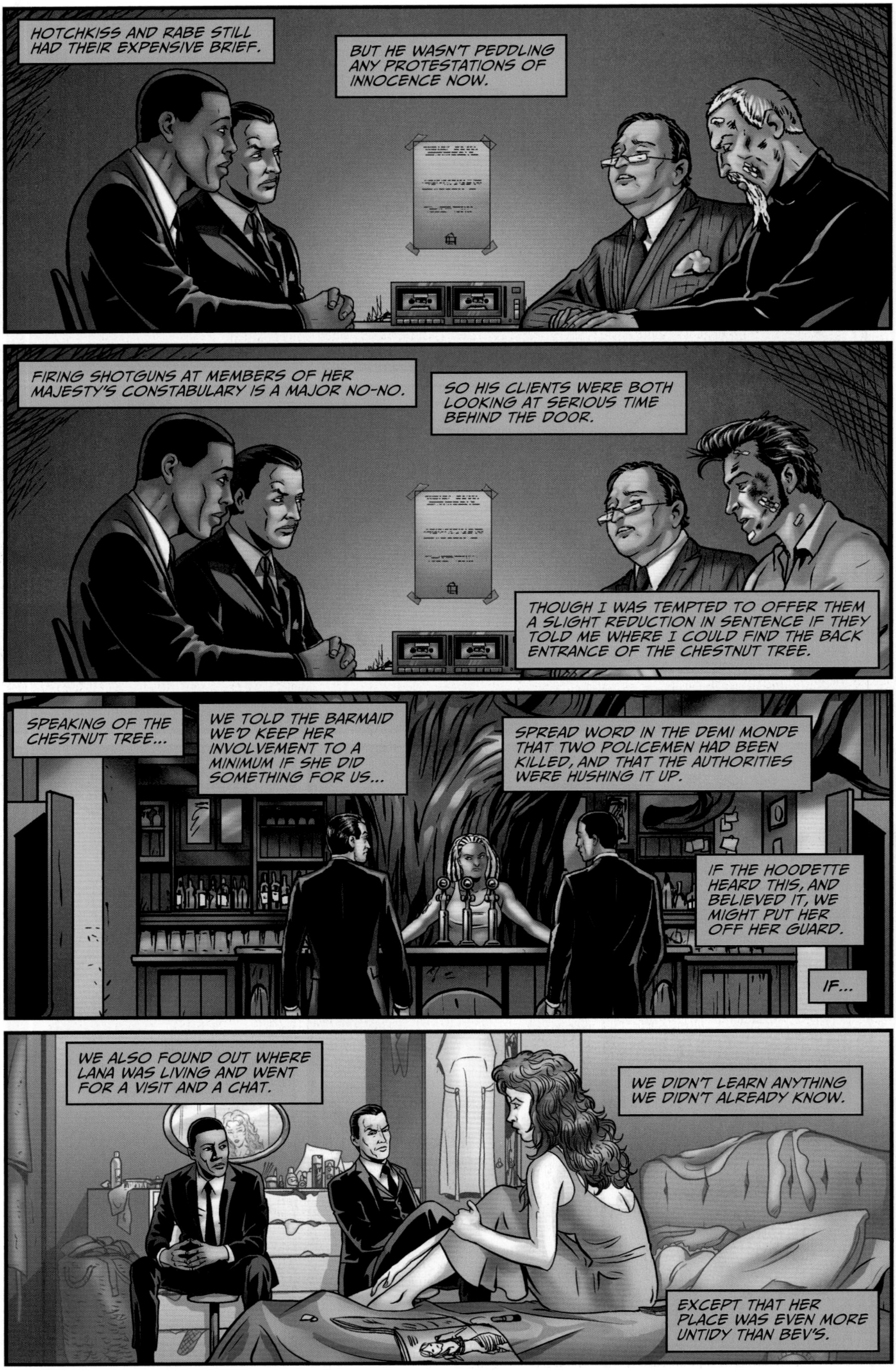
HOTCHKISS AND RABE STILL HAD THEIR EXPENSIVE BRIEF.
BUT HE WASN'T PEDDLING ANY PROTESTATIONS OF INNOCENCE NOW.
FIRING SHOTGUNS AT MEMBERS OF HER MAJESTY'S CONSTABULARY IS A MAJOR NO-NO.
SO HIS CLIENTS WERE BOTH LOOKING AT SERIOUS TIME BEHIND THE DOOR.
THOUGH I WAS TEMPTED TO OFFER THEM A SLIGHT REDUCTION IN SENTENCE IF THEY TOLD ME WHERE I COULD FIND THE BACK ENTRANCE OF THE CHESTNUT TREE.
SPEAKING OF THE CHESTNUT TREE...
WE TOLD THE BARMAID WE'D KEEP HER INVOLVEMENT TO A MINIMUM IF SHE DID SOMETHING FOR US...
SPREAD WORD IN THE DEMI MONDE THAT TWO POLICEMEN HAD BEEN KILLED, AND THAT THE AUTHORITIES WERE HUSHING IT UP.
IF THE HOODETTE HEARD THIS, AND BELIEVED IT, WE MIGHT PUT HER OFF HER GUARD.
IF...
WE ALSO FOUND OUT WHERE LANA WAS LIVING AND WENT FOR A VISIT AND A CHAT.
WE DIDN'T LEARN ANYTHING WE DIDN'T ALREADY KNOW.
EXCEPT THAT HER PLACE WAS EVEN MORE UNTIDY THAN BEV'S.

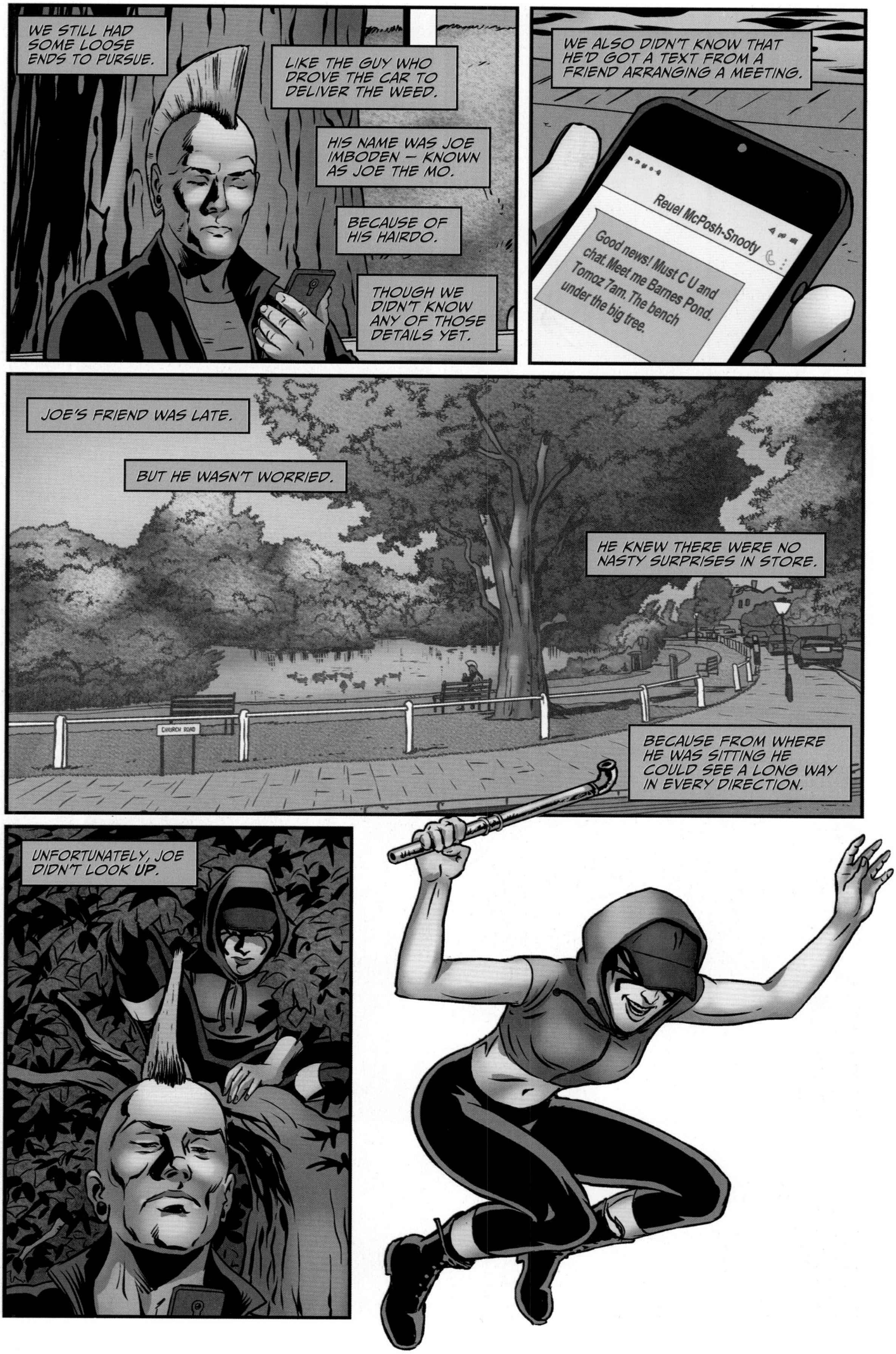
WE STILL HAD SOME LOOSE ENDS TO PURSUE.
LIKE THE GUY WHO DROVE THE CAR TO DELIVER THE WEED.
HIS NAME WAS JOE IMBODEN — KNOWN AS JOE THE MO.
BECAUSE OF HIS HAIRDO.
THOUGH WE DIDN'T KNOW ANY OF THOSE DETAILS YET.
WE ALSO DIDN'T KNOW THAT HE'D GOT A TEXT FROM A FRIEND ARRANGING A MEETING.
Reuel McPosh-Snooty
Good news! Must C U and chat. Meet me Barnes Pond. Tomoz 7am. The bench under the big tree.
JOE'S FRIEND WAS LATE.
BUT HE WASN'T WORRIED.
HE KNEW THERE WERE NO NASTY SURPRISES IN STORE.
CHURCH ROAD
BECAUSE FROM WHERE HE WAS SITTING HE COULD SEE A LONG WAY IN EVERY DIRECTION.
UNFORTUNATELY, JOE DIDN'T LOOK UP.

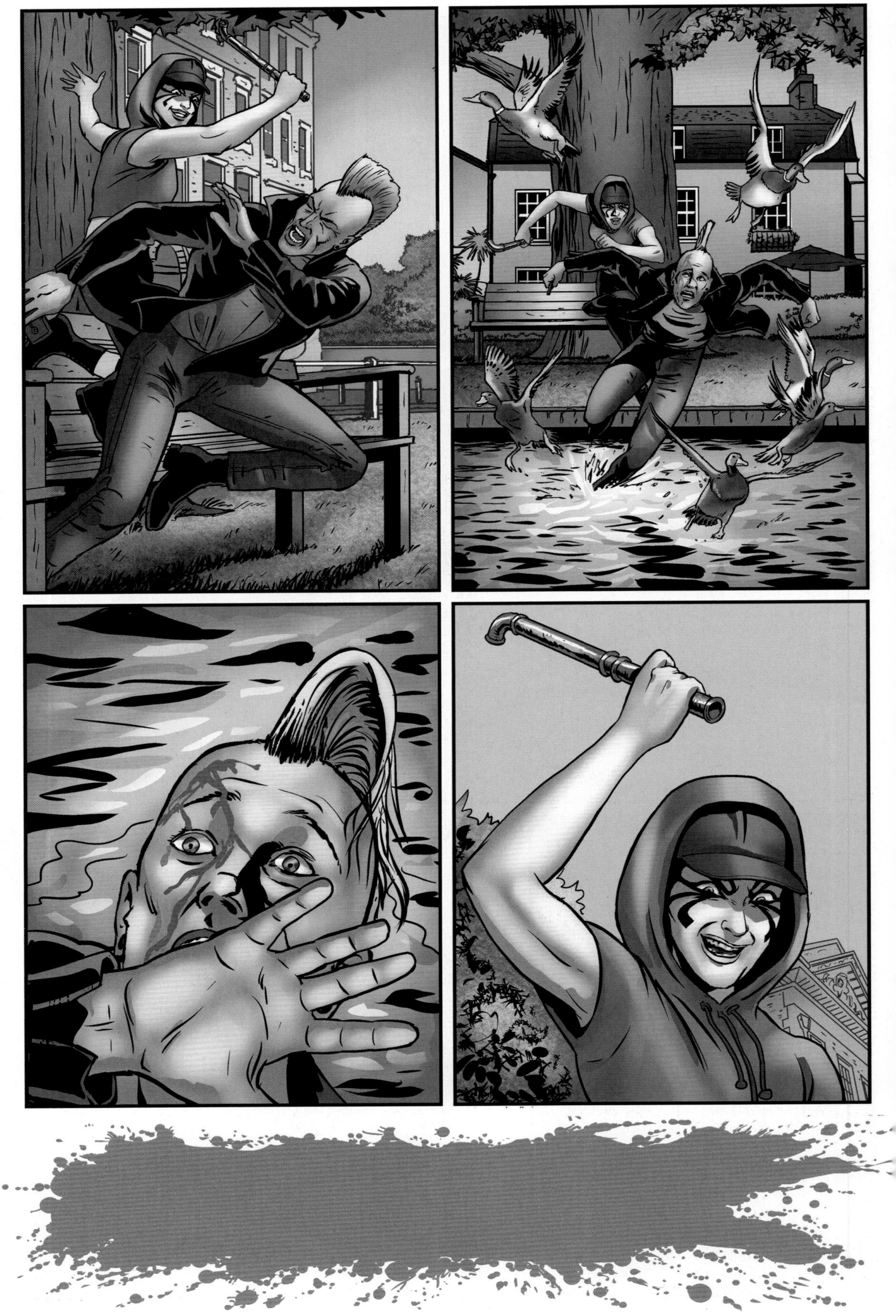

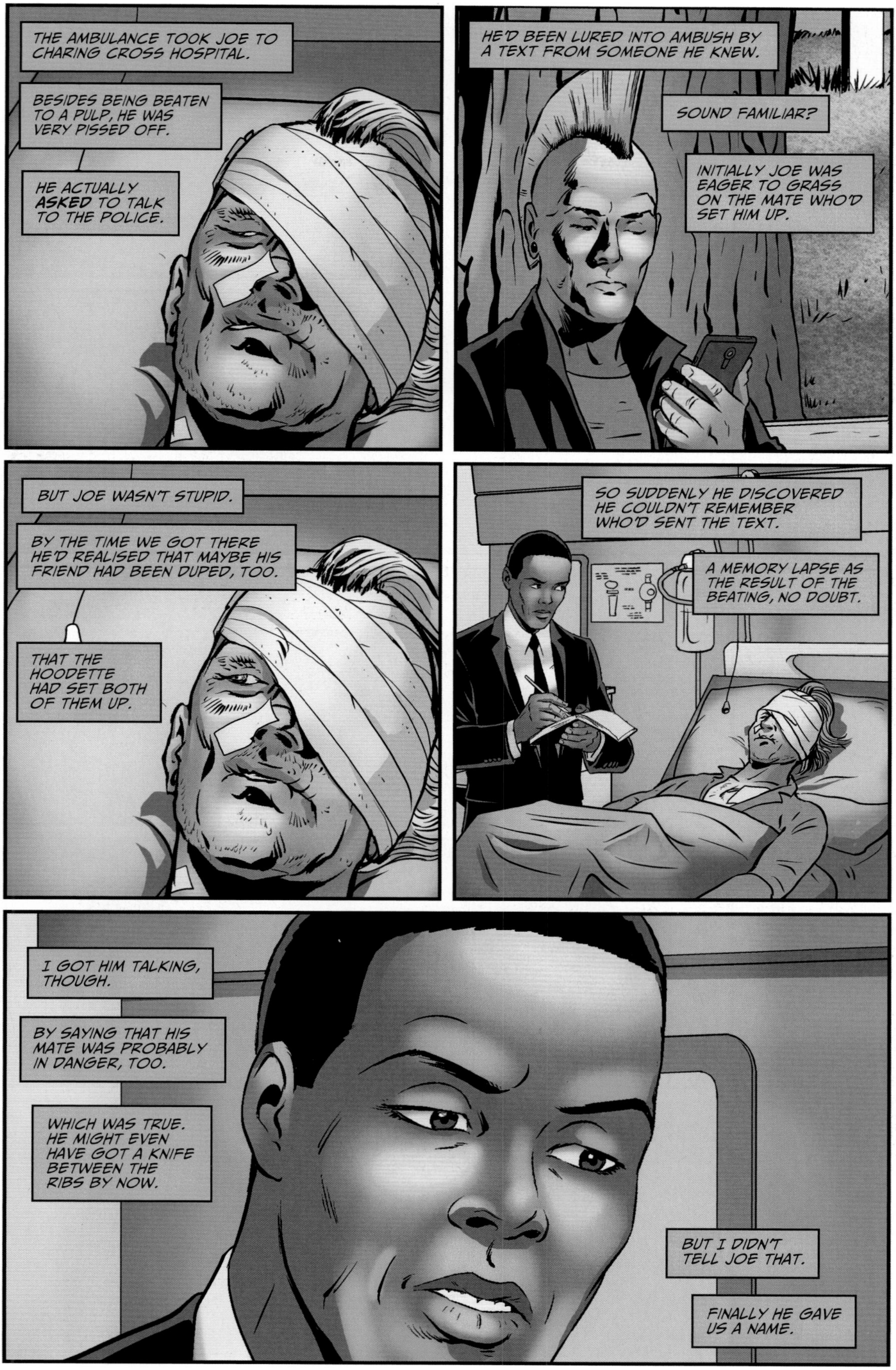
THE AMBULANCE TOOK JOE TO CHARING CROSS HOSPITAL.
BESIDES BEING BEATEN TO A PULP, HE WAS VERY PISSED OFF.
HE ACTUALLY **ASKED** TO TALK TO THE POLICE.
HE'D BEEN LURED INTO AMBUSH BY A TEXT FROM SOMEONE HE KNEW.
SOUND FAMILIAR?
INITIALLY JOE WAS EAGER TO GRASS ON THE MATE WHO'D SET HIM UP.
BUT JOE WASN'T STUPID.
BY THE TIME WE GOT THERE HE'D REALISED THAT MAYBE HIS FRIEND HAD BEEN DUPED, TOO.
THAT THE HOODETTE HAD SET BOTH OF THEM UP.
SO SUDDENLY HE DISCOVERED HE COULDN'T REMEMBER WHO'D SENT THE TEXT.
A MEMORY LAPSE AS THE RESULT OF THE BEATING, NO DOUBT.
I GOT HIM TALKING, THOUGH.
BY SAYING THAT HIS MATE WAS PROBABLY IN DANGER, TOO.
WHICH WAS TRUE. HE MIGHT EVEN HAVE GOT A KNIFE BETWEEN THE RIBS BY NOW.
BUT I DIDN'T TELL JOE THAT.
FINALLY HE GAVE US A NAME.

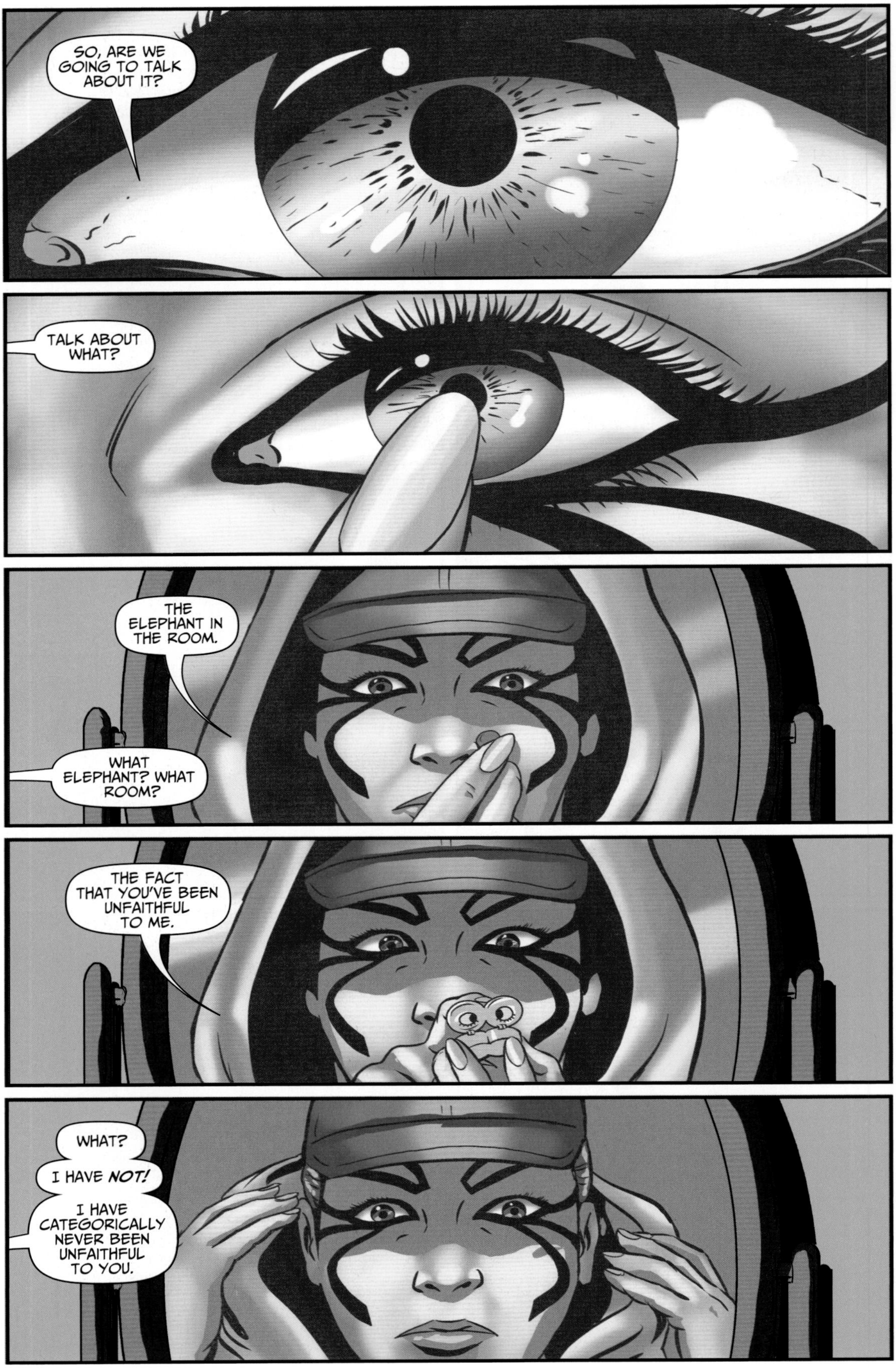
SO, ARE WE GOING TO TALK ABOUT IT?
TALK ABOUT WHAT?
THE ELEPHANT IN THE ROOM.
WHAT ELEPHANT? WHAT ROOM?
THE FACT THAT YOU'VE BEEN UNFAITHFUL TO ME.
WHAT?
I HAVE *NOT!*
I HAVE CATEGORICALLY NEVER BEEN UNFAITHFUL TO YOU.

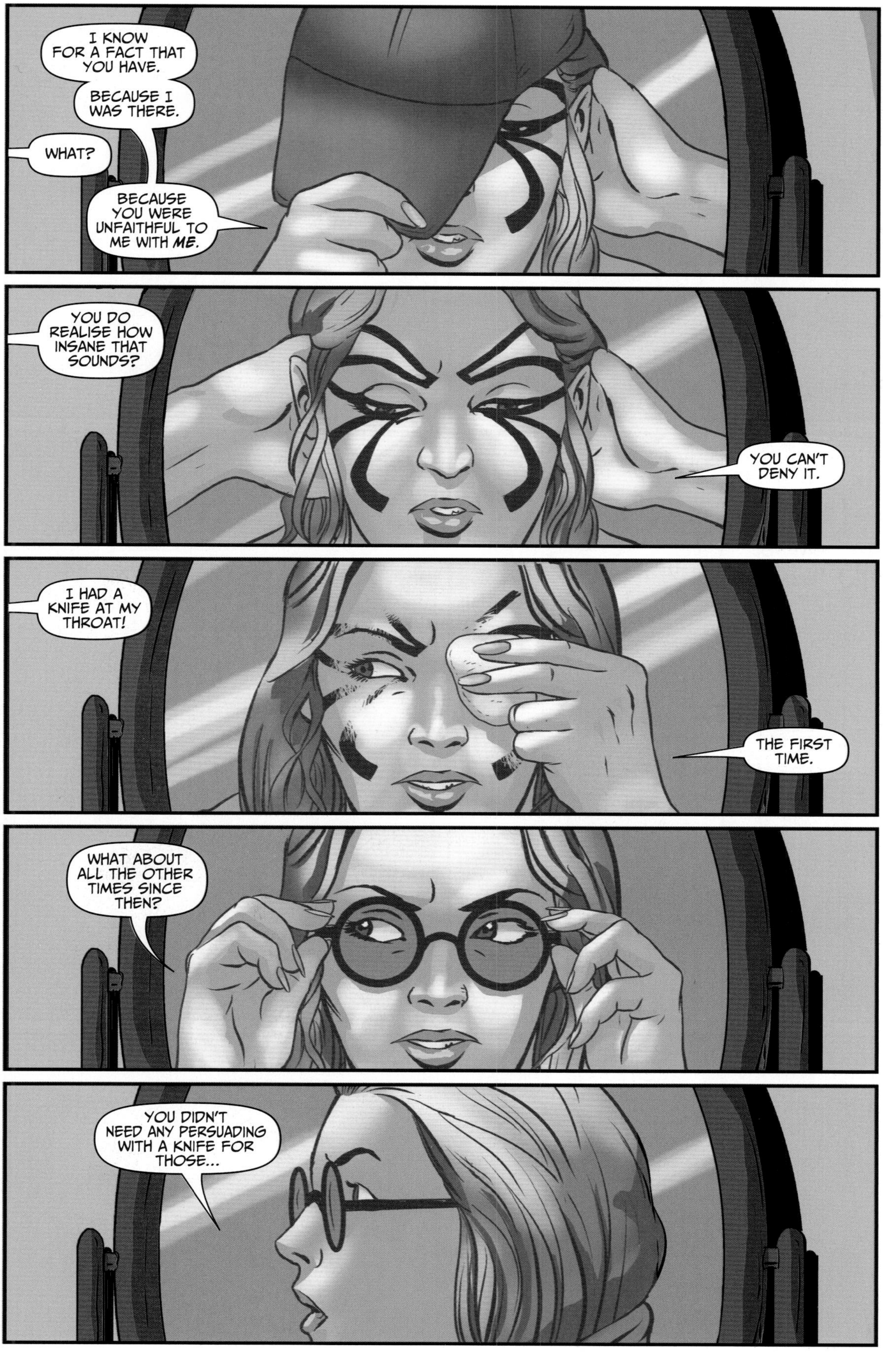
I KNOW FOR A FACT THAT YOU HAVE.
BECAUSE I WAS THERE.
WHAT?
BECAUSE YOU WERE UNFAITHFUL TO ME WITH *ME*.
YOU DO REALISE HOW INSANE THAT SOUNDS?
YOU CAN'T DENY IT.
I HAD A KNIFE AT MY THROAT!
THE FIRST TIME.
WHAT ABOUT ALL THE OTHER TIMES SINCE THEN?
YOU DIDN'T NEED ANY PERSUADING WITH A KNIFE FOR THOSE...

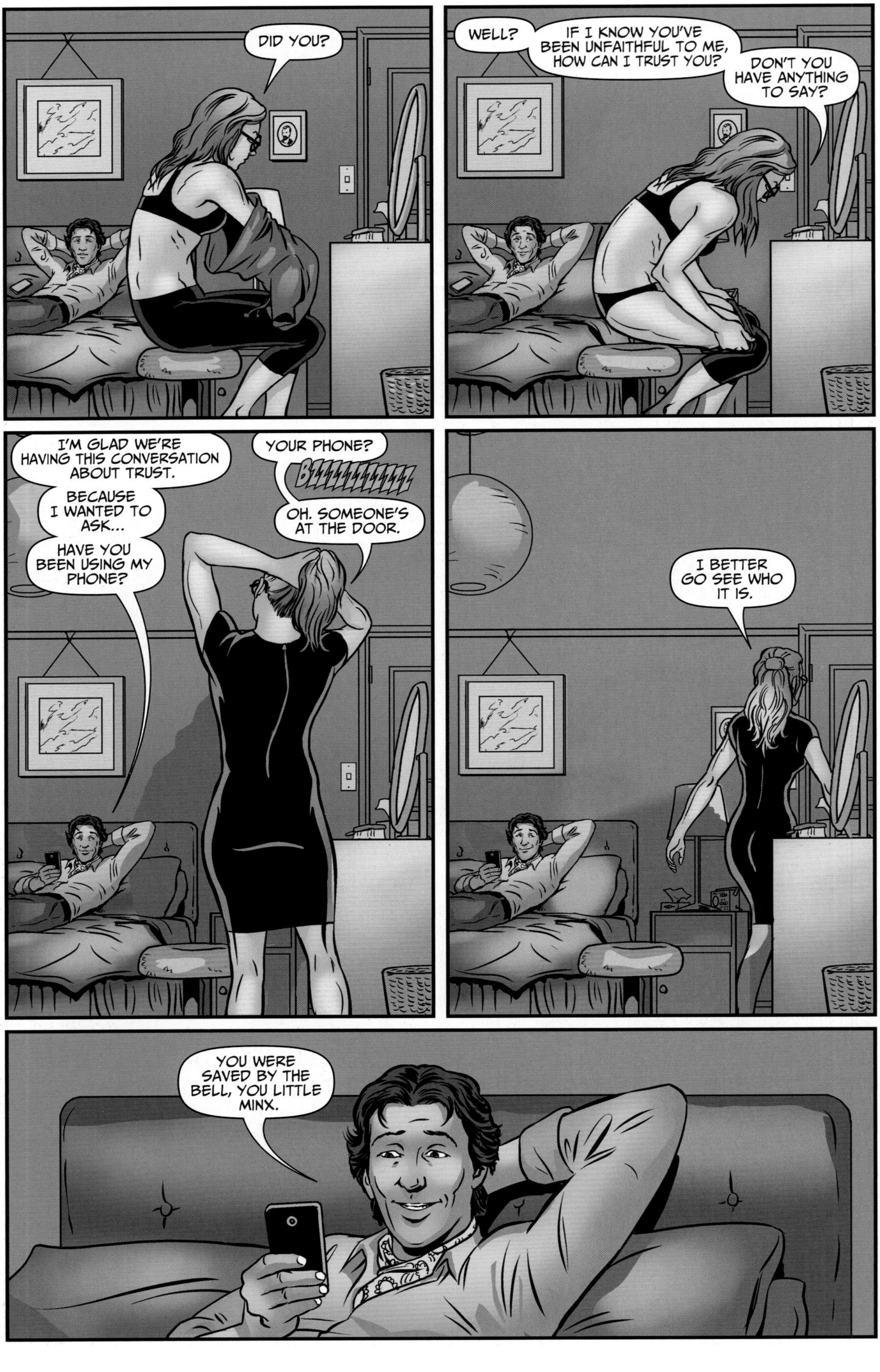
DID YOU?
WELL?
IF I KNOW YOU'VE BEEN UNFAITHFUL TO ME, HOW CAN I TRUST YOU?
DON'T YOU HAVE ANYTHING TO SAY?
I'M GLAD WE'RE HAVING THIS CONVERSATION ABOUT TRUST.
BECAUSE I WANTED TO ASK...
HAVE YOU BEEN USING MY PHONE?
YOUR PHONE?
BZZZZZZZZZZ
OH. SOMEONE'S AT THE DOOR.
I BETTER GO SEE WHO IT IS.
YOU WERE SAVED BY THE BELL, YOU LITTLE MINX.

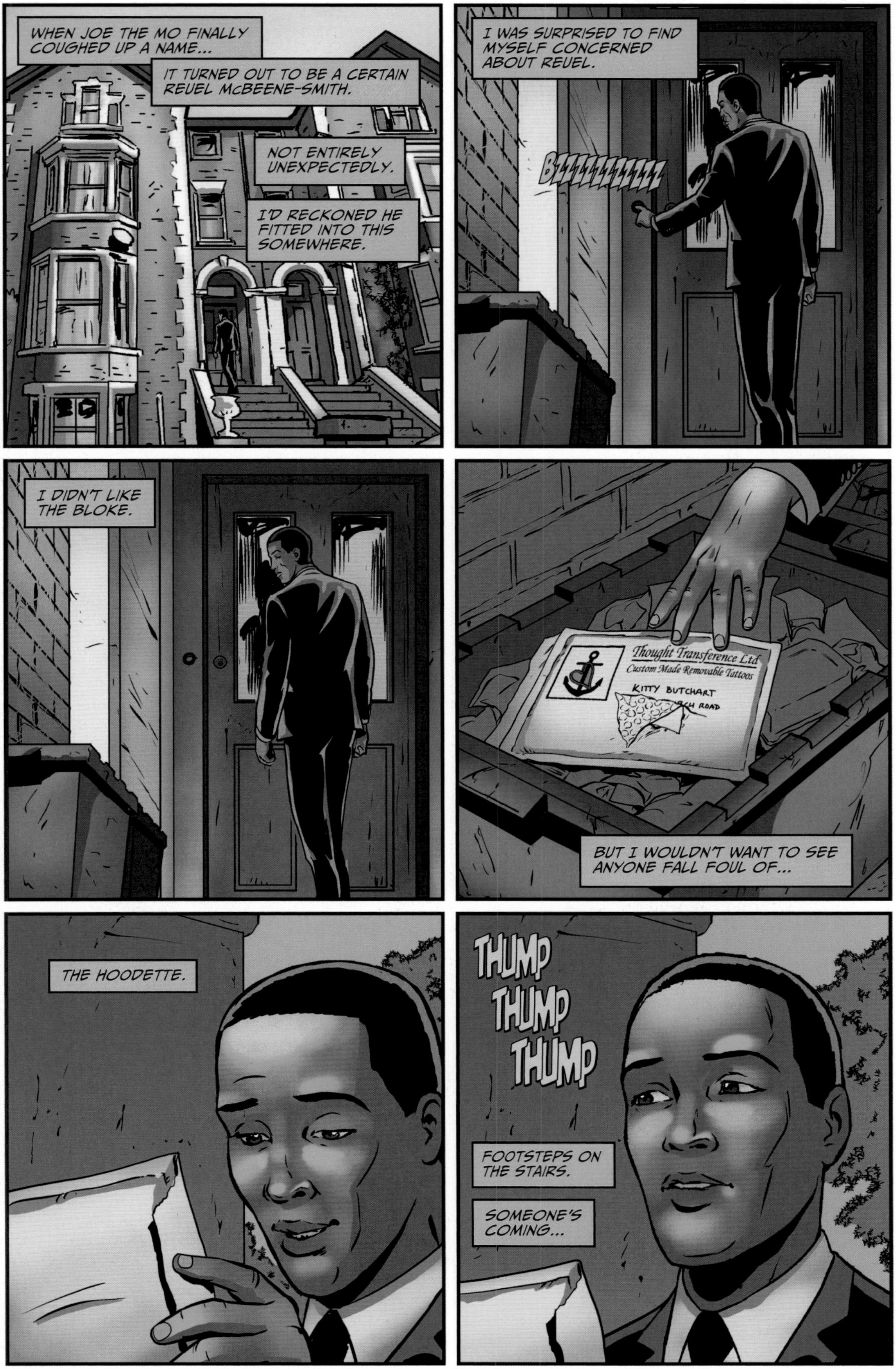
WHEN JOE THE MO FINALLY COUGHED UP A NAME...
IT TURNED OUT TO BE A CERTAIN REUEL McBEENE-SMITH.
NOT ENTIRELY UNEXPECTEDLY.
I'D RECKONED HE FITTED INTO THIS SOMEWHERE.
I WAS SURPRISED TO FIND MYSELF CONCERNED ABOUT REUEL.
BZZZZZZZZZZZ
I DIDN'T LIKE THE BLOKE.
Thought Transference Ltd
Custom Made Removable Tattoos
KITTY BUTCHART
BUT I WOULDN'T WANT TO SEE ANYONE FALL FOUL OF...
THE HOODETTE.
THUMP
THUMP
THUMP
FOOTSTEPS ON THE STAIRS.
SOMEONE'S COMING...

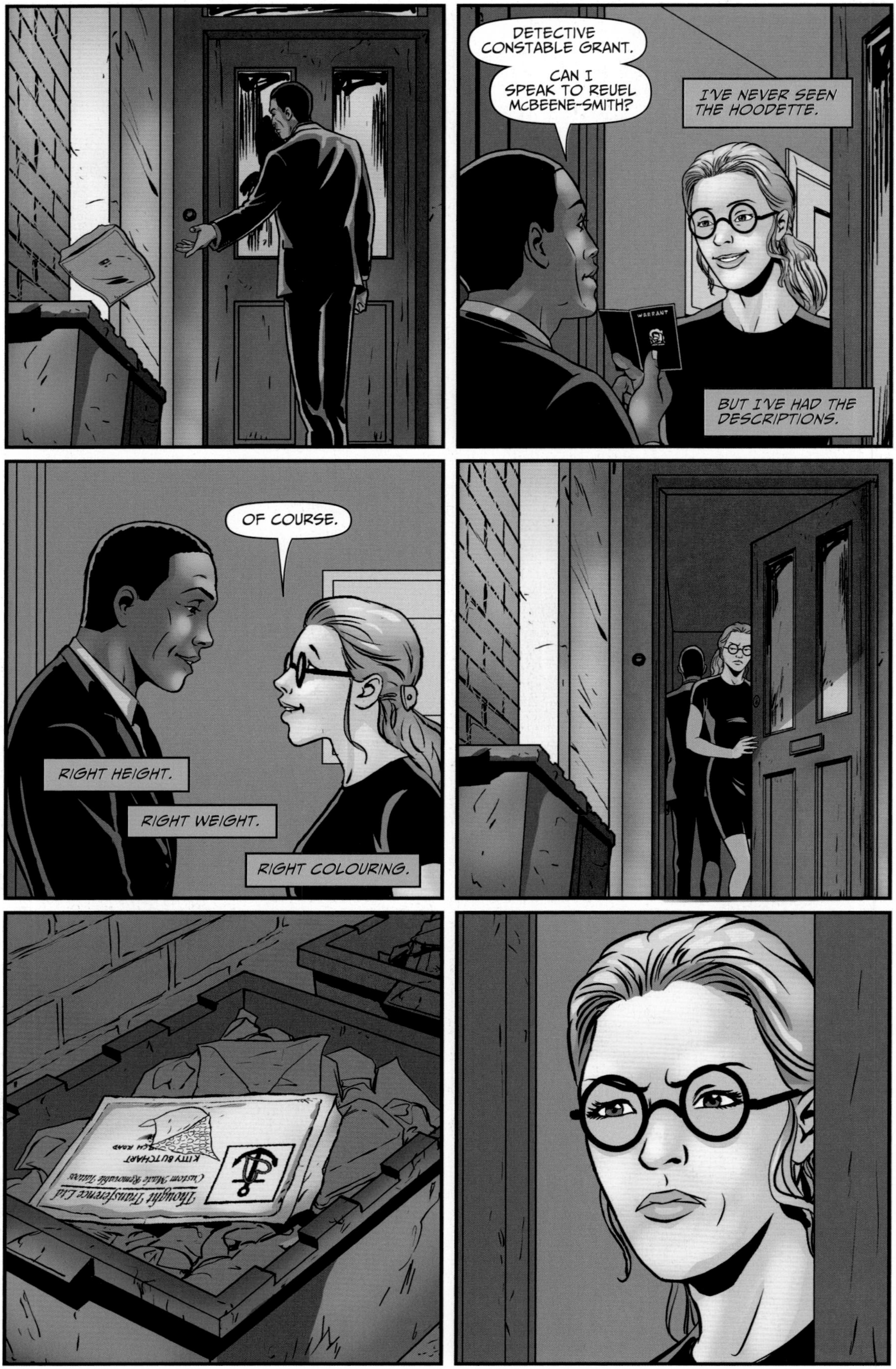
DETECTIVE CONSTABLE GRANT.
CAN I SPEAK TO REUEL McBEENE-SMITH?
I'VE NEVER SEEN THE HOODETTE.
WARRANT
BUT I'VE HAD THE DESCRIPTIONS.
OF COURSE.
RIGHT HEIGHT.
RIGHT WEIGHT.
RIGHT COLOURING.
Thought Transference Ltd
Custom-Made Removable Tattoos
KITTY BUTCHART

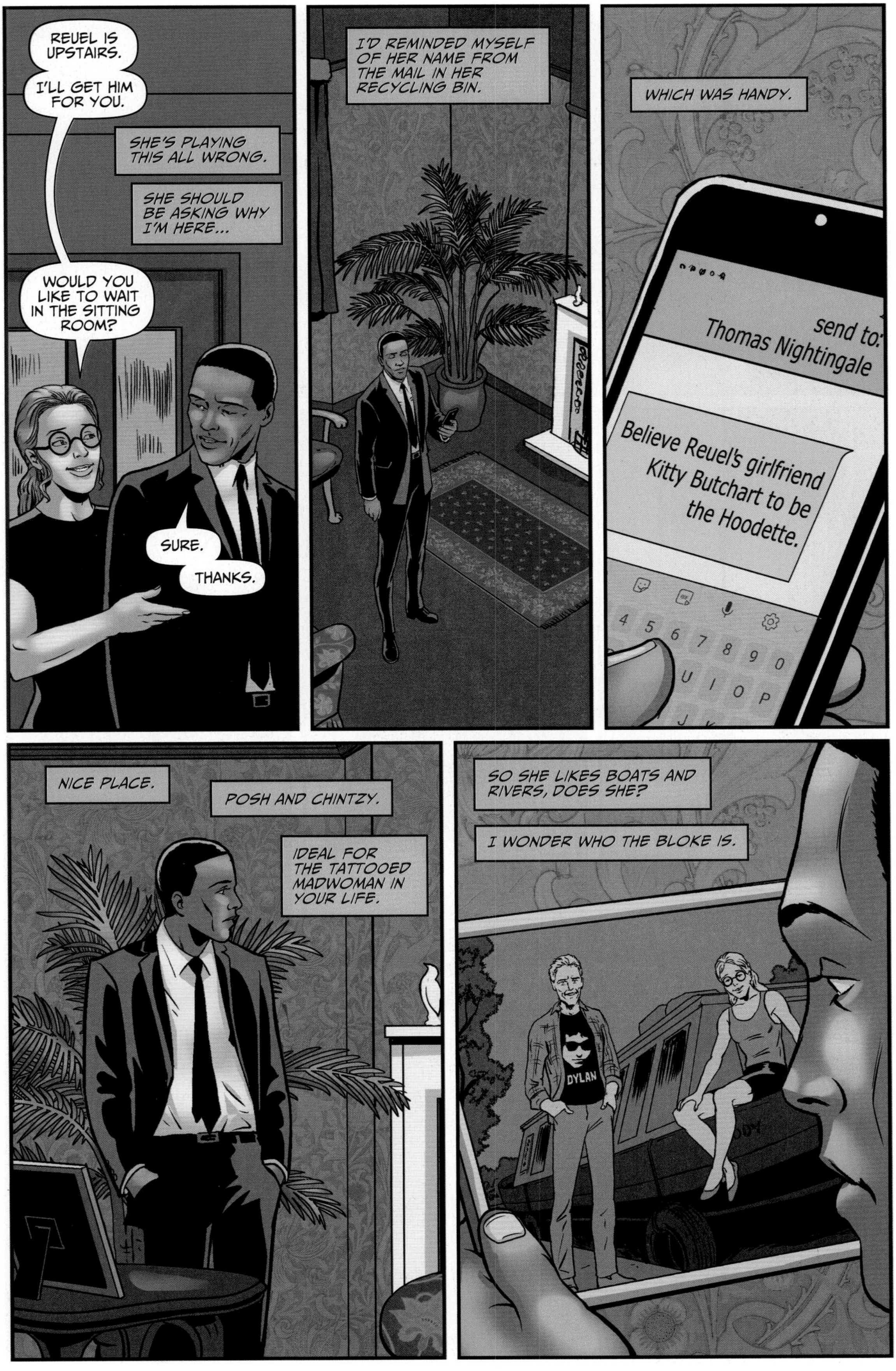
REUEL IS UPSTAIRS.
I'LL GET HIM FOR YOU.
SHE'S PLAYING THIS ALL WRONG.
SHE SHOULD BE ASKING WHY I'M HERE...
WOULD YOU LIKE TO WAIT IN THE SITTING ROOM?
SURE.
THANKS.
I'D REMINDED MYSELF OF HER NAME FROM THE MAIL IN HER RECYCLING BIN.
WHICH WAS HANDY.
send to: Thomas Nightingale
Believe Reuel's girlfriend Kitty Butchart to be the Hoodette.
NICE PLACE.
POSH AND CHINTZY.
IDEAL FOR THE TATTOOED MADWOMAN IN YOUR LIFE.
SO SHE LIKES BOATS AND RIVERS, DOES SHE?
I WONDER WHO THE BLOKE IS.
DYLAN

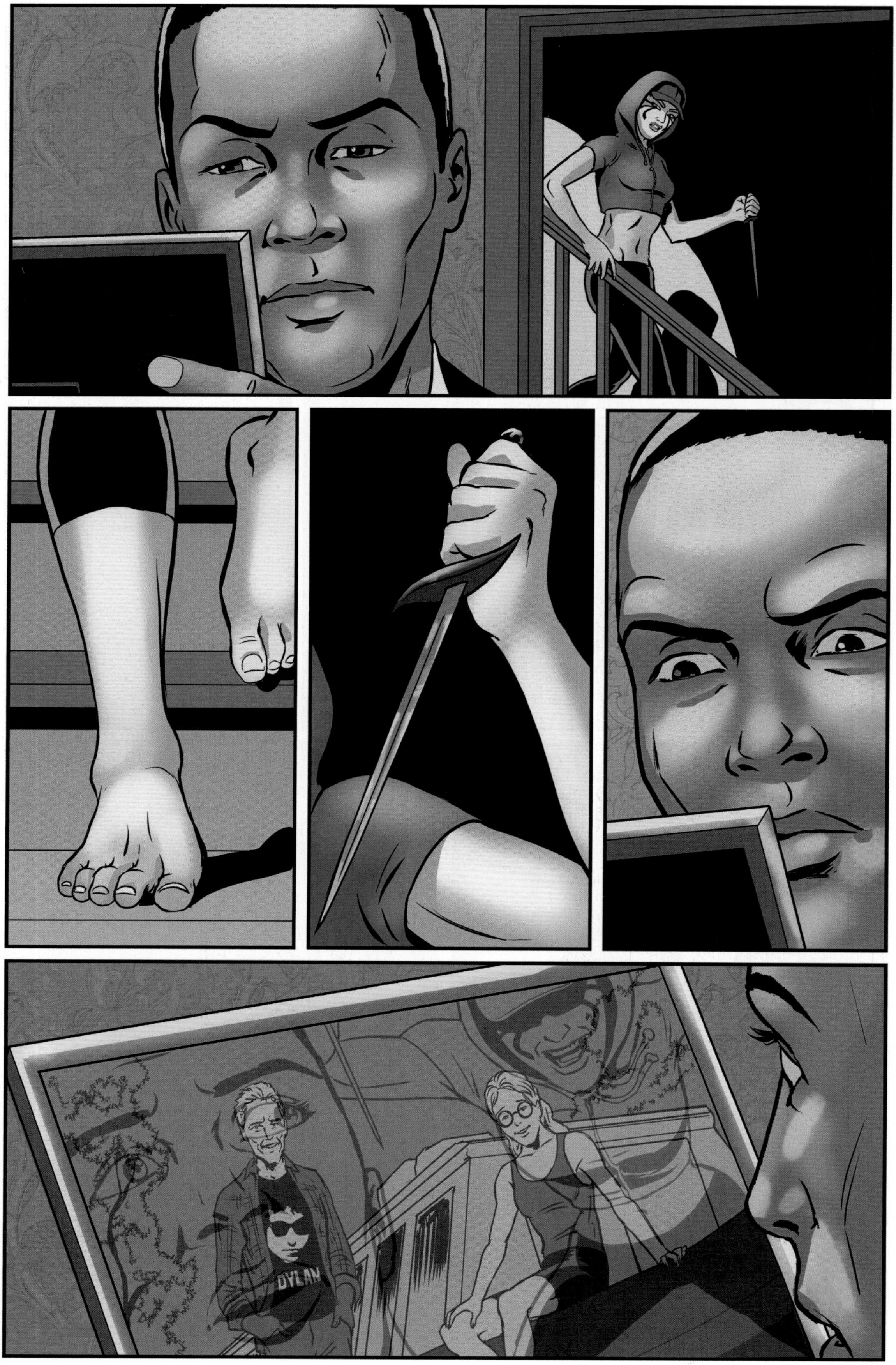
DYLAN

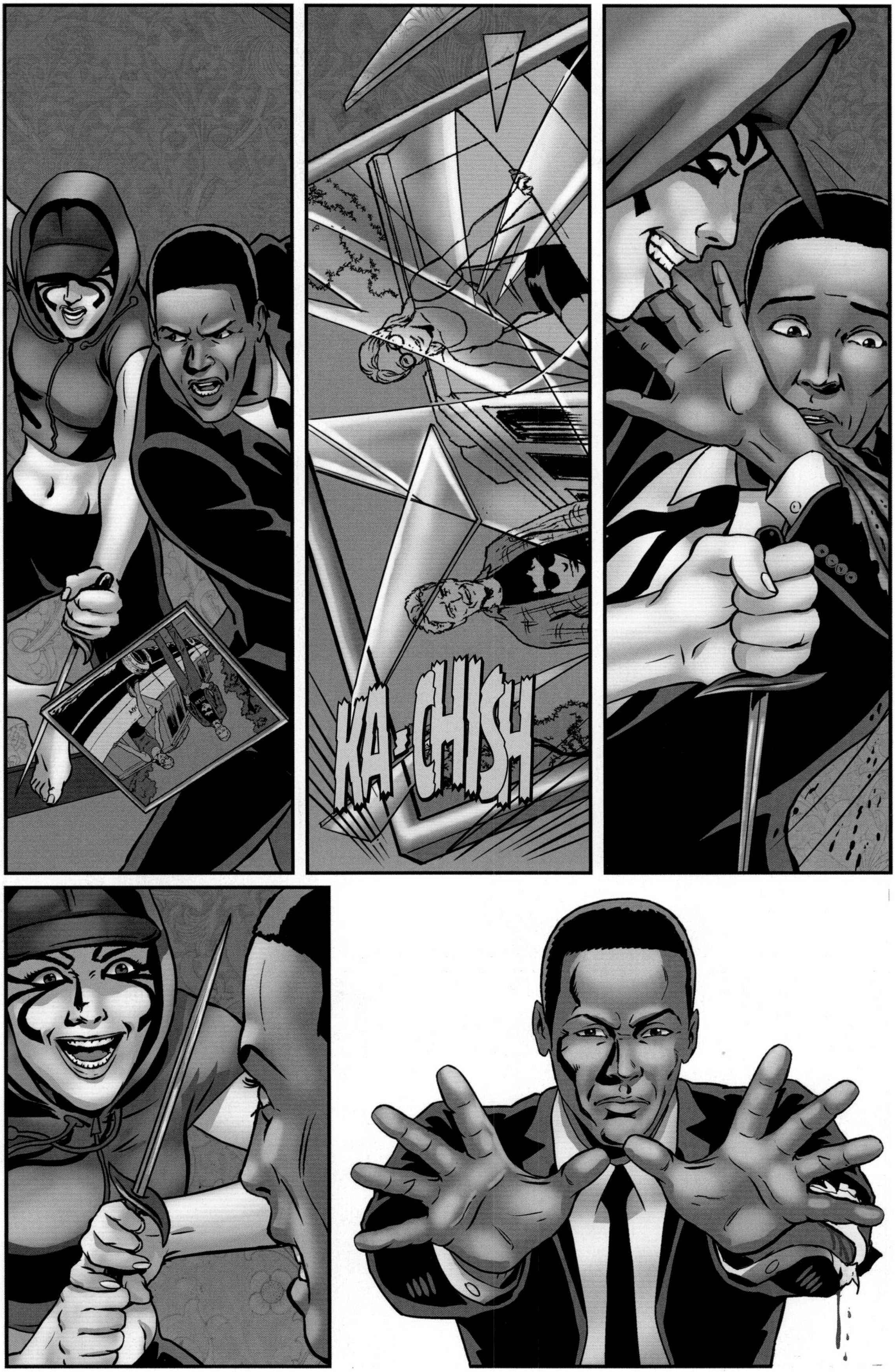
KA-CHISH

DROP THE KNIFE.

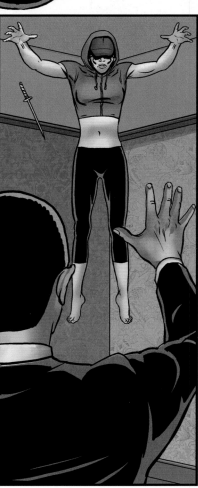

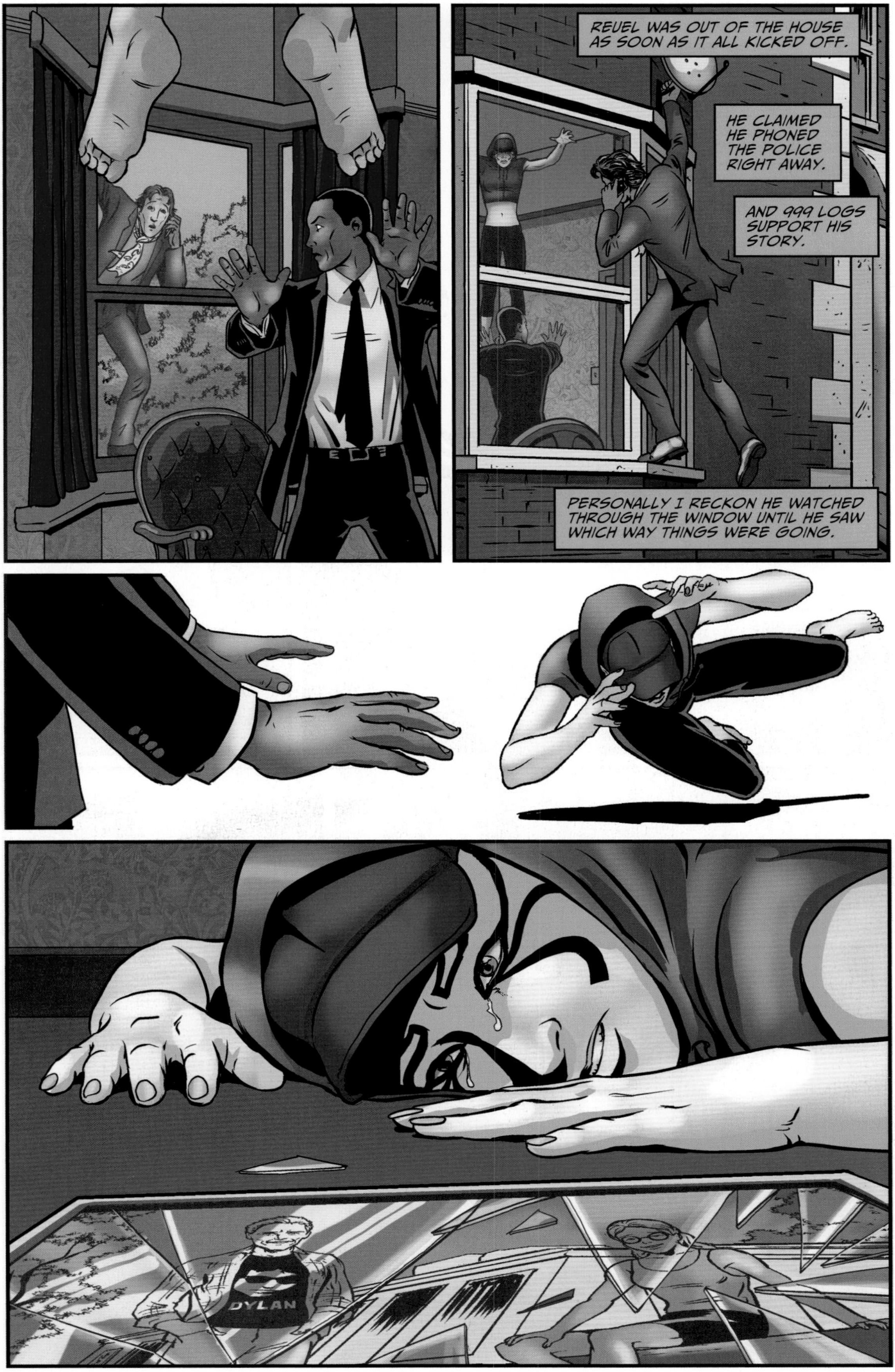
REUEL WAS OUT OF THE HOUSE AS SOON AS IT ALL KICKED OFF.
HE CLAIMED HE PHONED THE POLICE RIGHT AWAY.
AND 999 LOGS SUPPORT HIS STORY.
PERSONALLY I RECKON HE WATCHED THROUGH THE WINDOW UNTIL HE SAW WHICH WAY THINGS WERE GOING.
DYLAN

MEET JACOB HESKSHAW.

KITTY'S UNCLE JAKE.

SHE HAD ALWAYS HERO-WORSHIPPED HIM.

AND HE **WAS** PRETTY HEROIC.

OUTDOOR TYPE. LOVED TRAVEL AND ADVENTURE.

WHICH IS WHY IT WAS SO CRUEL...

WHEN A FALL WHILE ROCK CLIMBING...

LEFT HIM WITH BRAIN DAMAGE.

AND LOCKED-IN SYNDROME.

KITTY COULDN'T STAND THE THOUGHT OF HIM SPENDING THE REST OF HIS DAYS IN AN INTENSIVE CARE WARD.

IT WAS HER IDEA TO CONVERT A BOAT SO HE COULD LIVE ON IT.

JAKE HAD ALWAYS LOVED BOATS.

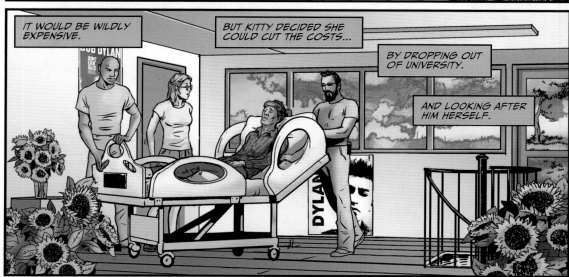

IT WOULD BE WILDLY EXPENSIVE.

BUT KITTY DECIDED SHE COULD CUT THE COSTS...

BY DROPPING OUT OF UNIVERSITY.

AND LOOKING AFTER HIM HERSELF.

SHE WAS FINDING OUT WHAT HARD WORK FULL-TIME CARE IS...

WHEN IT HAPPENED.

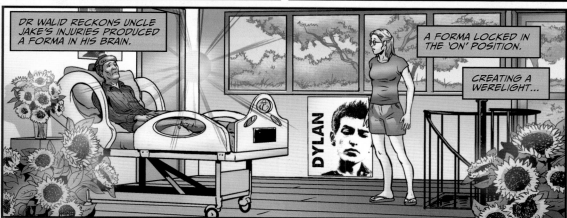

DR WALID RECKONS UNCLE JAKE'S INJURIES PRODUCED A FORMA IN HIS BRAIN.

A FORMA LOCKED IN THE 'ON' POSITION.

CREATING A WERELIGHT...

DYLAN

A PERPETUAL WERELIGHT.

LIKE SUNSHINE ON EVEN THE CLOUDIEST DAY.

LIKE THE SUNSHINE UNCLE JAKE LOVED.

DYLAN

AND, OH MY, HOW IT MADE PLANTS GROW...

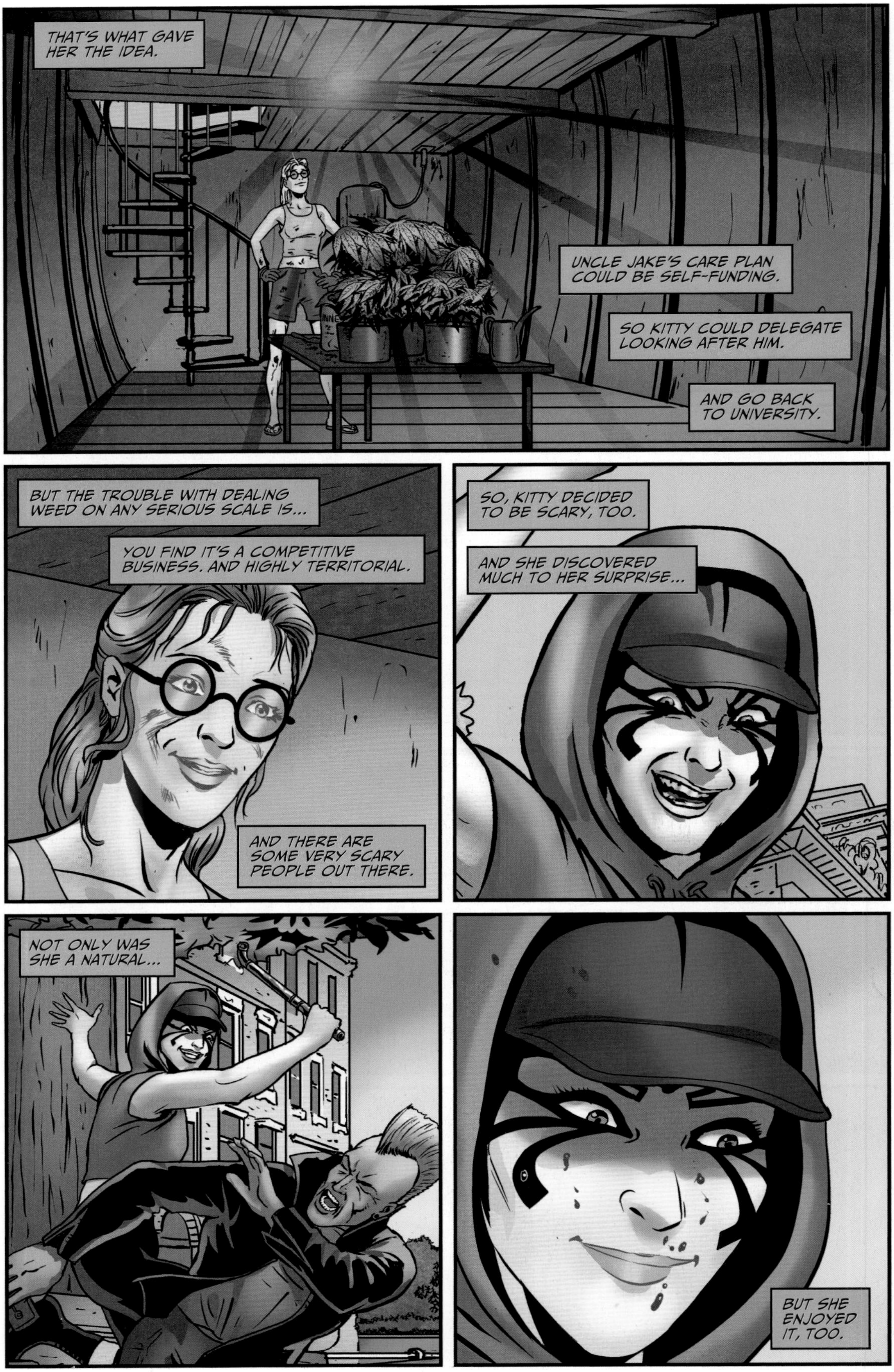
THAT'S WHAT GAVE HER THE IDEA.
UNCLE JAKE'S CARE PLAN COULD BE SELF-FUNDING.
SO KITTY COULD DELEGATE LOOKING AFTER HIM.
AND GO BACK TO UNIVERSITY.
BUT THE TROUBLE WITH DEALING WEED ON ANY SERIOUS SCALE IS...
YOU FIND IT'S A COMPETITIVE BUSINESS. AND HIGHLY TERRITORIAL.
AND THERE ARE SOME VERY SCARY PEOPLE OUT THERE.
SO, KITTY DECIDED TO BE SCARY, TOO.
AND SHE DISCOVERED MUCH TO HER SURPRISE...
NOT ONLY WAS SHE A NATURAL...
BUT SHE ENJOYED IT, TOO.

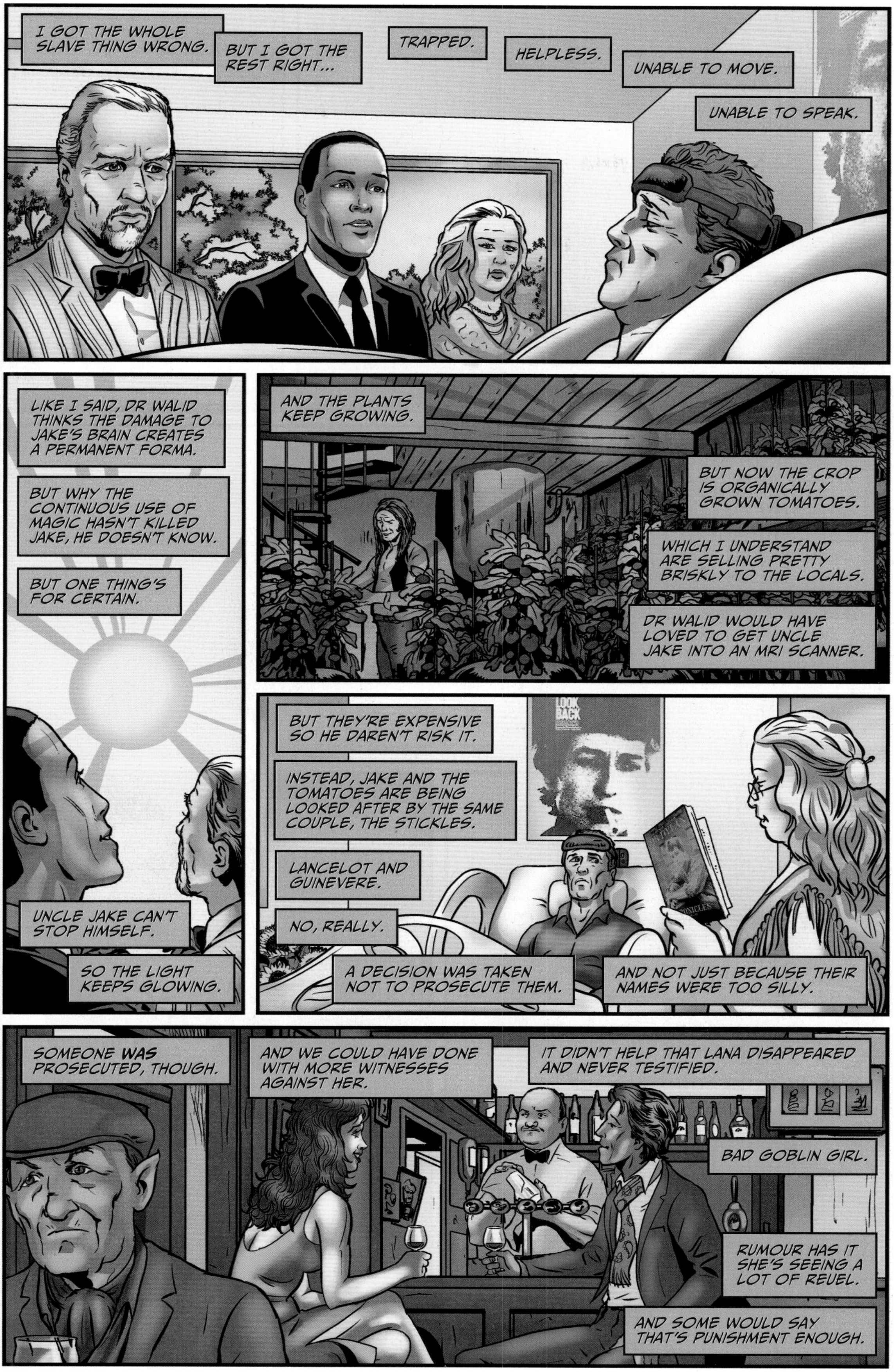
I GOT THE WHOLE SLAVE THING WRONG.
BUT I GOT THE REST RIGHT...
TRAPPED.
HELPLESS.
UNABLE TO MOVE.
UNABLE TO SPEAK.
LIKE I SAID, DR WALID THINKS THE DAMAGE TO JAKE'S BRAIN CREATES A PERMANENT FORMA.
BUT WHY THE CONTINUOUS USE OF MAGIC HASN'T KILLED JAKE, HE DOESN'T KNOW.
BUT ONE THING'S FOR CERTAIN.
UNCLE JAKE CAN'T STOP HIMSELF.
SO THE LIGHT KEEPS GLOWING.
AND THE PLANTS KEEP GROWING.
BUT NOW THE CROP IS ORGANICALLY GROWN TOMATOES.
WHICH I UNDERSTAND ARE SELLING PRETTY BRISKLY TO THE LOCALS.
DR WALID WOULD HAVE LOVED TO GET UNCLE JAKE INTO AN MRI SCANNER.
BUT THEY'RE EXPENSIVE SO HE DAREN'T RISK IT.
LOOK BACK
INSTEAD, JAKE AND THE TOMATOES ARE BEING LOOKED AFTER BY THE SAME COUPLE, THE STICKLES.
LANCELOT AND GUINEVERE.
NO, REALLY.
A DECISION WAS TAKEN NOT TO PROSECUTE THEM.
AND NOT JUST BECAUSE THEIR NAMES WERE TOO SILLY.
SOMEONE **WAS** PROSECUTED, THOUGH.
AND WE COULD HAVE DONE WITH MORE WITNESSES AGAINST HER.
IT DIDN'T HELP THAT LANA DISAPPEARED AND NEVER TESTIFIED.
BAD GOBLIN GIRL.
RUMOUR HAS IT SHE'S SEEING A LOT OF REUEL.
AND SOME WOULD SAY THAT'S PUNISHMENT ENOUGH.

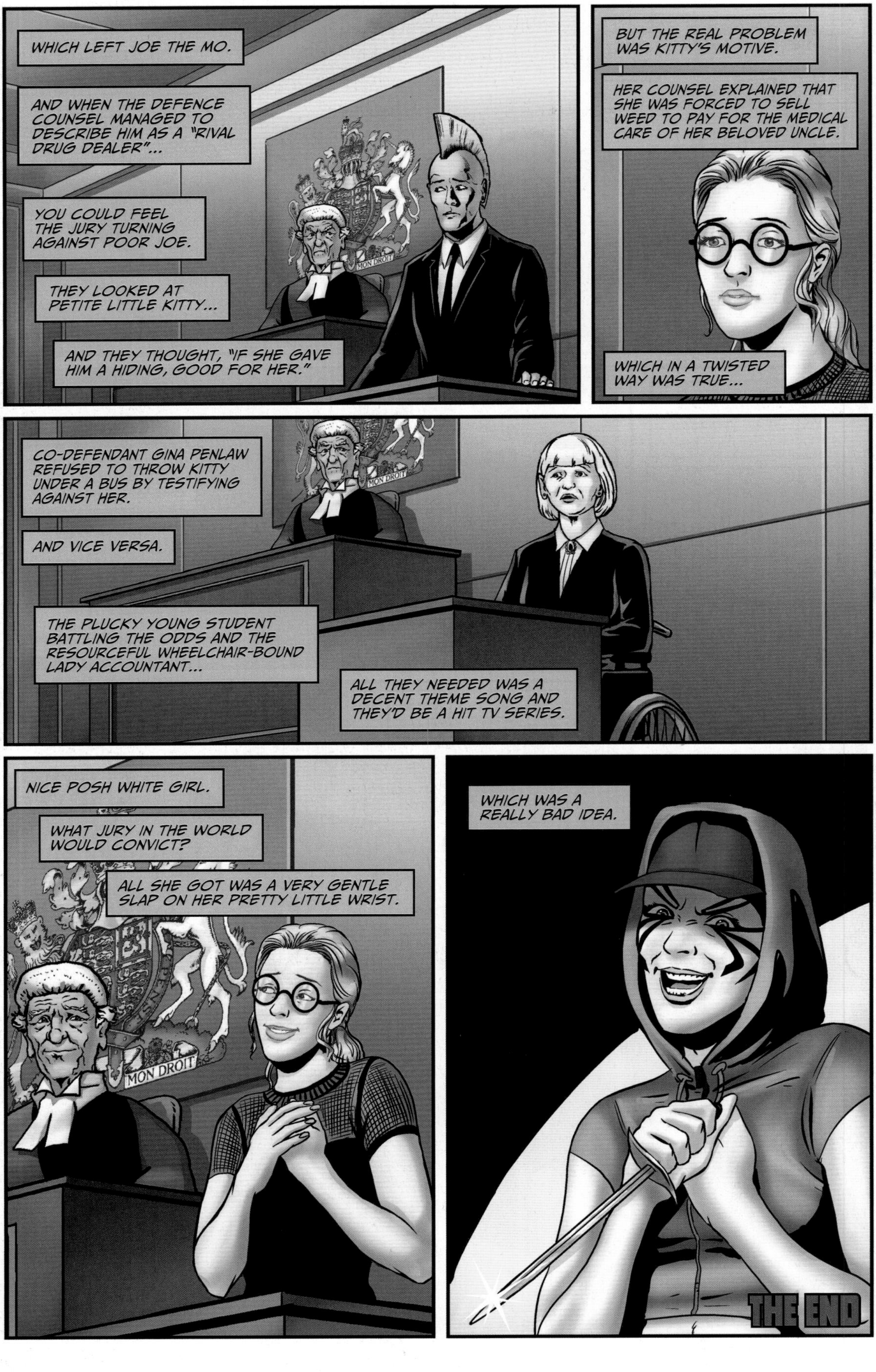
WHICH LEFT JOE THE MO.
AND WHEN THE DEFENCE COUNSEL MANAGED TO DESCRIBE HIM AS A "RIVAL DRUG DEALER"...
YOU COULD FEEL THE JURY TURNING AGAINST POOR JOE.
THEY LOOKED AT PETITE LITTLE KITTY...
AND THEY THOUGHT, "IF SHE GAVE HIM A HIDING, GOOD FOR HER."
MON DROIT
BUT THE REAL PROBLEM WAS KITTY'S MOTIVE.
HER COUNSEL EXPLAINED THAT SHE WAS FORCED TO SELL WEED TO PAY FOR THE MEDICAL CARE OF HER BELOVED UNCLE.
WHICH IN A TWISTED WAY WAS TRUE...
CO-DEFENDANT GINA PENLAW REFUSED TO THROW KITTY UNDER A BUS BY TESTIFYING AGAINST HER.
AND VICE VERSA.
THE PLUCKY YOUNG STUDENT BATTLING THE ODDS AND THE RESOURCEFUL WHEELCHAIR-BOUND LADY ACCOUNTANT...
ALL THEY NEEDED WAS A DECENT THEME SONG AND THEY'D BE A HIT TV SERIES.
NICE POSH WHITE GIRL.
WHAT JURY IN THE WORLD WOULD CONVICT?
ALL SHE GOT WAS A VERY GENTLE SLAP ON HER PRETTY LITTLE WRIST.
MON DROIT
WHICH WAS A REALLY BAD IDEA.
THE END

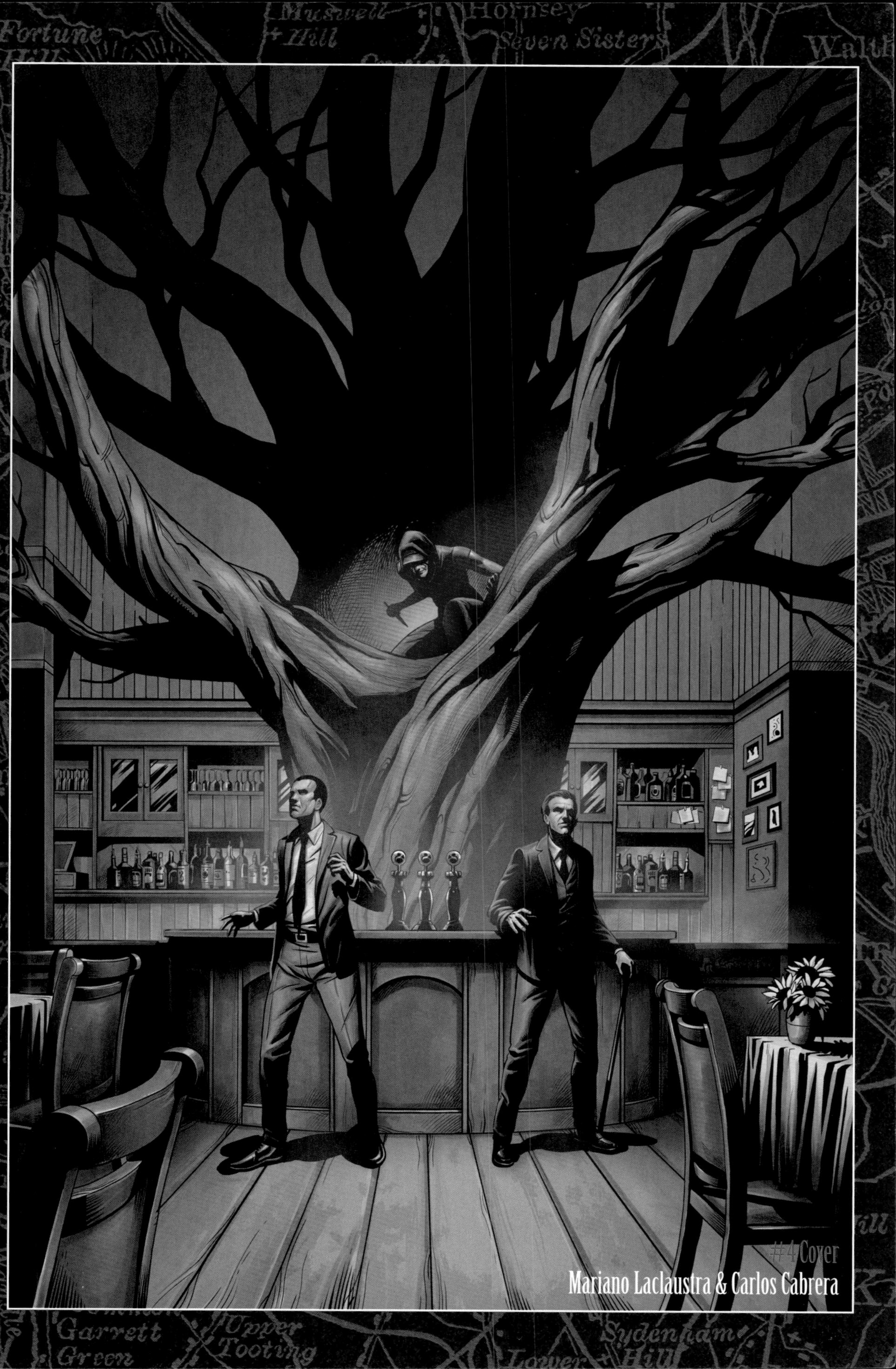
Fortune
Muswell
Hill
Hornsey
Seven Sisters
Garrett
Green
Upper
Tooting
Sydenham
Hill

#4 Cover
Mariano Laclaustra & Carlos Cabrera

TALES FROM SOUTHEND ON SEA

STARRING BEVERLEY BROOK

IN

"FAIR ADVANTAGE"

SCRIPT: CELESTE BRONFMAN
ART: BRIAN WILLIAMSON
COLOUR: LUIS GUERRERO

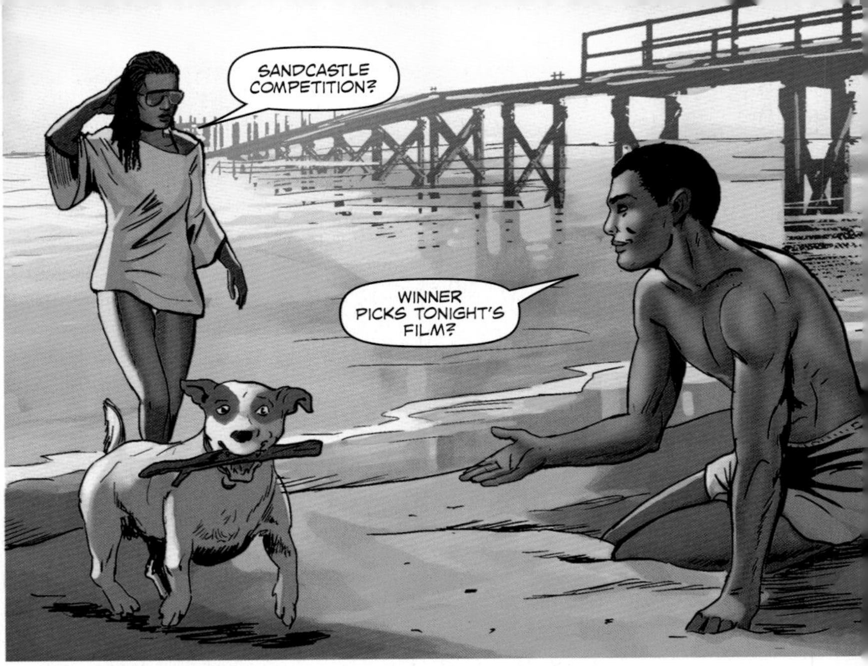
SANDCASTLE COMPETITION?
WINNER PICKS TONIGHT'S FILM?

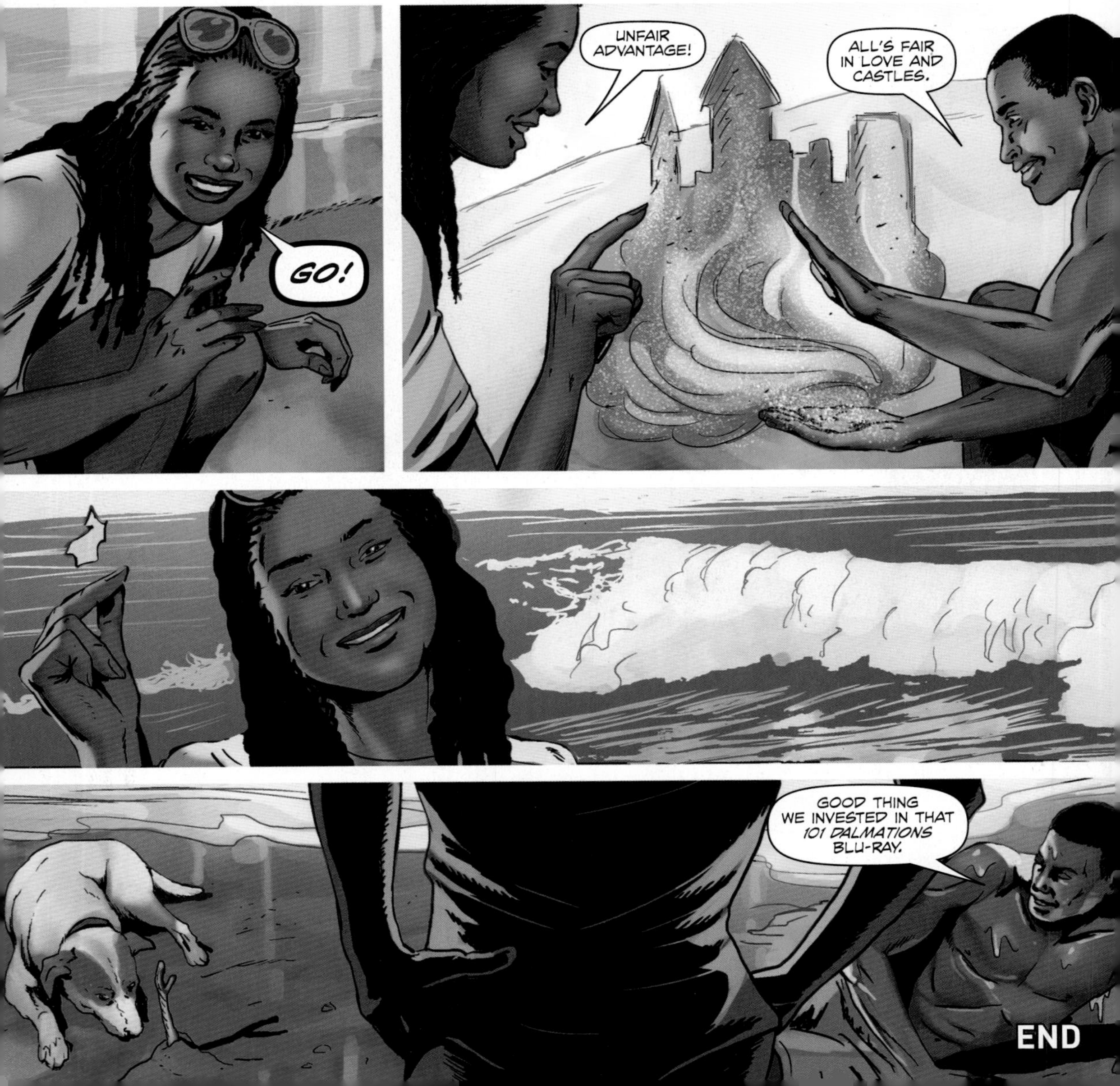
GO!
UNFAIR ADVANTAGE!
ALL'S FAIR IN LOVE AND CASTLES.
GOOD THING WE INVESTED IN THAT *101 DALMATIONS* BLU-RAY.
END

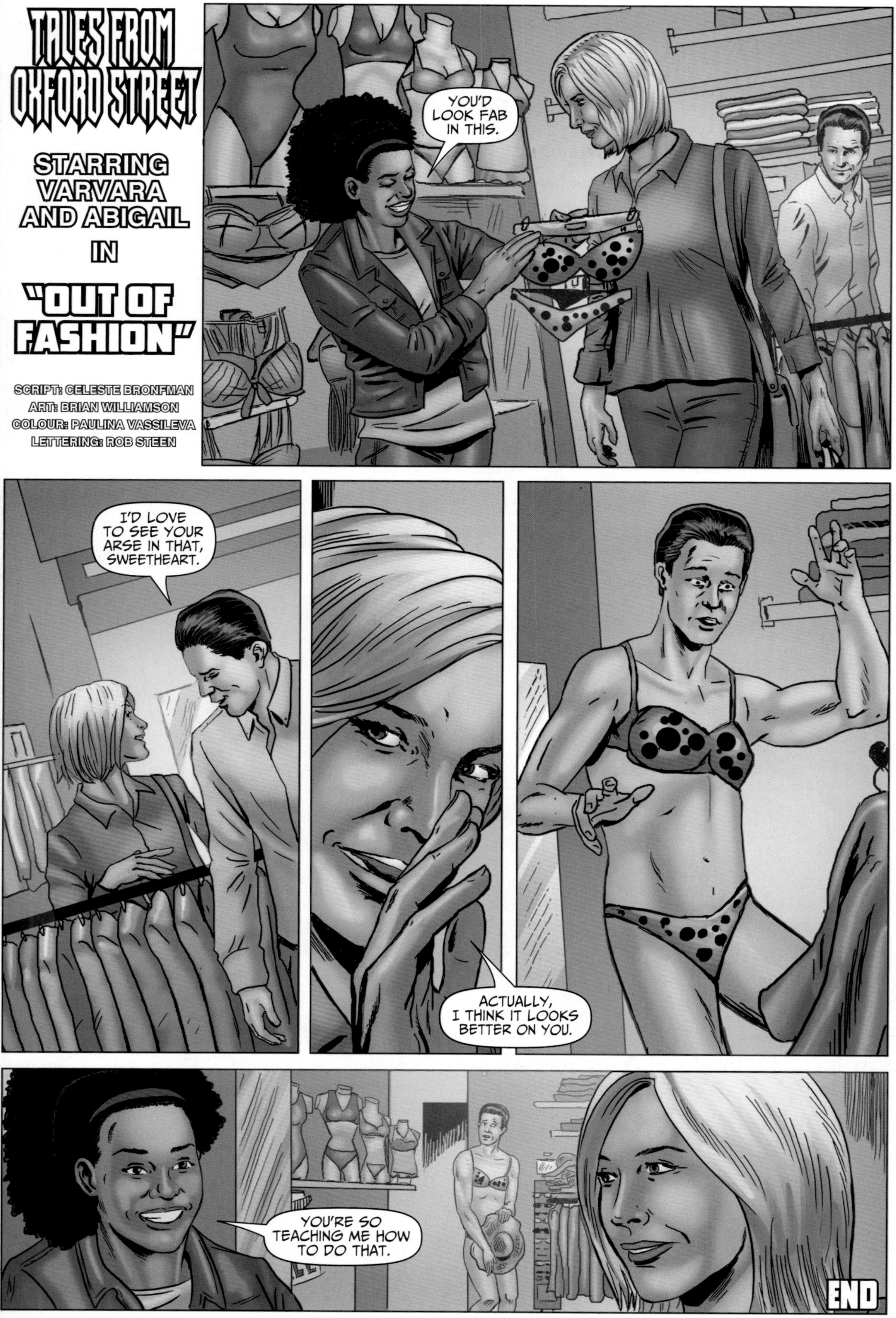
TALES FROM OXFORD STREET
STARRING VARVARA AND ABIGAIL IN
"OUT OF FASHION"
SCRIPT: CELESTE BRONFMAN
ART: BRIAN WILLIAMSON
COLOUR: PAULINA VASSILEVA
LETTERING: ROB STEEN
YOU'D LOOK FAB IN THIS.
I'D LOVE TO SEE YOUR ARSE IN THAT, SWEETHEART.
ACTUALLY, I THINK IT LOOKS BETTER ON YOU.
YOU'RE SO TEACHING ME HOW TO DO THAT.
END

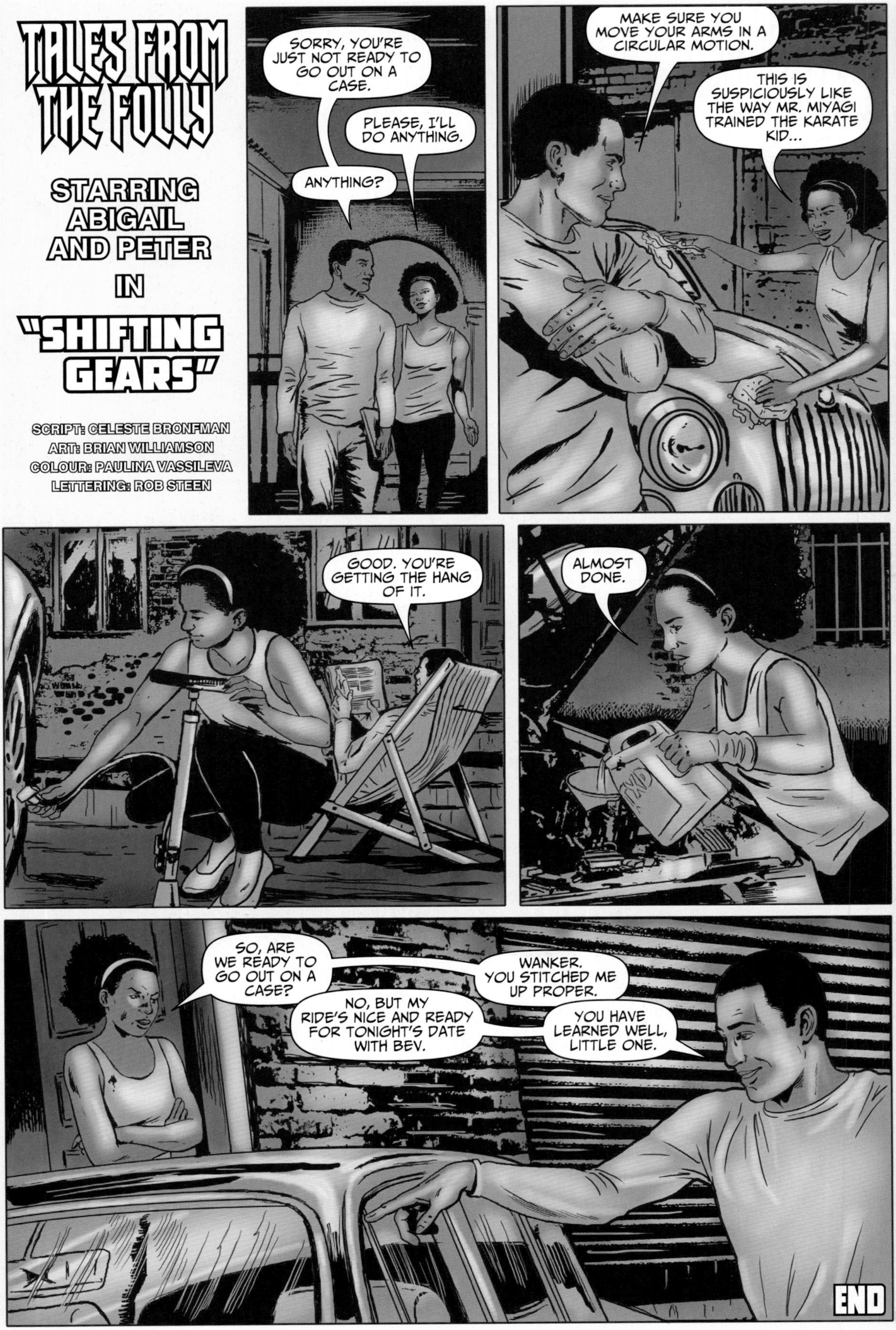
TALES FROM THE FOLLY
STARRING ABIGAIL AND PETER IN
"SHIFTING GEARS"
SCRIPT: CELESTE BRONFMAN
ART: BRIAN WILLIAMSON
COLOUR: PAULINA VASSILEVA
LETTERING: ROB STEEN
SORRY, YOU'RE JUST NOT READY TO GO OUT ON A CASE.
PLEASE, I'LL DO ANYTHING.
ANYTHING?
MAKE SURE YOU MOVE YOUR ARMS IN A CIRCULAR MOTION.
THIS IS SUSPICIOUSLY LIKE THE WAY MR. MIYAGI TRAINED THE KARATE KID...
GOOD. YOU'RE GETTING THE HANG OF IT.
ALMOST DONE.
SO, ARE WE READY TO GO OUT ON A CASE?
NO, BUT MY RIDE'S NICE AND READY FOR TONIGHT'S DATE WITH BEV.
WANKER. YOU STITCHED ME UP PROPER.
YOU HAVE LEARNED WELL, LITTLE ONE.
END

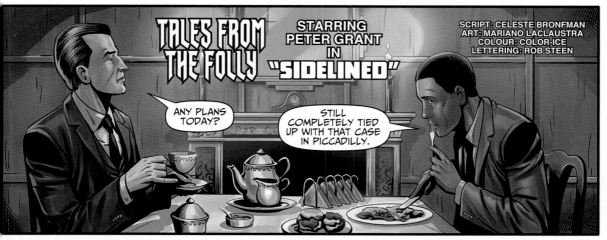

TALES FROM THE FOLLY

STARRING PETER GRANT IN "SIDELINED"

SCRIPT: CELESTE BRONFMAN
ART: MARIANO LACLAUSTRA
COLOUR: COLOR-ICE
LETTERING: ROB STEEN

ANY PLANS TODAY?

STILL COMPLETELY TIED UP WITH THAT CASE IN PICCADILLY.

SORRY, BOSS, BUT PRIORITIES ARE PRIORITIES.

00:00 ARS 0-0 AST

THE FA CUP

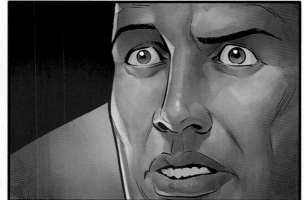

PETER-THIS SEAT COULD HAVE BEEN YOURS!

END

COVERS GALLERY

BEN AARONOVITCH   CARTMEL • SULLIVAN • GUERRERO

RIVERS OF LONDON

WATER WEED

ISSUE 1 – Cover
Alex Ronald

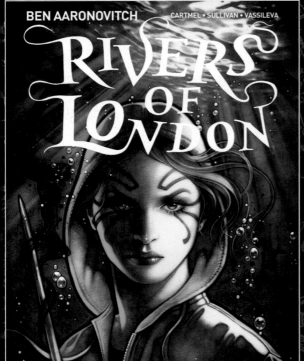

BEN AARONOVITCH   CARTMEL • SULLIVAN • VASSILEVA

RIVERS OF LONDON

WATER WEED

ISSUE 2 – Cover
Anna Dittmann

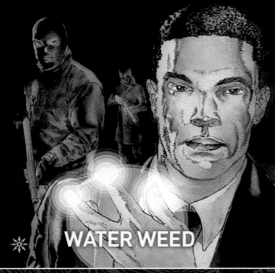

BEN AARONOVITCH   CARTMEL • SULLIVAN • VASSILEVA

RIVERS OF LONDON

WATER WEED

ISSUE 3 – Cover
Illeighstration

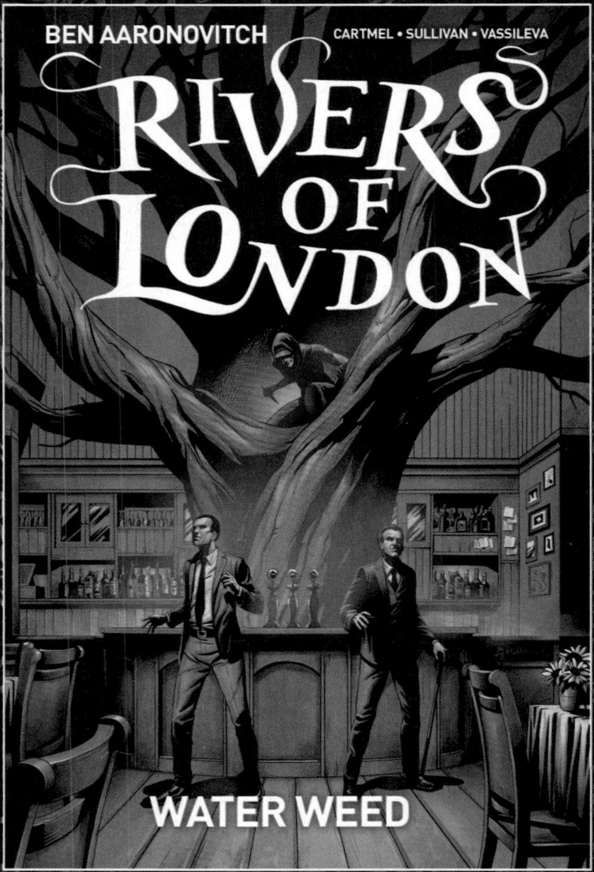

BEN AARONOVITCH   CARTMEL • SULLIVAN • VASSILEVA

RIVERS OF LONDON

WATER WEED

ISSUE 4 – Cover
Mariano Laclaustra & Carlos Cabrera

RIVERS OF LONDON READER'S GUIDE

The *Rivers of London* comics and graphic novels are an essential part of the saga. Though they each stand alone, together they add compelling depth to the wider world of Peter and the Folly!

This helpful guide shows where each book fits in the ever-growing timeline of the *Rivers of London* universe!

The Sunday Times Bestselling Peter Grant series
BEN AARONOVITCH
RIVERS OF LONDON
In the heart of the capital, a different world hides...

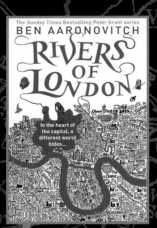

RIVERS OF LONDON / MIDNIGHT RIOT
Novel 1

BEN AARONOVITCH
MOON OVER SOHO

MOON OVER SOHO
Novel 2

BEN AARONOVITCH
The Sunday Times bestselling series
WHISPERS UNDER GROUND
If you've been on the Underground you know what horrors await . . .

WHISPERS UNDER GROUND
Novel 3

BEN AARONOVITCH
The Sunday Times Bestselling Peter Grant series
BROKEN HOMES
Stuff gets serious South of the River . . .

BROKEN HOMES
Novel 4

"A PERFECT BLEND OF CSI AND HARRY POTTER." – io9
RIVERS OF LONDON
BODY WORK
BEN AARONOVITCH • CARTMEL • SULLIVAN • GUERRERO

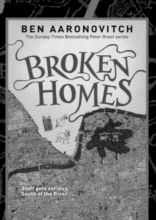

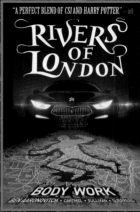

BODY WORK
Graphic Novel 1

FOXGLOVE
SUMMER
Novel 5

BLACK
MOULD
Graphic Novel 3

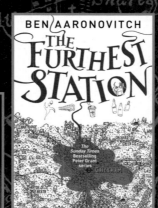

THE
FURTHEST
STATION
Novella 1

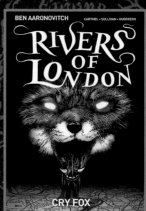

CRY FOX
Graphic
Novel 5

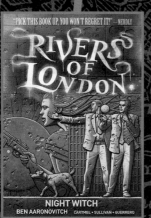

NIGHT
WITCH
Graphic Novel 2

THE HANGING
TREE
Novel 6

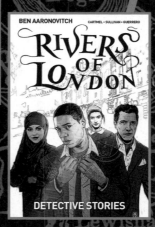

DETECTIVE
STORIES
Graphic Novel 4

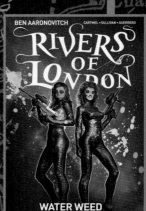

WATER WEED
Graphic Novel 6

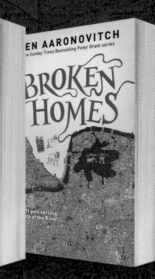
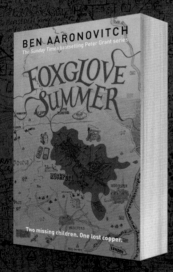

CREATOR BIOGRAPHIES

BEN AARONOVITCH

Ben is perhaps best known for his series of Peter Grant novels, which began with *Rivers of London*. Mixing police procedural with urban fantasy and London history, these novels have now sold over a million copies worldwide.

The latest Peter Grant novel, *Lies Sleeping,* is now available.

Ben is also known for his TV writing, writing fan-favourite episodes of *Doctor Who*; *Remembrance of the Daleks* and *Battlefield*.

He wrote an episode of BBC hospital drama, *Casualty*, and contributed to cult SF show, *Jupiter Moon*.

Ben was born, raised and lives in London, and says he will leave the city when they prise it out of his cold, dead fingers.

ANDREW CARTMEL

began a long and varied career in TV and publishing when he was hired as script editor on *Doctor Who* in 1986. He had a major (and very positive) impact on the final years of the original run of the TV show.

He has recently completed a comedy for the London stage, *Screwball*, and is also writing the *Vinyl Detective* series of crime novels for Titan Books; the fourth, *Flip Back*, will be available soon. In his spare time, he likes to do stand-up comedy.

LEE SULLIVAN

began his comics career at Marvel UK, drawing *Transformers* and *Robocop* for the US before moving on to *Judge Dredd* and *Thunderbirds* – and *Doctor Who*, for which he continues to draw, for a variety of publishers.

He played saxophone in a Roxy Music tribute band for a decade. He has dotted various Roxy Music-related gags through this series!

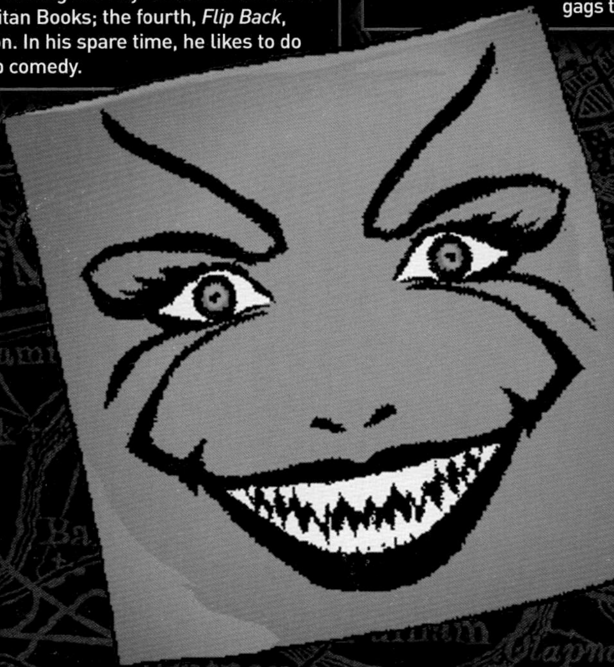

PAULINA VASSILEVA

is an illustrator of varied interests based in London. Originally from Bulgaria, she is a self-taught artist with a degree in graphic design and creative studies. In 2017, she collaborated with Rudra Purkyastha and Lyndon White in the acclaimed graphic anthology *Flirting With Death*, published by Untold Voyages.

LUIS GUERRERO

A native of Mexico, Luis has become a regular fixture at Titan Comics, colouring interiors and covers for a number of series including *Doctor Who, The Troop,* and *Mycroft Holmes,* as well as *Rivers of London*. Recently he has coloured for DC Comics on *The Flash*.